ROUTLEDGE LIBRARY EDITIONS: PEACE STUDIES

Volume 3

THE REBEL PASSION

THE REBEL PASSION

A Short History of Some Pioneer Peace-Makers

VERA BRITTAIN

Routledge
Taylor & Francis Group

LONDON AND NEW YORK

First published in 1964 by George Allen & Unwin Ltd

This edition first published in 2020
by Routledge
2 Park Square, Milton Park, Abingdon, Oxon OX14 4RN

and by Routledge
52 Vanderbilt Avenue, New York, NY 10017

Routledge is an imprint of the Taylor & Francis Group, an informa business

British Library Cataloguing in Publication Data
A catalogue record for this book is available from the British Library

ISBN: 978-0-367-21777-8 (Set)
ISBN: 978-0-429-29830-1 (Set) (ebk)
ISBN: 978-0-367-26175-7 (Volume 3) (hbk)
ISBN: 978-0-367-26187-0 (Volume 3) (pbk)
ISBN: 978-0-429-29190-6 (Volume 3) (ebk)

Publisher's Note
The publisher has gone to great lengths to ensure the quality of this reprint but points out that some imperfections in the original copies may be apparent.

Disclaimer
The publisher has made every effort to trace copyright holders and would welcome correspondence from those they have been unable to trace.

(Photo: Yevonde)

VERA BRITTAIN

This book is published to commemorate
the fiftieth anniversary of the
Fellowship of Reconciliation, founded
at Cambridge in December 1914, and
followed by the International Fellowship
in 1919.

THE REBEL PASSION

A Short History of
Some Pioneer Peace-makers

VERA BRITTAIN

London

GEORGE ALLEN & UNWIN LTD

RUSKIN HOUSE   MUSEUM STREET

PRINTED IN GREAT BRITAIN
in 11 point Juliana type
BY THE BLACKFRIARS PRESS LTD
LEICESTER

Pity is a rebel passion. Its hand is against the strong, against the organized force of society, against conventional sanctions and accepted Gods. It is the Kingdom of Heaven within us fighting against the brute powers of the world

> GILBERT MURRAY
> Introduction to *The Trojan Women,*
> translated from the Greek of Euripides

In every age God has scattered forerunners in the world. They are those who are ahead of their time and whose personal action is based on an inward knowledge of that which is yet to come

> ABBÉ DE TOURVILLE
> Letters of Direction. Thoughts
> on the Spiritual Life from the
> *Letters of Abbé de Tourville*

Preface

I owe the I.F.o.R. membership a sincere apology for the many errors and omissions which they are bound to find in this book.

When the idea of a history to commemorate the half centenary of the Fellowship was first discussed, it was hoped that some senior member who recalled its origins would undertake the task. As an occasional contributor to Fellowship publications, although I had never been concerned in the organization, I was asked to give a 'literary polish' to the completed manuscript. This, a matter of perhaps six weeks' revision, I agreed to do.

But when the preparations were complete none of the original members felt able to attempt the work involved and I was requested to take it over, though my knowledge of the F.o.R., especially abroad, was scanty, and I had two commissioned biographies to complete. I asked urgently that someone with fewer other commitments and more actual experience of the Fellowship should be invited instead, since my own connection with the pacifist movement has been chiefly as a member of the Board of *Peace News* and more recently as its Chairman. Alternatively, I suggested that the book should be a symposium, with each of the F.o.R. Centres writing its history in its own way. But this idea, for some reason still not clear to me, seemed unacceptable also, while my hopes of an effective substitute remained unfulfilled. Eventually I was persuaded to accept what has proved to be an even more formidable task than I anticipated.

It could not have been done at all without the help of several I.F.o.R. members whose qualifications in relation to the organization far exceed my own. For the supply of background material I am particularly indebted to the Rev. John Nevin Sayre, Percy W. Bartlett, and Muriel Lester; for extremely valuable and exhaustive research work on the Fellowship's numerous magazines, covering nearly half a century, to Miss Ethel Comber, who also helped me with personal impressions of individuals; for their recollections of I.F.o.R. leaders both past and present to the Rev.

Lewis Maclachlan, the Rev. Clifford Macquire, Mrs. Doris Nicholls and Mr and Mrs Sayre, and for biographical material on the Rev. Richard Roberts to his daughters Mrs Dorothy Knowles, Mrs Gwen E. P. Norman and Mrs Margaret P. MacVicar, and to President A. E. Kerr of Dalhousie University, Halifax, N.S.

I am particularly grateful to Jean Lasserre of the French Centre, Dr Heinz Kloppenburg and Frau Irmgard Schuchardt of the German Centre, and to the Secretaries of the Commonwealth Centres (including South Africa), for the concise, well-digested form in which they sent their information, thereby saving many hours of labour; to the members of the I.F.o.R. European Committee who checked the typescript last January and as far as possible brought it up to date; and last but far from least to the Rev. Philip Eastman, but for whose continuous help and encouragement I doubt if I should have persisted for the three years that the work has required.

Finally, I am much indebted to all those who allowed themselves to be 'interviewed' in various places, such as Canon C. E. Raven at his home in Cambridge, and the many I.F.o.R. leaders whom I met at Le Chambon in 1961. I wish I could have commanded the necessary space to incorporate more than a few scanty details from the life histories that I obtained from them, and from many other F.o.R. members to whom my gratitude is no less sincere because my limited allocation of words prevents me from enumerating them personally. I must however insist that none of those from whom I obtained information are in any way responsible for the selections that I have made from their stories or for the comments on their work, which for better or worse are my own.

VERA BRITTAIN
April 1964

Contents

ILLUSTRATIONS

Chapter 1

THE POLITICS OF COMPASSION

Politics are usually the executive expression of human immaturity. This is especially true of international politics in this twentieth century, which began as 'the Century of Hope', but now faces the possibility of going down to history as 'the Century of Hate'.

It opened with a bitter colonial conflict which is still responsible for the national and racial turmoil that smoulders in South Africa, throwing psychological tentacles of animosity across a turbulent world. But this limited war was a mere curtain-raiser for the unlimited fratricidal wars which wrecked human relationships for two fierce decades separated by twenty years of acrimonious truce, and left behind them the Cold War which has so long divided political mankind into two hostile camps.

Beneath these major manifestations of hate have lain for half a century the subsidiary hatreds which transform human brotherhood into sub-human enmity : the tension between white and non-white races; the inhumanity of the Nazis (and not the Nazis only) towards the Jews; the ferocious intolerance of the respective practitioners of different political creeds. Antipathy matched itself against antipathy, and he whose hatred expressed itself most ruthlessly became the loudly publicized leader of his own cause.

In such a period of moral decadence, the Christian who looks for inspiration to the Cross where love was crucified but not destroyed represents the revolutionary element in his own community, which at periods of maximum strain denounces him as a traitor, and in less dramatic intervals deprives him, with all the ingenuity in its power, of opportunities to bear witness to his faith. His profound impulse of love and pity becomes, as Professor Gilbert Murray called it, 'a rebel passion', not only fighting against the brute powers of the world, but seeking to establish in their place a new form of leadership inspired by different standards. Inevitably he becomes an object of distrust and suspicion to the 'accepted gods' whose authority he endeavours to dethrone, and penalties which vary from ignominy and deprivation to imprisonment and death will be imposed upon him.

One of the redeeming characteristics of our immature society, dominated by the childish but lethal emotions of fear, hatred and greed, has been the slowly growing Christian minority of men and women possessed by the rebel passion, who have accepted the retribution demanded by 'the organized force of society' (that is, the Establishments of their day) as their contemporary share in the Cross of Christ. This book endeavours to tell the story of some pioneer peace-makers—for the most part neither saints nor heroes, though a few have been both—in whose lives charity and compassion have played an organic part which has left them unimpaired by popular emotions and unmoved by the consistent opposition of power-wielding authorities.

They have seldom found their way to conspicuous worldly pedestals, but because the minds of at least some have been distinguished and prophetic, their unpublicized impact on their contemporaries has operated as a leaven which is gradually changing the thought of a generation in spite of the powerful ethics of the amoral State and the contrary standards of the conventional majority. They are a minority — in Isaiah's language a 'remnant' — whose thought speeds in advance of acknowledged values and thus keeps alive the vision of divine solutions for human problems (the Quakers' 'way of God for every situation'). In the words of the Abbé de Tourville, they are 'forerunners . . . who are ahead of their time and whose personal action is based on an inward knowledge of that which is yet to come'.

The major question of our day is whether their revolutionary influence, wherever it may be exerted, can operate in time to save their society from the suicidal consequences of its infantile malignities. 'The Christian,' wrote Professor G. H. C. Macgregor, 'must learn to live not as a baffled idealist but as a rebel against the world as it is.' But protest is only the beginning of his mission; his long-term purpose is to replace a decadent and corrupt society by one which creates the right atmosphere for moral impulses to grow. The substantial measure of achievement brought about by a few pioneers in the half-century covered by this story may perhaps encourage contemporary workers similarly moved by the rebel passion to join in the attempt to substitute spiritual foundations for the self-interested worldly standards which have brought mankind to the edge of the abyss, and to achieve this difficult purpose before the hour has grown too late.

'If there is one thing the world needs above everything it is Time,' the editorial of a large popular newspaper recently and unexpectedly asserted; 'Time for the human mind to adjust itself to what it has created.' The significant men and women of our day may well appear to the future to be those who have contributed to this adjustment, whether or not their names are blazoned in the big headlines.

The advance of science in the twentieth century has made hatred not merely a form of moral degradation, but a threat to the survival of mankind. A main contribution to international hatreds has come from militant nationalism and the national sovereignties created by it. Individuals moved by the rebel passion have learned to transcend frontiers and, in spite of war and man-made political obstacles, to link men and women across the world who subscribe to similar ideals.

Fifty years ago, as we shall see in Chapter 3, a group of citizens joined together to form a Fellowship of Reconciliation which by the end of the First World War had grown international, and became the uniting bond between groups of seekers from many countries who saw the communion that they were creating in terms of a society still to come. They did not visualize their movement in the shape of a new Church, for as de Chardin has written in *Le Milieu Divin*, 'the supernatural is a ferment, a soul, and not a complete and finished organism'. Rather it was seen as a witness within the Churches made by those who sought to interpret the Kingdom of God in terms of non-violence and sacrificial love.

The founders of the Fellowship sought individually and corporately to practice a ministry of reconciliation between man and man, class and class, nation and nation, believing all true

B

reconciliation between men to be based on reconciliation between man and God. This, rather than mere protest, was their purpose, for they were united in the belief that love as revealed and interpreted by the life and death of Jesus Christ was the key to a peaceful and attainable human order. Membership meant a quest for social justice and peaceful change by methods consistent with Christ's teaching, and hence involved the repudiation of war. The members sought less to put pressure on governments than to reach beyond the authority of the State to the failure of civilization, to heal the divisions in the human family from which this failure springs, and to draw together across all barriers of race, nationality, language and class many widely separated men and women linked by their characteristic interpretation of the New Testament.

In a leaflet entitled 'The Harsh Terms of Peace', Professor Howard Schomer, elected President of the International Fellowship of Reconciliation in 1959, commented on the 'soft-sounding' name of this body (derived from the words of St Paul in II Corinthians v, 18). He contrasted its gentle title with the costly sacrifice accepted by virile revolutionaries perpetually ready 'to stand up and be counted as unalterable friends of desperately imperilled human values' amid the strident passions of two great wars, and the fears and suspicions generated by the 'ghastly witch-hunt' precipitated in the United States after the initial alarms of the Cold War. The accepted obligation to 'speak truth' to the power wielded by amoral governments does not lead to popularity and an easy life in such recurrent crises as this twentieth century has imposed upon itself.

An article by Percy W. Bartlett, one of the first members of the Fellowship and the General Secretary of the British F.o.R. from 1925 to 1936, describes it as being from the start not only a Christian but an inter-church society. What made it, he asks, not merely a peace organization but a pacifist group (or, as we prefer to say today, a 'non-violent' community, owing to the prolonged popular confusion of pacifism with 'passivism'—i.e. standing aside and doing nothing in a challenging situation)? The answer seems partly to lie in the long history of pacifist thought within the churches, dating from the early days of Christianity when its practitioners were closest to the teaching of Jesus. In Him through the ages, and not least today, Christian pacifists have perceived the living embodiment of the rebel passion; the revolutionary leader who teaches reconciliation when the ethics of the Establishment demand not love but hate.

On September 17, 1960, when he dedicated the new headquarters of the International Fellowship in Finchley, London, Canon C. E. Raven described mankind as reaching its maturity only through the full knowledge of the Son of God — 'the measure of the stature of the fullness of Christ'. If we accept this interpretation of our God-ordained human destiny, we cannot help but regard war, the least inhibited expression of hate, as the extreme form of immaturity. Through it we press our claims, as children do, to the point of destruction. With its use of obsolete violence, war represents the supreme denial of Christ's teaching and the chief stumbling block to man's adoption of His methods. God's redemptive means of overcoming evil, the conversion of enemies into friends, becomes unattainable when we make a holocaust of those enemies, and put them beyond the reach of either friendship or repentance.

Just before the Second World War, Evelyn Underhill wrote that the Church was moving rapidly towards a moment in which, if she was to retain her integrity and spiritual influence, she must define (one might add 'unequivocally', since within recent years a number of skilfully ambiguous pronouncements have been made) her attitude towards war. When an atomic bomb fell on Hiroshima, that moment came. The problem of seeking and keeping world peace then ceased to be one great social concern amongst others; it became the dominant problem, for our failure to solve it means the end of seekers and solutions alike. Yet it is precisely here that the Christian comes into conflict with the State, for with the priority given to power the State enshrines immaturity in the seat of judgment. By not only permitting but encouraging a double standard of behaviour which the Christian as Christian cannot accept, it compels the rebel passion to become a revolutionary force.

Throughout history this revolutionary force has exerted an influence out of all proportion to its numbers. The handful of religious rebels who stood up for three centuries with unimpaired principles against the pagan might of Imperial Rome found, for example, their modest counterpart in the little Bedford church of John Bunyan, composed of humble local citizens 'very zealous according to their light', which became the heart and symbol of the values established by the Puritan Revolution. The light which illuminated their hearts is the same light that gives the 40,000 members of the International Fellowship their place in history.

What meaning, we shall ask, attaches to their fifty years of witness for this catastrophically menaced age, in which human beings, still helpless, face a situation where the mature qualities of wisdom and judgment are demanded to their maximum? This story of a scattered but united group of modern rebels will perhaps show that they have relevance for today in terms of that search for the Kingdom of God which may embody the secret of human survival both spiritual and physical.

We may well find that, in Goethe's words, 'Man is only creative when he is truly religious; without religion he becomes merely repetitive and imitative'. And we may conclude, with even more reason than Goethe, that the time for the repetition and imitation of past human errors has gone by, and that our society must try the harsh and painful path of charity and compassion where alone sacrifice achieves a creative end.

Chapter 2

PEACE-MAKING EXPERIMENTS
BEFORE 1914

Long before the Fellowship of Reconciliation was founded, a number of concerned citizens in several countries had been working for international amity. We need not go back so far as the seventeenth century 'Grand Design' of Sully, the great minister of Henry IV of France, or the *De Jure Belli et Pacis* of Hugo Grotius, published in 1625 as an answer to the anarchy created in Central Europe by the opening period of the Thirty Years War, to realize that a strong impulse towards peace, beginning with the Napoleonic Wars, existed during the century preceding 1914.

In an article on Nuclear Warfare published in *The Witness* (USA) for May 26, 1960, the Rev. John Nevin Sayre, the veteran American churchman and pacifist who for many years was Chairman of the New York Fellowship of Reconciliation, has written of 'the creative moving of the spirit in search of life breaking through the obstruction of military thinking and habit which has been shared by mankind generally for centuries'. Military thinking and habit of course had its strong influence during the immediate pre-war decade; Britain's Lord Roberts and Lord Kitchener, for example, spent the years between the Boer War and the First World War doing their best to make their equable fellow-citizens become war-minded, owing to the prevalence of conscription in Europe and their fear lest the sheer weight of the growing national military machines would break down the precarious balance of power between the Triple Alliance and the Triple Entente. But the endeavours made to preserve friendly relationships, and the popular expectation that these would continue indefinitely, dominated the international

scene to a degree never realized for years even by the survivors
of the young generation which bore the burden of the 1914
conflict, and certainly unknown to their modern successors apart
from a few students of history.

The first English-speaking peace societies arose directly after
the Napoleonic Wars, even though governments then regarded
war, or the threat of war, as a normal right of policy-making.
An article by Bertram Pickard on 'Friends and the Organisation
of Peace', published in *The Friend* for March 10, 1961, described
the century and a half since 1815 as divided, as though by a
great watershed, by the First World War and the League of
Nations. After the foundation of the League, governments began
to agree that war should be ended rather than modified, and
undertook, at least in theory, to renounce their freedom to make
war.

A number of conspicuous Quakers contributed their thinking
to the peace testimony of the nineteenth century. According to
an unpublished manuscript by Percy W. Bartlett, these included
Jonathan Dymond (1796-1828), who wrote a well-known 'Essay
on War'; William Allen (1770-1843), a founder of the London
Peace Society; Joseph Sturge (1793-1859), the first person to
propose the holding of international peace congresses; and John
Bright (1811-1889). Before the Schleswig-Holstein conflict of
1864-6, Joseph Sturge led deputations to the governments of
Germany and Denmark hoping to avert war, and John Bright,
as M.P. for Birmingham, made a moving speech against the
Crimean War in 1857.

Between 1815 and 1914 Bertram Pickard shows that there were
two distinct but overlapping movements towards peace. The first
concerned itself with the reasons for abolishing war, which was
seen as inconsistent with the Christian spirit and the true
interests of mankind; the second and later movement was both
more proletarian and more international, laying its emphasis on
social justice and political freedom. Throughout this century the
peace movement was a recognizable entity, with its co-ordinating bureaux and conferences quite unrelated to government
bodies. By 1914 about 500 separate organizations were included
within the peace movement as such.

Many of these arose in the United States, where as early as
1793 an enterprising free Negro from Baltimore named Benjamin

Bannecker had produced a 'Plan of a Peace Office', published in *Bannecker's Almanack*. In 1863, sixty years after Bannecker's death, an article in the *Atlantic Monthly* described him as 'the most original scientific intellect which the South has yet produced'. His plan, though much of it was naïve and fantastic, bore some resemblance to more recent proposals.

A hundred years before the Fellowship of Reconciliation began, a New England Congregational minister, the Rev. Noah Worcester, started a forty-page magazine called *The Friend of Peace*, not dissimilar from the contemporary American publication *Fellowship*. An early issue published the Constitution of the Massachusetts Peace Society, which took over the magazine. The numerous Christian ministers who belonged to the Society found it a convenient repository for their religious articles, though it also published occasional political commentaries. In 1829 the Society became an auxiliary of the newly established American Peace Society, and *The Friend of Peace* was eventually rechristened *The Calumet*.

By 1835 peace organizations had arisen in most of the States, and *The Calumet* had given way to *The Advocate of Peace* as the organ of the American Peace Society. Throughout the Civil War, though many ardent abolitionists among the Society's members supported Lincoln and the Union armies, *The Advocate* firmly maintained its pacifist outlook. When the war ended a new organization called the Universal Peace Society, which included the social reformer Lucretia Mott among its members, published an eight-page monthly called *The Bond of Peace*. The President of this Society was Arthur H. Love, who held this office from the beginning until his death in 1913.

After three years the Universal Peace Society supplanted its monthly magazine with a new radical journal, *The Voice of Peace*. An early contributor was Julia Ward Howe, author of the famous 'Battle Hymn of the Republic'. In 1883 the journal again changed its name to *The Peacemaker and Court of Arbitration*, edited by Henry S. Clubb. Its Vice-Presidents for 1884-5 included Clara Barton, the founder of the American Red Cross. All these endeavours must have been influenced, however unconsciously, by the European thinking of the period, which might be briefly described as a struggle between the ideas of Hegel and those of Kant.

Early in the sixteenth century Machiavelli, the Florentine author of *The Prince*, had exalted the unchristian character of the prevailing statecraft into a theory of political necessity, and represented man as a mere means to the State's ends. Two centuries later, Frederick the Great of Prussia discovered to his cost the dual pressures of ethics and political opportunism; though he disliked the work of Machiavelli he found himself compelled to follow him by 'political necessity', and in his own *Testament Politique* to justify his acts of violence by 'Reason of State'.

In 1795, nine years after the death of Frederick, Immanuel Kant (1724-1804), who held the Chair of Philosophy at the University of Königsberg, published his famous *Essay on Perpetual Peace* (*Ewige Friede*). For Kant, as Professor Heering, Doctor of Theology at Leyden University, has stated in *The Fall of Christianity* (1928), there was only one ethical standard—that to which conscience testified.

In Professor Heering's own view, the Church had steadily retreated since the days of Constantine before the encroachments of the State, the claims of which had come to dominate nineteenth-century thought owing largely to the work of Hegel (1770-1831), the greatest German philosopher of the post-Kantian period. Hegel, a Conservative thinker with an overwhelming intellect, created the philosophy of might; the State, powerful and therefore free, was his political ideal. For him it represented 'the visible, concrete Godhead'. Following Hegel, Johann Gottlieb Fichte (1762-1814), of the University of Jena, gave the State a practical meaning by seeing it as national life; to this German school, later interpreted by Heinrich von Treitschke (1834-96) and Friedrich Nietzsche (1844-1900), who died insane, the State was all and the individual human being a mere cog, an object of contempt.

Lone voices such as that of Bertha von Süttner, who wrote *Die Waffen Nieder* ('Lay Down Your Arms') after the wars of 1866 and 1870, had little chance to make themselves widely heard in the predominating Hegelian climate. But the type of thinking to which she gave expression was responsible for the numerous peace societies of the period, and found an echo in the work of the Dutch philosophers who, by the twentieth century, had departed from Hegel. These, besides Heering, included Professor H. Krabbe, for many years an enthusiastic advocate of the theory that the State is simply an instrument of justice, and Professor Leo Polak of Gröningen (eventually a Second World War martyr to the Nazi policy of exterminating the Jews), who as late as 1915 was insisting that war is essentially "a settlement of differences *not* by justice but by might". This outlook, and that of the peace societies, contributed to the relative serenity which gave a deceptive optimism to the international atmosphere of the year 1900.

In spite of the European tension created by the Franco-Prussian War, the imperialistic Jingoism of the struggle in South Africa, and the growing Anglo-German naval rivalry, the turn of the century, compared with the anxieties of our own menaced generation, appeared to many members of the contemporary public to be the threshold of a secure and beneficent age. Germany, it was true, had a young, vainglorious and ambitious ruler who tended to take too much into his own hands, but the Emperor William II, as historians have now established, was no warmonger. Britain, looking anxiously across the North Sea, eventually made the complicated war preparations described in Lord Hankey's *Memoirs*, but these precautionary measures, inspired by fear, did not mean any official desire for a 'showdown'.

Nobody in fact wanted war except for a few anarchic minorities in the turbulent countries of South-East Europe, which like all such restless groups, hoped that a major conflagration would somehow work out to their own advantage. The Hague Peace Conferences of 1899 and 1907, initiated in 1892 by Czar Nicholas II of Russia, fitted the hopes and expectations of the majority better than Lord Roberts's depressing demand for conscription and the Lloyd George - Churchill policy of naval armaments, which between them cast an incongruous and unwelcome shadow over that easy, prosperous age.

The Hague Conferences led to a general study of international law, developed procedures for conciliation, and established the Permanent Court of Arbitration to provide a substitute for war. Andrew Carnegie, the Scottish-American millionaire, gave £500,000 for the erection of that sadly ironic monument to human hopes, the Palace of Peace at The Hague, where the Court and various conferences met. One of the first Judges appointed to the Court was Sir Edward Fry, the father of Margery, Ruth and Roger Fry and their three sisters.

Writing of this period half a century later, Percy W. Bartlett found it difficult to convey the paradox which arose from the fact that two opposing statements were both true: first, that the 1914 war broke on the world as a surprise; secondly, that the foreign and military policies of the previous decade made it inevitable. Though the idealism which produced the Hague Conferences lowered the temperature of international suspicion, it was simultaneously raised by the braggadocio which accompanied Germany's military enterprises, and at the end of the decade by the Balkan Wars, largely disregarded as the serious warning that they should have been.

The Anglo-German naval rivalry, intensified by the Entente Cordiale between Britain and France, compelled politically-conscious persons to seek means of preventing a disastrous and undesired war. This task seemed especially urgent after a Press-engineered panic in 1909 caused the Dreadnoughts of the period, in spite of their relatively limited destructive power, to stir apprehensions similar to those more justifiably roused today by nuclear weapons. The growing threat brought a Christian concern, shared by Church leaders, radical M.P.s, and some representatives of municipal institutions, to counter it as far as possible across barriers and frontiers by moral strength and undaunted collaboration. Since Germany had now replaced France as the potential enemy in any war involving Britain, these efforts were concentrated on the creation of understanding between the two peoples.

A few other areas, such as Scandinavia and Holland, had well-established peace movements at this time, but these were too small to affect international policy, and the United States joined only sporadically in projects originating in Britain. The responsibility for drawing dedicated Christians together therefore fell mainly upon the minority British peace movement, combined with several leading Churchmen and Quakers, and a few publicists in both Britain and Germany. On the English side the initiative was taken by Joseph Rowntree, a Friend and Member of Parliament who, with Barrow Cadbury, largely financed the Christian Radicals in the House of Commons; and in Germany by F. Siegmund-Schültze, the Pastor of the Church at Potsdam who was closely in touch with the Kaiser, and is still today an outstanding member of the Fellowship of Reconciliation.

In 1905 an Anglo-German Conciliation Committee invited Archbishop Davidson of Canterbury to sign an address protesting at the mere thought of conflict between Britain and Germany. Dr Davidson agreed with the text but would not sign, giving as his reason that he did not wish to lend colour to the idea of strained relations. In her *Life of Geraldine S. Cadbury*, Janet Whitney relates that the following year a British Committee for the Study of Municipal Institutions invited a party of German mayors from Cologne, Dresden, Aachen and other cities to visit London. On the final day they travelled by special train to Birmingham to see Bournville, and discussed Anglo-German relations as well as industrial topics.

A history of the Ecumenical Movement by Ruth Rouse and Stephen C. Neill describes a Memorandum drawn up in 1907 to give expression 'to the Christian conviction that arbitration should be used as a means of settling conflicts between nations'. A special deputation presented this Memorandum to the Hague Conference, led by L. Allen Baker, M.P., who was especially interested in the exchange of visits. In the summer of 1908 the Seventeenth Universal Congress for Peace met in London, and about 130 German Churchmen arranged a visit to England to coincide with it. At Buckingham Palace King Edward VII and Queen Alexandra received a deputation from the Congress which included some of the German guests. The Congress itself adopted a resolution 'recognizing how greatly the world's peace depends upon the amicable relations between our two countries'.

Another endeavour to interest Archbishop Davidson in these attempts at reconciliation occurred in 1909, when Dr Scott Lidgett, President of the Free Church Council, asked him to consider the possible issue of a joint statement by Church leaders deploring the current talk about inevitable war. Again he refused to sign, on the ground that they must not be accused of political action, but he supported the idea of sending a representative group of British Churchmen to Germany to return the visit of 1908. On this occasion Dr Spiecker, the chairman of the German Committee, and its secretary, Dr F. Siegmund-Schültze, came to England in a specially chartered Hamburg-Amerika liner, *The Meteor*, to take the British party to Hamburg. It amounted to over 100 delegates, including four Anglican Bishops, several Roman Catholics, and five members of the Society of Friends led by Joseph Allen Baker and Barrow Cadbury.

The Kaiser welcomed his guests at Potsdam, and addressed them as 'gentlemen and brothers'. Subsequently Dr Siegmund-Schültze edited a souvenir volume recording their visit on behalf of the Churches' Committee for Promoting Friendly Relations between Great Britain and Germany. Archbishop Davidson accepted a copy of this publication, and wrote, in acknowledging it to John R. Ellis, a Quaker member of the group, 'It is in this kind of way, I believe, that public opinion or rather public sentiments, will be best elicited, consolidated, and made effective'.

In February 1911, representatives of the German Churches' Committee visited England. With them, besides Dr. Spiecker, came Professor Harnack of Berlin, a celebrated New Testament scholar. In the company of the Archbishop they visited Buckingham Palace, and on February 5th attended Divine Service in the private chapel where the King and Queen were present. Next day a meeting at the Queen's Hall, where the Archbishop presided, formed a British section of the 'Associated Councils of the Churches of the British and German Empires for fostering friendly relations'. Willoughby Hyett Dickinson, later Lord Dickinson of Painswick, became secretary of this Committee, and the Treasurers were Lord Kinnaird and Barrow Cadbury.

The late Stephen Hobhouse, in his autobiography *Forty Years and an Epilogue,* has recorded that various private groups arranged hospitality for these visiting parties. He himself, being fluent in German, was one of the hosts; others included Leonard and Kate Courtney, who had been leaders of the 'pro-Boer' party a decade earlier. Various small organizations, such as the Peace Committee of the Society of Friends and the Church of England Peace Society, also joined in these gestures of friendship. Most of them, foreshadowing the later International Fellowship of Reconciliation, had small 'opposite numbers' in a few continental countries.

Three years before the outbreak of war, a transatlantic visit by J. Allen Baker and F. Siegmund-Schültze to attend a Conference stirred a parallel interest in the United States, where the long-established American Peace Society was now growing conservative. The numerous clergymen among its founder-members in 1829 had long given place to realistic business executives, industrialists, and bankers, of whom the best known was Andrew Carnegie. At this time the more radical Universal Peace Society still existed, but in 1913 the death of Arthur H. Love brought the organization and its periodicals to an end.

In 1911 the Powers had been considering a draft Arbitration Treaty prepared by the United States, though relations between Britain and Germany were already strained and the Balkan Wars about to begin. Even then the peace endeavours continued, and J. H. Rushbrook edited a quarterly magazine, *The Peacemaker*, for the British Council of the Associated British and German Churches. A Conference to study Anglo-German understanding took place at the Guildhall in December 1912, and in 1913, when the Kaiser's demi-Jubilee was celebrated in Germany, the Associated British and German Churches presented an address of congratulation. Present there were both F. Siegmund-Schültze, who enjoyed the Kaiser's confidence, and Andrew Carnegie, who made to the Kaiser the first offer of a large sum to be used for the preservation of peace. Eventually he was persuaded to increase his gift to two million dollars.

Two aspects of these persevering but foredoomed peace efforts may be contrasted with the subsequent work of the Fellowship of Reconciliation. One was the belief that peace could be enforced by a league of many law-abiding nations confronting an 'aggressor', which was later developed in the constitutions of both the League of Nations and the United Nations. Another theory put its trust in the efficacy of 'police work' under international control, but later events were to reveal the illusory basis of these optimistic assumptions. In this twentieth century the unanimous agreement of 'righteous' nations has seldom been attainable, while the wars in Korea and Katanga showed, even more clearly than the Suez campaign, how quickly international 'police work' becomes indistinguishable from war.

In the United States Andrew Carnegie's substantial gift was used to establish the Church Peace Union, with Frederick Lynch as secretary. Through the Union invitations were sent out for an international conference of about 150 Churchmen, to be held

in Constance at the beginning of August 1914. War between
Germany and France, and Germany and Russia, was already
beginning as the Conference gathered. After telegraphing
appeals to the heads of the belligerent States, it was compelled
to break up, but succeeded in first forming the World Alliance
for Promoting International Friendship through the Churches,
later absorbed in the World Council of Churches and the (joint)
Churches' Commission on International Affairs. It was also a
precursor of the Fellowship of Reconciliation, since F. Siegmund-
Schültze and Henry T. Hodgkin, a founder of the British
Fellowship, were both present.

It is not quite clear how much the Fellowship owed to a draft
statement subsequently issued as a leaflet by the Society of
Friends, sent to Berlin, and circulated by F. Siegmund-Schültze
to German Church leaders and others. After the Conference had
ended, Henry Hodgkin and Dr Siegmund-Schültze travelled to
Cologne, there to be parted by the outbreak of war.

When they bade each other farewell, Siegmund-Schültze gave
his companion a pledge: 'Whatever happens, nothing is changed
between us'. Though they could not meet during the war years,
they managed to keep in touch and to discover other Christians
who, like themselves, refused to support the war and felt themselves divinely summoned to a ministry of reconciliation.

Chapter 3

THE I.F.o.R. 1914-39

In August 1914 the war that nobody wanted and everybody had prepared for flooded the world like a dark deluge. Historians such as Professors G. P. Gooch and Sidney B. Fay eventually concluded that the conflict was mainly the offspring of fear, and its immediate cause the hasty Russian mobilization which the Kaiser vainly endeavoured to check by frantic telegrams to the Czar. At first the waters of the storm submerged only Europe, but within a year many of the earth's remoter areas were feeling its force.

An immediate denunciation of the German invasion of Belgium, and the subsequent recruiting campaign, frustrated early protests against British involvement, though conscription did not come until 1916.

In an article published in Lansbury's *Labour Weekly* for March 7, 1925, George Lansbury recalled how men and women who had written and talked internationalism for twenty-five years were swept off their feet by the disingenuous 'scrap of paper' appeal to emotion. Though crowds gathered in London's Trafalgar Square on August 3rd to shout 'Down with the war', most of them two days later had been deceived by the Press into believing that 'honour' compelled them to take part.

The Society of Friends did what they could. Early in August, under Henry T. Hodgkin, just back from Constance, they drew up a 'Message to Men and Women of Goodwill' of which 475,000 copies were printed. On August 8th this message appeared as a paid advertisement in nine leading newspapers, and a copy, referred to in the previous chapter, reached Germany and was circulated there.

The message began by patriotically recognizing that 'our Government has made a most tremendous effort to preserve peace'—a view now substantially accepted, though the *Memoirs* of Lord Hankey, published in 1960, show that Britain was involved in detailed preparations for war long before 1914. It went on to make six main points: (1) The conditions which created the catastrophe were essentially unchristian; (2) Christians must not therefore forsake Christ, who was being crucified afresh; (3) obedience to His teaching involved courage 'in the cause of love and in the hate of hate'; (4) the gigantic folly now enveloping mankind would mean a stupendous task of reconstruction at the war's close; (5) to achieve this task the war should not be carried on vindictively, and must be ended as soon as possible; (6) faith and confidence in God would alone bring the fulfilment of His purpose 'after all the desolation and sorrow that lie before us'.

Six weeks later, at a Friends Conference in Llandudno, Arnold S. Rowntree, a Quaker M.P., discussed some of the policies which might have prevented the war. His suggestions included a recognition of the German fear of 'the Russian menace'; an effort to understand the four million German Social Democrats who wanted peace; an endeavour to establish a Federation of European States; and an attempt by 'the wider Church' to get in touch with Germans such as Harnack and Eucken who had themselves been fighting the philosophy of force. His speech echoed that of his Quaker colleague T. Edmund Harvey, who had said in the House of Commons on August 3rd: 'This war, for the great masses of the countries of Europe and not for our country alone, is no peoples' war. It is a war that has been made . . . by men in high places.'

For individuals among these peoples, the crisis had meant no estrangement; though the sense of corporate guilt weighed heavily on many who did not accept the war but still felt responsible, convictions pondered in isolation by those who could not follow the shouting crowds brought creative decisions even in the first year. Among the Friends at Llandudno were two future founders of the Fellowship of Reconciliation, Henry Hodgkin and Richard Roberts. In the American magazine *Fellowship* for January 1943 Richard Roberts described, in the middle of the Second War, the compulsions which moved him at the beginning of the First, and eventually led to the establishment of the F.o.R.

HENRY T. HODGKIN

RICHARD ROBERTS

LILIAN STEVENSON

LEYTON RICHARDS

Plate 1

CHARLES RAVEN

GEORGE LANSBURY

PERCY BARTLETT

MURIEL LESTER

Plate 2

In July 1914 Richard Roberts, then Minister of the Presbyterian Church at Crouch Hill, which had then perhaps the
largest evening congregation in North London, had attended the
first conference of the newly-formed Presbyterian Fellowship at
Swanwick in Derbyshire. He expected the existing international
tensions to be diplomatically resolved as many preceding crises
had been, but when he was at Swanwick war was declared.
Intending to preach at his own church on the first Sunday of the
conflict he promptly returned to London, but the prepared
address was never delivered. As he rose to give it, he noticed
that a group of young German business lads who attended his
church every Sunday were not there, and felt petrified by the
realization that the British and German members of his congregation might soon be killing each other on distant battle-
fields. He brought what seemed to him an appalling development before his hearers, and knew when he left the church that
as a Christian minister he could take no part in the war.

By telephone he summoned some younger ministers and lay-
men whom he knew to meet him at his empty house on Crouch
Hill. His guests included Dr W. E. Orchard, Edwyn Bevan and
Dr G. K. Bell, later Bishop of Chichester. It was a bewildered
gathering; none of them had considered the Christian attitude
to war since the Boer War over a decade ago. They expected
enlightenment from Henry Hodgkin, but he was as puzzled as
the rest. Only two certainties seemed clear to them; first, that
Britain was bound in honour to help France; secondly, that war
was unchristian.

They decided to meet again and to publish a series of Papers;
as editor they chose William Temple, later Archbishop of York
and of Canterbury. The first issue stated: 'The war remains in
the deepest sense a challenge to Christian thought', and
explained that the papers attempted to reach a truer understanding of Christianity and the Church.

Richard Roberts soon discovered a strong inclination towards
pro-war propaganda developing among their group; he and
Henry Hodgkin found themselves in a hopeless minority. Dr
Hodgkin's mind was now made up; the following March he was
to declare in an address to the annual meeting of the National
Free Church Council at Manchester: 'This war . . . is showing
us, in a very lurid light, how utterly unchristian a thing war

C

is . . . I for one cannot understand the position of my fellow Christians who frankly call men to arms in the name of Christ.'

The two friends did not immediately leave the group, but ceased to attend. Instead they invited all the people whom they knew shared their convictions to meet at a house in Pimlico called the Collegium, where a Quaker, Lucy Gardner, presided over a loosely-organized body of forward-looking persons. With time their number grew until the makings of a comprehensive association appeared. Their attempt to work out a mutually acceptable Christian pacifist philosophy had at first little ground for encouragement; the existing Peace Society in London had accepted the war as inevitable, and gave no light. But at last their search seemed to show a solid basis of agreement, capable of being stated. At this stage they called the Conference which met at Cambridge University, and formed the Fellowship of Reconciliation in the last four days of 1914.

Among 130 persons who gathered for that fateful New Year were several men and women well known in both England and America; besides Henry Hodgkin and Richard Roberts, they included George Lansbury, W. E. Orchard, Maude Royden, Leyton Richards and Lucy Gardner. One evening they sat far into the night to consider what their name should be, and next morning the description 'Fellowship of Reconciliation' was brought forward and adopted.

In his *Fellowship* article Richard Roberts explains that the word 'Reconciliation' was chosen partly to avoid confusion with the London Peace Society, but also to suggest that peace was much more than the absence of war. It was a method of waging war on war — 'the art and practice of turning enemies into friends'. Jesus was its chief exemplar, and its classical statement appeared in St Paul's Second Epistle to the Corinthians: 'If any man be in Christ, he is a new creature; old things are passed away; behold, all things are become new. And all things are of God who hath reconciled us to Himself by Jesus Christ, and has given to us the ministry of reconciliation.' (II Corinthians v, 17-19.)

This passage implies that reconciliation is a universal principle, to be practised in all departments of life; in store, office, workshop and home. The members of the newly-formed Fellowship saw it as God's will that men should be reconciled to Him and to one another; and at Cambridge they drew up a five-point document, later known as 'The Basis', which expressed their common convictions:

1. 'That Love, as revealed and interpreted in the life and death of Jesus Christ, involves more than we have yet seen, that it is the only power by which evil can be overcome, and the only sufficient basis of human society.'

2. 'That, in order to establish a world-order based on Love, it is incumbent upon those who believe in this principle to accept it fully, both for themselves and in their relation to others, and to take the risks involved in doing so in a world which does not as yet accept it.'

3. 'That, therefore, as Christians, we are forbidden to wage war, and that our loyalty to our country, to humanity, to the Church Universal, and to Jesus Christ, our Lord and Master, calls us instead to a life service for the enthronement of Love in personal, social, commercial and national life.'

4. 'That the Power, Wisdom and Love of God stretch far beyond the limits of our present experience, and that He is ever waiting to break forth into human life in new and larger ways.'

5. 'That since God manifests Himself in the world through men and women, we offer ourselves to Him for His redemptive purpose, to be used by Him in whatever way He may reveal to us.'

Those who drew up this statement did not put it forward as final. What they wished to see was not a common creed, but one spirit animating a living body. To this end they laid down three general principles: first, that the Fellowship would work constructively for reconciliation, and not spend its energies in mere protest; secondly, that its purpose was to bring into being a new order based on Christian principles; thirdly, that members should work out the implications of membership in their own lives, and not be tied to a stereotyped programme. The Fellowship was thus immediately distinguished from other peace and pacifist organizations, for the founders realized (as we are still realizing in this nuclear age) that most men are incapable of learning from experience, and can be saved only through grace divinely bestowed.

The second principle explained that the testimony of the Fellowship related especially to war because its origin came from an international crisis. But those who drafted it understood (like Gandhi when he founded his school, Nai Talim, for education in non-violence at Sevagram in the Central Provinces of India) that the law of love is violated in many other ways. Industrial strife, colonial exploitation, and commercial competition are all forms of violence, though war is the most extreme.

The Fellowship 'basis' involved a total change in the values by which men lived and by which the majority still live today. Its members resolved not only to present Christianity as a creative way of life, but immediately to reach through neutrals to like-minded people on the other side of the conflict.

It was a hard undertaking in wartime, when it would certainly involve not only unpopularity, misrepresentation and isolation, but official suspicion and even persecution. Those who foresaw these consequences had good reason; in August 1915, the offices of the pacifist *Labour Leader* were raided by the police, and in two wars pacifists were to become accustomed to constant police supervision. Yet, whatever possibilities lay in the logic of events, those who attended that first F.o.R. meeting subsequently testified to the feeling of light emerging from darkness which came when each found himself or herself to be no longer alone. By November 1915, 1,550 members had registered.

In view of the inevitable influence of time upon the use and effect of words the unmodified survival of this basic statement through fifty years seems remarkable, especially when we consider the normal human reaction of the reserved Anglo-Saxons to emotional expressions. 'I always feel suspicious when I hear the word "love"', a dedicated political pacifist recently remarked to the author of this book, who agreed that the expression 'love' is impaired by sentimentalities and hypocrisies. On the rare occasions when we are able to respond to the formidable New Testament injunctions to love our enemies and love our neighbours as ourselves, few of us could honestly say that we feel an emotional affection towards either an enemy or a neighbour (though we may be deeply stirred by a neighbour's special happiness or particular tragedy).

One difficulty arises because in the English language 'love' is an umbrella word, covering a whole series of different emotions. Where English has one word, the richer Greek has three—*eros* (sexual passion, hardly ever used in the New Testament), *philia* (friendship), and *agape* (charity or good will). When Jesus said 'Love your enemies', the actual words used in the Greek are *agapate tous echthrous humon.* The Fellowship founders used the word 'love' in the sense of *agape,* the persistent charity which Jesus showed towards his friends, his enemies, and those whom 'respectable' society judged and condemned—publicans and sinners, the adultress, the prostitute, the despised Samaritan and the dying thief.

In the autumn of 1915 Henry Hodgkin, as secretary of the Friends' foreign missions, went over to America and addressed a hundred meetings on 'the reinterpretation of Jesus Christ in the light of present world conditions'. In November he was invited to a Conference at Garden City, Long Island, to consider the meaning of the words 'Love your enemies' in a world at war.

At this time the United States was still neutral, but strong popular feeling favoured her participation in the war, and thoughtful persons felt compelled to define their position. On November 11th and 12th the Conference formed an American Fellowship, which published a leaflet containing the following paragraph:

'The distinctive note of the Fellowship is its repudiation of war and commitment to a way of life creative of brotherhood . . . Membership implies such a dedication to the practice of the principle of love as the inviolable law of personal relationships and the transforming power of human life that any use or countenance of the war method by those who belong is impossible.'

One thousand members enrolled in the United States before and during the war, which for them began on April 6, 1917. American participation brought an outbreak of intolerance which weighed heavily on the young Fellowship. Its members soon found themselves fighting for liberty of thought, speech and the right to meet. Many went to prison as conscientious objectors after severe sentences at courts-martial; others worked in reconstruction units or as chaplains. In April 1917 the American *Advocate of Peace* magazine had carried a statement by the leaders of the F.o.R. opposing America's entry into the war, but when war was declared this publication, which had stood so firmly by its pacifist principles during the Civil War, supported the government.

In 1916 Richard Roberts and, for a brief period, Leyton
Richards, another F.o.R. founder, followed Henry Hodgkin to
America. During the same year the new movement was taken
to Holland by Cornelis Boeke, where a 'Brotherhood in Christ'
arose. Two years later a small group came together in Stockholm
and formed a 'League for Christian Citizenship' in which radical
social reform was allied with the witness against war. In Denmark a group known as *Kristeligt Fredsforbund*, founded in
1913, became affiliated with the Fellowship.

The members of the British F.o.R. found the churches to
which they belonged gradually shaken by catastrophe from their
dull pre-war lethargy. One of the first to manifest a revolutionary
spirit was London's St Martin-in-the-Fields, where a young ex-
chaplain called H. R. L. Sheppard returned physically shattered
from a brief experience at the front to become Vicar of the now
famous church in Trafalgar Square. Soon he was keeping its
crypt open all night for soldiers returning from France and
civilians caught by Zeppelin raids, which caused little damage
though the small bombs that they dropped seemed terrifying to
contemporary Londoners.

Hitherto only the Suffragettes had challenged the right of
established conventions to go on existing, but the new Vicar of
St Martin's was to join and eventually to lead those who ques-
tioned the compatibility of Christianity and war. Many of his
fellow clergy then preached recruiting sermons, and some even
used the skeleton addresses officially prepared for them.

The only refugee problem was that of the Belgians; no displaced persons existed apart from the inhabitants of battle areas,
and there were no dictators to deserve the exaggerated accusations levelled at the Kaiser. Several anti-German raids followed
the sinking of the *Lusitania* in 1915, and angry mobs looted
shops owned by Germans and Austrians.

The long casualty lists eventually brought conscription. After
it came tribunals for the relatively few and much-abused war
resisters; men who refused to fight were sent under guard to
their regiments and then transferred to civil prisons. Little
understanding of the conscientious objector was shown even in
England; still less revealed itself in Germany and the rest of the
Continent. No radio or television helped to form public opinion;
instead, British citizens saw war posters which showed either

an anxious man being asked by his small son: 'What did you do in the Great War, Daddy?' or a tough-looking soldier beckoning to passers-by above the caption: 'He's happy and comfortable. Are you?' The public were also exposed to lurid propaganda stories, such as those of violated Belgian nuns, crucified soldiers, and the 'corpse factory'. All these were disproved ten years after the war by Arthur Ponsonby's well-known classic, *Falsehood in Wartime*.

Against this background, the Fellowship of Reconciliation began to do its work. Though its members were isolated, they could meet more frequently than the overworked citizens of the nineteen-sixties. Travel was cheaper, and there were fewer demands on the time of leaders and thinkers. Household work was still done for the well-to-do by the poor, though towards the end of the war munition factories had absorbed most of the domestic helpers, and middle-class housewives, to their astonished resentment, found themselves doing their own domestic work with much less casual competence than is customary today.

On the Fellowship's return from Cambridge, a Central Committee, with Henry Hodgkin as chairman and Lucy Gardner as secretary, was formed to carry on for a year. For a time they continued to meet at the Collegium, but this proved to be too inaccessible. As Lucy Gardner could not leave her duties to go daily to an office, both a secretary and an office had to be found. Eventually the Fellowship established itself in Red Lion Square, Bloomsbury, where its rooms had once been used by William Morris and D. G. Rossetti. Henry Hodgkin invited Richard Roberts to be secretary, and as his relations with his church had sharply deteriorated owing to his attitude towards the war, he accepted the offer and began work on July 1, 1915.

The staff still consisted of the secretary and a typist, occasionally augmented by voluntary workers. One of the first volunteers was Lewis Maclachlan, the highly intelligent sardonic Scot who subsequently, for many years, edited the magazine *Reconciliation*. Another early volunteer was George Llewellyn Davies, a banker from Wales who as a Territorial Army officer became convinced of the evils of militarism and resigned his commission. When he recalled this handsome young man many years afterwards, a phrase 'the sun in splendour' came into

Richard Roberts' mind. Many other would-be members wrote from towns and churches where they had thought themselves alone in their belief that the war could not be supported on Christian grounds. Now they knew themselves to be, not solitary eccentrics, but part of a larger whole. Some found difficulty in formulating an intellectual presentation of their faith, and looked to the F.o.R leaders to guide them.

In December 1916, after Asquith had resigned as Prime Minister and a more vigorous Win-the-War administration had been formed under Lloyd George, Leyton Richards, afterwards minister of Carr's Lane Congregational Church, Birmingham, succeeded Richard Roberts as British General Secretary. Richard Roberts had then received a call to become minister of the Church of the Pilgrims in Brooklyn, N.Y., and Leyton Richards had just returned from a four months' visit to America where he followed up Henry Hodgkin's work. At that time Woodrow Wilson had been re-elected to the Presidency owing to a liberal use of the slogan 'Woodrow Wilson Wins Without War', and the cinemas echoed to a popular song, 'I didn't raise my boy to be a soldier'.

It was not then possible for the Fellowship to begin its basic missionary work by sending 'apostles' of reconciliation to other countries, though 'the art and practice of turning enemies into friends' was part of its technique from the beginning. Its first tasks therefore appeared to lie in attempts to influence public opinion and to help victims of war, such as the stranded enemy nationals threatened by mob violence. Some members joined the Friends' groups working among refugees or civilians in devastated areas; others succeeded in getting messages through to Christians in Germany. Some of these were published in *Die Eiche*, a German quarterly magazine, for January 1917, and included a balanced leaflet drawn up by the Fellowship after the sinking of the *Lusitania*.

When conscription began in Britain in 1916 and in the United States in 1917, many F.o.R. members refused military service. In Britain about 600 went to prison, to help furnish the total of approximately 16,000 imprisoned during the war. Older members not liable to the call-up co-operated by attending courts-martial, visiting prisoners, sending out circulars containing advice, founding an emergency fund to help the families of the men involved, and periodically taking joint action with the No Conscription Fellowship and the Friends' Service Committee.

No detailed figures exist of Continental war-resisters at this time, as the only effectively organized movement was in Britain. But in Germany, Austria, Hungary, Bohemia and even France, there were men who refused to fight and received treatment similar to that of British conscientious objectors. In Hungary, where many Nazarenes declined to serve in the Army, whole-sale shootings occurred.

The Fellowship published a sequence of books by Christian thinkers, re-stating the fundamental religious basis of peace-making, called *The Christian Revolution Series*, and in October 1915 founded a brown-covered thirty-two-page monthly magazine 'of Christian thought and practice', *The Venturer*. Its name was suggested by a passage from F. W. H. Myers' popular poem *St Paul*:

> 'Lo, as some venturer, from his stars receiving
> Promise and presage of sublime emprise,
> Wears evermore the soul of his believing
> Deep in the dark of solitary eyes.'

The first issue included articles by W. E. Orchard, Henry Hodgkin, Richard Roberts and Maude Royden, and the monthly notes were contributed by H. W. Horwill, a Fellowship member and one of the best journalists in London. The little magazine breathed a naïve idealism which seems pathetic today, but its first editorial correctly estimated the significance of the times: 'The war is the nemesis and the end of an age . . . This is the most terrific and the most critical hour since Calvary . . . It is very little of the old world that we shall carry over into the new . . . The task before us is none other than the creation of a new world.'

Few would-be peacemakers realized in 1915 how grimly like the old this new world would become.

Between 1916 and 1918 several unofficial efforts were made to end the war by negotiation. These seldom reached the ears of the public. The best-known arose from a memorandum circulated in November 1916 by Lord Lansdowne, a member of the Cabinet, who had been responsible for the *Entente Cordiale* in 1904. According to Lloyd George's *War Memoirs*, he made no

actual constructive proposals, but within the next few weeks
the contents of his memorandum, followed in 1917 by a letter
to the *Daily Telegraph*, became vaguely known, and led to some
anti-war demonstrations.

One of these (described by Frank Hancock, a F.o.R. member
who took part, in *Reconciliation* for January 1962) occurred in
April 1917 in Victoria Park, Bow, after a procession from
Canning Town. Those who joined included Mrs. Despard, the
sister of Sir John (later Lord) French; Sylvia Pankhurst; Muriel
Lester; Rosa Hobhouse; and Marian Ellis, later Lady Parmoor.
The meeting was broken up by soldiers and hostile civilians, but
even to convinced non-pacifists the efforts of Lord Lansdowne
and his incongruous East End supporters appear in a different
light today.

Three months later a number of Swedish Christians invited
the Pope and twenty-five Protestant communions to attend a
Church Conference of Neutrals in Upsala. The American
Federal Council of the Churches agreed that it was 'not advisable'
for the Council to take part, but a more positive response came
from Britain, which in November 1917 set up a 'British Council
for promoting an International Christian meeting', with several
prominent supporters. *The Venturer* later described this Conference, held in December 1917 and attended by representatives
of Denmark, Holland, Norway, Sweden and Switzerland, as 'a
great source of strength to us and our brethren'.

An even less publicized endeavour was reported by Professor
George D. Herron in a remarkable article called 'A Golden
Bridge Unbuilt', which appeared in *The World Tomorrow* (the
American predecessor of *Fellowship*) in December 1921. This
article described a meeting on February 3, 1918, between George
Herron himself, Colonel William Godson, the American Military Attaché at Berne, and Professor Heinrich Lammasch, the
last Prime Minister of Austro-Hungary. They discussed a peace
to be obtained, under the mutual auspices of President Wilson
and the Emperor Karl, through the withdrawal of Austria from
the war and her initiation of a European programme according
to Wilsonian principles.

This noble effort by Lammasch — whom Professor Herron
described as 'one of the world's last statesmen and most saintly
personalities'—failed owing to the emperor's inability to play

his part. The story recalls the unavailing struggle of the Swedish industrialist, Berger Dahlerus, described in his book *The Last Attempt*, to prevent the outbreak of the Second World War by non-stop periods of negotiation between Germany, Sweden and Britain in the last days of August 1939.

No further endeavour to end the war seems to have occurred until the Armistice itself, which since November 1918 has meant for Christians not only the tragedies of that epoch, but the rebirth of the peace movement during the years in which a growing number of men and women realized that participation in war was inconsistent with their religious faith.

The Fellowship perceived from the beginning that truth and brotherhood would have to be carried across frontiers as soon as possible when the war ended. One of its first members to go to Germany was Oswald Garrison Villard, grandson of William Lloyd Garrison and editor of the American *Nation*, who was also to find himself 'Inside Germany' in the autumn of 1939. To the displeasure of President Wilson when the Peace Conference was sitting at Versailles and the defeated enemy were being starved by the naval blockade, Mr Villard got through to Berlin in February 1919.

To coincide with his visit *The World Tomorrow* published an editorial on 'World Chaos and Versailles', and in June he himself contributed an article called 'Germany in Collapse'. He began by recording that, when he entered Berlin, he saw on its dead walls a coloured lithograph which for him symbolized the fallen nation's demoralization. It showed a young woman dancing with a skeleton above the legend: 'Berlin, don't you see who your partner is? It is death.'

In December 1919 a two-page Christmas Appeal for the starving children of Austria and Germany appeared in the magazine. It need hardly be said that, at this date, attempts to stir the 'rebel passion' on behalf even of the children of a defeated nation were rare indeed.

In October 1919 fifty men and women from ten countries, including those recently at war, met at Bilthoven, near Utrecht. Invitations had been sent to them in the names of Henry Hodgkin and Cornelis Boeke, a Dutch violinist who had been forced by British antagonism against foreigners to leave England when war began. With his English wife he established a gaily-painted 'Brotherhood House', and here the Conference gathered. Thence was to come the impulse which carried the F.o.R. message to over twenty nations. Those present included F. Siegmund-Schültze from Germany, Mathilda Wrede (a Finnish Margery Fry), Pierre Cérésole from Switzerland, Henry Hodgkin and Leyton Richards from Britain, and Noble Elderkin, the Western secretary of the American F.o.R.

The delegates took meals together under the pines, and exchanged impressions of the war years. It soon became clear that convictions similar to those of the British and American F.o.R. leaders had grown independently in many countries. Of this Conference Lilian Stevenson, who was present, has written: 'No effort was made to achieve unity, for unity was a central fact . . . We met as strangers; we parted a Fellowship.' Together the delegates faced the grim legacies of the war; their sense of corporate guilt subsequently appeared in a message entitled 'The Way' drawn up on German initiative and sent out after the Conference. The key sentence ran: 'We all stand condemned before God. None can cast a stone at his brother.'

This Conference formed the 'Movement Towards a Christian International', changed after some years to 'International Fellowship of Reconciliation'. When it ended a group of delegates travelled round Holland, and held meetings in six towns which included Amsterdam, Rotterdam, and The Hague.

In July 1920 a second Bilthoven Conference of sixty people from sixteen countries brought the movement in touch with three categories of experience not represented at the first meeting—the Youth Movements of Germany and Switzerland, groups from the Roman Church, and the Eastern Christians who had delegates present. Clashes of temperament within this diverse assembly symbolized the restlessness and unsatisfied longing which dominated the post-war world. But these two conferences, with their 1914 predecessor, laid the foundations of the I.F.o.R. The second was followed by a reconciliation tour through the chief German cities by five delegates, Dutch (Boeke), British (Oliver Dryer), French (Leon Revoyre), German (Walter Koch), and American (John Nevin Sayre). Great plans were made, but there was little money to carry them out.

The work of the I.F.o.R. came to be directed by a Council of twelve or fifteen members, and an Executive of about nineteen which carried on between the Council meetings. The national centres elected their own representatives to the Council. The international office, linking both the centres and the members in countries where no centre existed, was first established at Bilthoven and in 1921 transferred to London with Oliver Dryer as secretary. In 1929 it moved to Vienna under Donald Grant, where a centre for Eastern and Central Europe had become necessary.

One delegate to Bilthoven had been an Austrian Roman Catholic priest, Max Josef Metzger (later martyred by the Nazis), who with another Catholic priest, Johannes Ude, had preached anti-war sermons in Graz. Metzger founded a religious society, 'Das Weisse Kreuz' ('the White Cross') and organized—still at that date without official interference—an international Committee of leading Catholics who sent peace testimonies to the Pope and the Emperor. At Bilthoven he became a founder of the I.F.o.R., and set up a special secretariat for peace work in the Catholic Church. Of this Kaspar Mayr acted as secretary until his transfer to the London office in 1924. From that time onwards attempts were made to win Catholics for the I.F.o.R., and until 1934, when the Nazi movement put an end to the work, Conferences were held in Luxemburg, Berlin, Warsaw and Cracow, and speaking tours organized in the main Polish towns.

In 1933 Pasteur Henri Roser became I.F.o.R. secretary, and the frustrated Vienna office went to Paris. Five years later it moved again to London under Percy Bartlett.

Inevitably the post-war work of the I.F.o.R. related itself to the social efforts of the Churches. In Britain these had found a focus in the United Summer Schools organized by Lucy Gardner at the S.C.M. Conference House at Swanwick; thence came the 1924 C.O.P.E.C. Conference in Birmingham which tried, without reaching agreement, to face the challenge of pacifism. Throughout Europe, only a minority within the Churches accepted the pacifist convictions which led them to urge that the Church should be faithful to what seemed to them to be the real meaning of the Cross, and should not allow its pulpits, as in 1914, to become recruiting platforms.

By 1928 the British magazine *Reconciliation* was hopefully

recording that 'since 1914 the mind of the Church has been changing', but safe respectability still appeared to be its policy for all but the few.

Occasionally those few exerted an influence out of all proportion to their numbers. In 1924 the German Catholic peace movement expressed at its Conference the view that, though there might be a righteous war in theory, 'actually the conditions are wanting which Catholic ethics lays down for a war to be sanctioned'. In the same year, thirty Dutch clergymen opposed to war founded the association *Kerk en Vrede*.

During 1925 a Union of Anti-Militarist Clergymen was formed in Switzerland which in August 1926 issued an international Anti-Conscription Manifesto. This followed a proposal in 1924 to form a society in France for the legal recognition of conscientious objectors, a petition signed by 40,000 people in Switzerland demanding the introduction of alternative service, and a Government Bill in Finland for the same purpose.

The seventy distinguished signatories of the Manifesto included C. F. Andrews, Norman Angell, Einstein, Gandhi, Romain Rolland, Bertrand Russell, Tagore, and H. G. Wells. It contained the statement: 'It is humiliating to human dignity to compel men against their will . . . to sacrifice their lives or to kill others'. A British move followed in 1927 with a Peace Letter submitted to the Prime Minister by Arthur Ponsonby, Under-Secretary for Foreign Affairs in the first Labour Government, in which the 128,770 signatories refused their support to any war. In 1928, 135 ministers of the Dutch Evangelical Lutheran Church declared war to be opposed to the fundamental principles of Christianity.

Among lay peace bodies at the opening of the inter-war era, the International Peace Bureau, which had organized many pre-war peace conferences, found itself unable to cover the numerous groups drawn into the orbit of the League of Nations. Such co-ordinating societies as the National Peace Council achieved some valuable work, but the new and active League of Nations Union did not readily co-operate with the older organizations, or pretend to be pacifist. Leading pacifists such as Mrs H. M. Swanwick, who occasionally worked with it, were not popular among its conservative officials.

The Fellowship, in addition to its pacifist education, began a comprehensive programme of social work which continued between the wars. Immediately after Bilthoven its members joined Friends and others in feeding hungry Austrian, German and Russian children. When the need for this relief ended, the I.F.o.R. initiated a series of Youth Camps and Summer Schools for younger leaders at Oberammergau in 1926, Vaumarcus above Lake Neuchâtel in 1927, and Sandwich on the Kent coast in 1928. In May 1924, *The World Tomorrow* published a challenging article on the international youth movement by Devere Allen, later editor, with his wife Marie, of the American news sheet *Worldover Press*. This early work forged continuous links with the developing I.F.o.R. Youth Movement of today, typified by the travelling embassies of the young Catholics, Hildegard and Jean Goss-Mayr.

Political and industrial mediation also formed part of the Fellowship's work. Political intervention included a mission to Ireland during the period of tension with England which preceded the establishment of the Irish Free State, and a Friendship Mission to Central America in 1927. Industrial mediation found ample scope in the prevalent unemployment and distress among English and Welsh miners, particularly during the coal dispute which led to the General Strike in 1926. Similar work was done at the time of hosiery and textile strikes in New York State in 1930 and 1931, and among unemployed Liverpool dock labourers in 1927.

Immediately after Bilthoven, the Fellowship began to organize goodwill tours and to appoint travelling secretaries, such as John Nevin Sayre, André Trocmé, Muriel Lester, Henri Roser and Percy Bartlett. One of the earliest international reconstruction units inspired by the Fellowship worked under Pierre Cérésole in a devastated area near Verdun, where the inhabitants typified the human disillusionment that the war had brought to France.

A typescript by John Nevin Sayre records a tour made in 1921, and the reconciliation work which he observed in Europe. He describes the collection of clothing for Austria which he saw in the British F.o.R. office; his own international mission of popular reconciliation, carried out with four colleagues in sixteen German cities where neither national patriots nor local police interfered with the speakers; the Verdun experiment in which a Swiss, a Dutchwoman, three Germans and a Hungarian rebuilt the homes of French peasants and restored the shell-blasted fields; and the work of British Beatrice Hoysted in Vienna, where over forty Austrians joined the F.o.R.

Many later tours carried the Fellowship's message to Scandinavia, Central Europe and Poland, and even to such difficult pioneer areas as the Baltic States and the Balkans. From these travels grew the sequence of international conferences which the I.F.o.R. arranged in the twelve years that followed the war.

The first large international Conference brought 200 delegates from twenty nations and many communions to Sonntagberg, a hill-top amid the Austrian Alps. Among them were representatives from far countries such as India, Burma, and Ukrainia. Together they examined the implications of their faith, and sent a message 'to the Churches and Christians in all lands' asking the Church to 'call fearlessly for a policy of complete forgiveness towards enemies past and present'.

In 1923, 200 came together at Nyborg in Denmark to discuss social and political problems. Many Scandinavians attended, and Leonhard Ragaz of Switzerland, who was also there, noted in his book *Mein Weg* 'a very mixed company', which included Dr Metzger from Graz and Professor Hermann Hoffmann from Breslau. 'Because of the motley presented by the existing Fellowship,' he recorded, 'it was a big problem to find a common ground.'

The fifth Conference in 1924 at Bad Boll in Würtemberg was therefore restricted to 100 in the hope of responsibly discussing the Fellowship's foundations. This time the eighty delegates, including three from Bulgaria, represented seventeen countries. Professor Ragaz was again present and again critical. ('I tried to get the Fellowship back to its Bilthoven origin . . . For days did we fight for these things in the pavilion in the great park.') Eventually, because 'truth became more and more important than reconciliation', he broke with the Fellowship. This episode illustrated the difficulty experienced by post-war international movements discussing fundamentals in reaching agreement, but the Conference did eventually issue a statement on the religious basis of their deliberations.

Two years later the Fellowship met at Oberammergau, the Bavarian home of the Passion Play, where 220 delegates from twenty-four nations discussed the disarmament difficulties of

JOHN HAYNES HOLMES

NORMAN THOMAS

PAUL JONES

JOHN NEVIN SAYRE

Plate 3

KEES BOEKE

NATANAEL BESKOW

PIERRE CERESOLE

PREMYSL PITTER

Plate 4

Western Europe and the minority problems of south-eastern countries. Present also were forty-four students of international affairs, carefully chosen for their expert knowledge whether they belonged to the Fellowship or not.

This period was one of European tension, especially between Stresemann and Mussolini; it did not then become acute because both Austria and Germany were disarmed. The growth of nationalism was not peculiar to Italy; Spain, Greece, Roumania and Bulgaria had all tried to initiate dictatorships, and Germany, France and Poland were beginning to demand them. In March 1926 the Editor of *Reconciliation*, who saw disarmament as the chief solution for Europe's problems, pertinently asked: 'What will happen when the fearful horrors of the last war have been forgotten and the now impoverished peoples have regained their strength if in the meantime the powers of reconciliation do not prevail?' The reader of the nineteen-sixties, who knows the answer, can only comment: 'What indeed!'

Four years after the Oberammergau Conference, the Fellowship experimented by establishing a hostel there for the four months' duration of the Passion Play. Local permission was obtained owing to the favourable impression left by the 1926 gathering, and 1,170 visitors from fifteen countries eventually passed through this hostel. The majority were strangers to the I.F.o.R., who thus became acquainted with its work. In the interval further conferences had been held at Vaumarcus (1927) and Lyons (1929), and in 1931, 140 persons met at Lunteren in Holland to discuss Disarmament, Treaty Revision, Christianity, and War.

The Vaumarcus Conference in French Switzerland was an International Youth Camp which commemorated the 700th anniversary of St Francis of Assisi. Two hundred young people discussed 'St Francis and the Youth of Today', and the speakers included Max Josef Metzger, whose hymn, 'O *Seliger Tag*', the Conference, led by him at the piano, sang on the morning of his departure. Among those present were Premysl Pitter from Czechoslovakia, Henri Roser and André Trocmé from France, and Kaspar Mayr from Vienna. The young delegates concluded by dedicating themselves to God round a great fire laid on the hillside.

The hopes of that time centred in youth movements and

D

international conferences; the long marches which expressed
these enthusiasms foreshadowed the marches that began forty
years later in protest against the development of nuclear weapons.
In all discussions a potential clash was apparent between the
conservatives who looked for salvation from peace-building
institutions such as the League of Nations, and the radicals who
relied on an individual determination to renounce violence.

During 1928 the I.F.o.R. office moved to Vienna, where owing
to the 'continued breakdown' of Oliver Dryer, Kaspar Mayr
took charge until the arrival of Donald Grant in 1929. At this
time the original Kellogg proposals, acceptable to the peace
movement, were being modified by European reservations which
turned the plan into a distant relative of the original.

In February 1932, a year distracted by economic catastrophe
and the rise of Europe's formidable new nationalisms, the
Geneva World Disarmament Conference began. On its opening
day the I.F.o.R. started a Youth Crusade which 'marched for
disarmament' across France and Germany by several routes con-
verging on Geneva. Protestants and Catholics from all over
Europe co-operated in this demonstration; 150 meetings were
held *en route* for audiences sometimes as large as 1,600. When
the march reached its goal, 50,000 people had heard its international team of French, German, English, Dutch and Belgian
speakers.

Finally twelve representatives presented the Crusade Petition
to Arthur Henderson, the President of the Conference. It called
for the recognition of total disarmament as the goal of all states,
and ended with the words: 'We refuse . . . to take part in a
new war whose victims will be youth'.

But the times were now resistant to such initiatives. In
October, after deputations from the Churches and the Trade
Union Congress had expressed disquiet at the slow progress of
the discussions, Germany left the Conference. In November the
'economic blizzard' in the United States, following the Wall
Street crash of 1929, carried Roosevelt and the Democrats to
power. Even in these lean years, the American F.o.R. managed
to give over $8,500 to the work of the Fellowship in Europe.

January 1933 saw Hitler's election as Chancellor, which began
the sequence of events that led—uninterrupted by any example
of enlightened statesmanship save the unofficial Embassies of

Reconciliation between 1936 and 1938—by stages covering six years to the Second World War.

In the sinister light of these events the Youth Crusade might appear to have failed, but its tradition remained to inspire the young marchers of a distant future.

The nineteen-thirties witnessed the decline of the League of Nations, undermined by its continuing reputation as a body which perpetuated the *status quo* established at Versailles. Its authority was finally wrecked by the persistent abstention of the United States, the refusal of Great Britain to interfere with the Japanese adventure in Manchuria, the breakdown of the Disarmament Conference, Hitler's re-introduction of conscription and re-occupation of the Rhineland in 1936, its flaccid detachment from the Spanish Civil War, and its failure to prevent aggression in China, Abyssinia, Austria and Czechoslovakia.

Throughout these darkening years only two sources of light penetrated the gloom. The first was the growing influence of Mahatma Gandhi, and the second the great experiment made by the I.F.o.R. in creating the Embassies of Reconciliation.

Gandhi had come from India to London in 1931 to take part in the Round Table Conference. From Muriel Lester's East End settlement, Kingsley Hall, where he was staying, he broadcast a message attributing the moral influence of India's struggle to 'the fact that the means adopted by us . . . are not bloodshed, not violence, nor diplomacy as one understands it nowadays. They are purely and simply truth and non-violence'.

Thenceforth it became clear that a spiritual technique for resisting evil and achieving social transformation had again come into the world. The same principles inspired the Embassies of Reconciliation, which even at that late hour might have averted war had the I.F.o.R. initiative been powerfully backed by any important Government.

That noble failure was preceded by some less radical but useful endeavours to create an appropriate atmosphere for conciliation. In 1932, 1935 and 1937, three small Conferences were held at Bentveld (Holland), Knocke (Belgium) and Zürich (Switzerland). The last was intended to facilitate personal contacts between Italian friends of the I.F.o.R. and members in Switzerland, France and Austria, but no Austrians came because travel permits were refused. The German Fellowship had 'voluntarily' dissolved itself in 1933.

In Britain the experiment known as the 'Christ and Peace Campaign' linked pacifist with non-pacifist Christians in a series of large public meetings which ended with a Conference at Oxford in 1931. At the suggestion of the F.o.R. in 1934, the various denominational Peace Fellowships united in a body known as the Council of Christian Pacifist groups, which co-operated with the Fellowship in holding further demonstrations. The whole effort culminated in August 1935 with a letter from George Lansbury to *The Times*, in which he urged that the Archbishops and the Pope should call a solemn convocation, representing every phase of religious thought, to meet in Jerusalem, and from Mount Calvary call a Truce of God and bid the war spirit rest.

The following year the I.F.o.R. began its new initiative in areas where the political situation had become most critical. The Embassies of Reconciliation were at first organized by the Rev. Nevin Sayre, Canon C. E. Raven, the Rev. Henry Carter, Dr F. Siegmund-Schültze, and Percy W. Bartlett, who acted as secretary. Others who joined the movement later included H. Runham Brown, Barrow Cadbury and T. Corder Catchpool. The 'Embassies' first operated from Red Lion Square and then opened an office in Victoria Street, which eventually moved to Gray's Inn Road.

After George Lansbury's letter to *The Times*, he travelled to the United States and conferred with President Roosevelt on the issues he had raised. He now agreed to become a 'peace ambassador' to the Prime Ministers of France, Belgium, Denmark, Norway and Sweden, and after these journeys announced his willingness to go to Berlin. This visit occurred in April 1937, when George Lansbury spent over two hours in confidential discussion with Hitler, and said directly afterwards: 'I got what I went for'. Hitler had declared that Germany would take part in a new world peace conference, and an agreed statement was issued to the Press: 'Germany will be very willing to attend a conference and take part in a united effort to establish economic co-operation and mutual understanding between the nations if President Roosevelt or the head of another great country will take the lead in calling such a conference'.

A cautious statement followed from the British Prime Minister, Neville Chamberlain, that Britain would also join the suggested conference 'provided that it was adequately prepared and gave promise of success'. Subsequently George Lansbury visited Rome and had two conversations with Mussolini, who assured him that he was anxious to maintain peace. He explained that his intervention in Spain was not due to any desire for territory, but to the fear of a Communist government being set up in the Mediterranean. Later George Lansbury and other members of the group travelled to Spain, Warsaw and Prague, while Percy Bartlett addressed meetings in America to discuss reconciliation in the Far East. In December George Lansbury, Henry Carter and Percy Bartlett again went to Prague and Warsaw, and also visited Vienna.

The following year, 1938, the same group went to the capitals of South-Eastern Europe, largely to discuss the long-awaited Report by M. van Zeeland, the Belgian Prime Minister, on the causes of the current strangulation of international trade. George Lansbury and his colleagues had hoped that M. van Zeeland would speak in London, but though a big public meeting was held, the impression made was frustrated by the indecisive policy of the British government shown in the resignation of Anthony Eden, and by the German occupation of Austria. Even then George Lansbury did not abandon his endeavours, but sent a telegram to Hitler reminding him of their conversation twelve months earlier. He also telegraphed again to both Hitler and President Benés of Czechoslovakia during the Munich crisis, and at the end of October begged President Roosevelt to invite European statesmen to meet him round the conference table.

It was not then known that in January 1938 (as both Sir Winston Churchill and Lord Templewood later recorded) the President had suggested a general peace conference which Neville Chamberlain rejected without even consulting the Foreign Affairs Committee of his Cabinet. The fact that Roosevelt made another last-moment effort to get an international conference in April 1939, and invited the dictators to pledge themselves to abstain from further aggression for ten years in return for economic benefits, may well have owed a good deal to George Lansbury's undaunted persistence.

From the middle of 1938 onwards Continental pacifists passed through a time of severe testing, but the I.F.o.R. Council, meeting at Lunteren in the Munich period, resolutely adopted a budget totalling £2000. The still existing confusion (not yet dead in the nineteen-sixties) of pacifism with 'passivism' and 'appeasement' did not make life easier for F.o.R. members in any country as the shadow of war again descended on Europe.

Chapter 4

THE I.F.o.R. 1939-64

When the Chinese Ambassador in London, Quo Tai Chi, was asked in 1939 to comment on the outbreak of war, he said: 'The sky is black with chickens coming home to roost'. Quoting this remark in a booklet some years later, the American pamphleteer Kirby Page observed that 'Hitler merely lighted the match which he threw into the European bonfire of explosives'.

Towards the end of the second decade of embittered truce, the victims of totalitarianism flooded the democratic countries. John Nevin Sayre, visiting Europe in 1938 to preside at the Lunteren Conference, recorded after travelling through fifteen countries that dictatorship and militarism had 'driven our comrades into new catacombs and set us the severe task of maintaining unbroken friendship with them'. Two years later the I.F.o.R. agreed to his proposal that Stockholm should act as one of several wartime centres for the Fellowship, and a F.o.R. Refugee Committee brought Jewish and other fugitives from Germany and Austria to the United States.

Nine months after war broke out, all Western Europe seemed to be on the move. A document dated September 1940 reported that 5,000 refugees were crowded into tiny Le Chambon, the village home of André Trocmé.

The delegates who met in the Lunteren woods had decided to move the I.F.o.R. office to London; 'it seemed best to have our headquarters in the country which appears to have the greatest resources in Christian pacifism that might be mobilized'. In December 1940 this office at 16 Victoria Street was completely demolished, though nobody was hurt. The Society of Friends offered accommodation at their own headquarters, and the office moved there for the duration.

Even more than the First War this second catastrophe, with its many helpless victims, brought a painful conflict of loyalties to many pacifists. Some brilliant and inspired exponents, such as Maude Royden, found themselves compelled to put the State before their faith. Many who stood by their convictions became conscientious objectors, to whom the War Resisters' International was to give unique service. Even within the totalitarian countries, 496 resisters were known to the Fellowship. In Britain the total eventually reached over 64,000, of whom a large number belonged to the F.o.R. Many of these went to prison.

Meanwhile thousands of interned foreigners filled British camps in the Isle of Man and elsewhere. One F.o.R. member, Dr Walter Zander, described his experiences as a Jewish 'enemy alien' in a leaflet entitled 'The Power of the Spirit in Internment'. Even in India a member of the former German F.o.R., Lies Gompertz, who had gone to Calcutta as a maternity nurse, found herself interned at Darjeeling.

Some distinguished British citizens also became 'suspect'. In June 1960 the Americans granted a visa to Professor G. H. C. Macgregor for a visit to the United States, but the British exit permit was refused. Appropriately the I.F.o.R. *Newsletter* for March 1941 quoted Aristophanes: 'From the murmur and subtlety of suspicion with which we vex one another, give us rest'. Four years earlier, in *The New Testament Basis of Pacifism*, Professor Macgregor had himself written of 'the gradual paganizing of the mind of the whole community' when the State sought to usurp God's position, imposing conformity through deprivations and penalties upon its intellectual and moral dissenters. By such methods the British Government repudiated the very ends for which it professed to be fighting.

The events of the Second War disrupted communications far more completely than the First between 1914 and 1918. The I.F.o.R. *Newsletter* for March 1941 reported that airmail letters from England to Switzerland were taking two or three weeks, and ordinary letters to other countries from three to nine months when they arrived at all. News of Continental I.F.o.R. leaders filtered slowly through, sometimes by word of mouth. The London office collected these fragments of information and periodically published the *Newsletter*, which took several months to reach some of its scattered recipients. Early in 1940 it also organized Pacifist Service Units which undertook club and community work and the care of 'problem families', and supplied thirty-six young volunteers for anti-typhus training to prevent the spread of typhus in the event of bacteriological warfare. The Pacifist Service Units continued as 'Family Service Units' after the war.

In September 1940 Pasteur Henri Roser wrote that he and his wife, after escaping from Paris during the German advance, had decided to return to their suburban settlement at Aubervilliers, because 'our place is among our people where they are most unfortunate, and perhaps the most in spiritual danger'. Another letter received via Cook's Agency from 'our friend W.M.' (Wilhelm Mensching) in Germany reported that he could still work 'in almost exactly the old way, and I should like to do even more in the service of our brethren and of our common Father'.

The Fellowship learned in March 1940 that its members in Holland had not then encountered any special trouble, though all regular activities were impossible. Danish workers had revived their Christian Peace Fellowship, which disappeared after the invasion. Neutral Sweden had held a F.o.R. Conference, addressed by Dr Natanael Beskow, in August 1940. That year, as the December 1941 *Newsletter* recorded, the American F.o.R. leader Douglas Steere had visited Stockholm. Sweden, wrote Dr Siegmund-Schültze, was 'very living', but its pacifist activities were hampered by its consciousness of Finland's adjacent struggle for freedom. Earlier the death had been reported to the British office of its devoted chairman in Czechoslovakia, Frau Pavla Moudra, aged seventy-nine.

The Canadian Fellowship lamented the official exclusion of London's *Peace News*, thus depriving them of help from 'the score of men and women whose weekly messages have kept the fires of faith in a better way of life burning brightly'. Australian sympathy was conveyed through the Women's International League for Peace and Freedom; New Zealand's Christian Pacifist Society, its membership increased from 370 to 680 during eighteen months of war, announced in December 1941 that its President and Secretary had both been in prison for publicly preaching pacifism. India recorded constitutional deadlock; from China an American missionary applauded 'the steadying influence' of the *Newsletter*; in Japan many Christians suffered from totalitarian persecution.

At the Stockholm Conference Natanael Beskow had declared the war situation to be 'unfavourable for Christianity', yet in America the Federal Council of the Churches had established a special commission to study 'the Bases of Just and Durable Peace', and the F.o.R. reported that between August 1940 and August 1941 nearly 4,000 new members had joined the Fellowship. Dr Harry Emerson Fosdick of Riverside Church, New York, and President Albert W. Palmer of Chicago Theological Seminary alike continued to maintain that war was irreconcilable with Christian teaching.

The British F.o.R. also announced an increase of nearly 1,000 new members in eleven months to counter 129 resignations. In London the Anglican Pacifist Fellowship had taken charge of the shelters in St Martin's Crypt, and a Hungerford Club had been formed on Donald Soper's initiative for men and women unsuited to ordinary shelters. The Council of Christian Pacifist Groups had organized a public meeting for Canon Raven, Pastor Franz Hildebrandt and Dr Soper, while the International Voluntary Service for Peace, no longer free to journey abroad, was doing reconstruction work in bombed towns or helping with agriculture and forestry.

During 1940, when tension began to mount in the Far East, the Embassies of Reconciliation had sent Anne Seesholtz, former National Y.W.C.A. Student Secretary, to Japan and China. Floyd Schmoe, later to direct 'Houses for Hiroshima', was also sent to Hawaii to study Japanese-American relations. Throughout the war the idea of a Far Eastern office, in Calcutta or Chungking or both, continued to haunt I.F.o.R. deliberations. After Pearl Harbour brought America into the conflict, F.O.R. groups protested to the Government regarding its ruthless policy of Japanese-American evacuation from the West Coast, and helped the evacuees by guarding their property, storing furniture, and visiting the relocation camps (see Chapter 2).

Through 1942, owing to scarce and unreliable news from the Far East and elsewhere, the mental fog deepened until it lay like a blanket over the extended wartime scene. Nevertheless an article by F. Ernest Johnson in the *American Journal of Sociology* for November 1942 emphasized the contrast between the response of the American Protestant Churches to the outbreak of war in 1941 and their attitude in 1917, when according to Professor Ray H. Abrams in *Preachers Present Arms* (1933), all but about seventy clergy conformed to the secular pattern. A postscript by the Editor (E. Stanley Jones) of the first American edition (1943) of Professor Heering's *The Fall of Christianity* stressed the integrity of most Christian pacifist leaders in face of the new challenge, and testified to the effectiveness of pacifist education between the wars (see Appendix, p. 226).

The F.o.R., especially in America, now saw its work as a threefold effort. First, it sought by inter-church mediation to find ways of ending the conflict; secondly, to help conscientious objectors; and thirdly, to keep the real nature of war continuously before the consciences of its fellow citizens.

The American Selective Service Act of 1940 had provided alternative outlets for registered conscientious objectors in Civilian Public Service camps. Thousands of young men chose 'non-combatant' service, and some 16,500 others accepted 'work of national importance'. About a quarter of these worked in the country's under-staffed mental hospitals. But the Selective Service law had many weaknesses which made its provisions unacceptable to convinced objectors. Before the war ended about 6,000 had been sentenced to prison terms, including five F.o.R. secretaries—Roger Axford, Caleb Foote, Alfred Hassler, Bayard Rustin and Glenn Smiley.

In Occupied Europe the imposition of the British food blockade caused acute suffering from undernourishment, especially to children. The countries hardest hit were Greece, Belgium and Poland. In Britain a small pacifist Food Relief Campaign managed, despite some tension, to work co-operatively with the larger non-pacifist Famine Relief Committee under the Bishop of Chichester. Some eminent non-pacifists, such as Clare Boothe Luce, supported the Famine Relief movement in the United States, and the American F.o.R. set up a Food for Europe Fund. It also published a British plea for Europe's famished children, *One of These Little Ones*. By 1945, famine relief campaigners were already occupied with plans for feeding half-starved Europe.

Government policies as pitiless as the food blockade included 'obliteration' bombing—a first instalment of genocide—against which pacifists consistently protested. In Britain a Bombing

Restriction Committee with a Quaker Chairman, Corder Catch-pool, resolutely published pamphlets giving details of the civilian suffering caused by saturation raids. During November 1943 a British traveller carried to New York a booklet written by Vera Brittain for this Committee, and showed it to the F.o.R.

Its secretaries, J. N. Sayre and A. J. Muste, debarred by war-time communications from consulting the author, changed its quiet title, *Seed of Chaos* (from a couplet by Alexander Pope) to the more sensational *Massacre By Bombing*, and persuaded twenty-eight religious leaders to support the writer's plea for compassion. The results, thanks to uneasy American consciences, were also sensational, for the publication and its author were widely discussed by the u.s. press and radio, and attacked in some 200 articles which went all the way from expostulation to furious denunciation.

Years afterwards, in 1961, came a remarkable sequel, when a short book, *Science and Government*, by Sir Charles Snow, revealed that a profound conflict about saturation bombing had divided the two leading scientists involved, Sir Henry Tizard and F. A. Lindemann (later Lord Cherwell). An official publica-tion, *The Strategic Air Offensive against Germany 1939-45*, also disclosed that Winston Churchill himself had desired to call off 'the bombing of German cities simply for the sake of increasing the terror'.

Terror had of course been engendered in many other ways, notably by the ferocity of the propaganda which 'wrote down' the traditional value of such words as charity, magnanimity, and pity (translated into 'squeamishness'). One form of 'psycho-logical warfare' by pacifist writers consisted in attempts to restore the integrity of these words, and to mitigate the brutality of the press. Towards the war's end not the least destructive purpose of its noisy clamour was 'unconditional surrender'—which, when the demand succeeded, was to leave the defeated enemy without a government, and eventually to present the former Allies with the recalcitrant problems of a divided Ger-many and an isolated Berlin.

On April 25, 1945, the international conference foreshadowed at Yalta met in San Francisco—described by one disillusioned journalist as 'San Fiasco'—and established the United Nations. This body was at least to prove more accessible than the League of Nations to the non-governmental organizations wishing to consult it, which included the Society of Friends.

In November 1944 the first General Secretary of the British F.o.R., Lucy Gardner, had died in England. Another pioneer, Richard Roberts, passed away in Canada while the Conference was sitting. With the end of the war in Europe came news both good and bad of other I.F.o.R. members. Dr Siegmund-Schültze, arrested twenty-seven times in the First War, had survived exile during the Second, but Max Josef Metzger, discovered in his 'Una Sancta' centre at Meitlingen, had unwittingly entrusted a private political document to a spy of the secret police and was subsequently executed by the Nazis. Some thousands of F.o.R. members had suffered internment or imprisonment for their convictions, and over eighty had died in gas chambers, concentration camps or on Nazi scaffolds. The membership had nevertheless reached 30,000, from fifteen countries. Ten years later the movement had spread to thirty countries and numbered 40,000.

Early in August 1945 American airmen dropped atomic bombs on Hiroshima and Nagasaki, and confronted the Fellowship, like all humanity, with a military problem of incalculable dimensions. Nuclear warfare was genocide, crudely pitiless. Five years later Canon Raven wrote in *The Theological Basis of Christian Pacifism* regarding nuclear research: 'This triumphant vindication of human faith and patience was proclaimed to the world by the two great Christian democracies in terms of the annihilation of a city'.

After the war the I.F.o.R. was steadily to increase its worldwide protest against nuclear weapons, but in 1945 the enormous task of post-war reconstruction, and especially that of feeding the famished, appeared more urgent. In July 1946, *Fellowship* published an article, 'How it Feels to be Starved', describing an experiment by thirty-six conscientious objectors who had acted as 'guinea-pigs' for the University of Minnesota.

As early as August 1945 exit permits again became available to British pacifists, and in that month Percy Bartlett and Henry Carter attended the summer Conference at Saanen in Switzerland. A wave of deep emotion swept over the gathering when

Henry Carter extended his hand to Dr Siegmund-Schültze, saying: 'I greet you, my brother in Christ'.

One of the first experiments in post-war reconciliation, supported by many F.o.R. members, began in September 1945 when
the British publisher Victor Gollancz founded the organization
'Save Europe Now', and issued an 'Appeal' for the '8,000,000
homeless nomads milling around Berlin'. By the end of the
month 10,000 postcards had come from people willing to cut
down their own rations. When Vera Brittain described this
movement, which involved help for Germany, at the Nobel
Institute in Oslo only five months after the German occupation
of Norway had ended, the crowded audience broke into applause.
During that visit she obtained many details of Norway's non-
violent resistance against the Nazis, especially by women
teachers, which has since become famous.

In October 1945 the Fellowship mourned the death of a great
Swiss personality, Pierre Cérésole, founder of *Service Civile*. On
his release in May from a period of wartime imprisonment, he
had suffered a serious heart attack from which he never
recovered (see Chapter 9).

Between January and April 1946, the Rev. Nevin Sayre made
a three months tour of twelve Western European countries and
addressed fifty-seven meetings. Everywhere he found appalling
but not total destruction; 'Germany and the Germans still exist'.
More spiritually sinister seemed the intensified nationalism in
every European country, the hostility between collaborationists
and non-collaborationists, the bitter divisions within Germany's
population, and the exhaustion of diminished food stores everywhere by hungry refugees.

In March he presided at the first post-war I.F.o.R. Council in
Stockholm. This represented, in effect, a rebirth of the movement and a gathering of its most dynamic leaders. Natanael
Beskow, F. Siegmund-Schültze, Charles Raven, Wilhelm
Mensching, G. J. Heering and Henri Roser were all present, and
fifty delegates from twelve countries gave moving reports of
their wartime experience. Wilhelm Mensching obtained permission to leave Germany only at the last moment, and received
a memorable greeting from an English delegate when he arrived
late and penniless after a long night journey.

Dr Siegmund-Schültze, speaking of the 'terrible things' done in Germany (where Naziism had destroyed his own twenty years' work in East Berlin), appealed to his colleagues to face realistically the demoralization brought by war to European civilization. The Council saw its future work in terms of the threefold challenge to Christian pacifism by the post-war world, the Nation-State, and the non-pacifist Church.

In September 1946 Canon Raven acted as host for a meeting of the European executive at Christ's College, Cambridge, where it was reported that Council membership had been re-established with the Fellowships in seventeen countries. By this time the travelling I.F.o.R. secretaries, who now included André Trocmé, had resumed their work, and Muriel Lester had left for India, China, and the United States.

At the Executive meetings in January and September 1947, *Kerk en Vrede* announced a membership of 1,800 though the Dutch Church was still hostile, and Nevin Sayre described a tour of Central and South America. Pasteur Henri Roser reported that French people were still too tired to listen to the message of reconciliation, while Dr Siegmund-Schültze spoke of the widespread spiritual collapse in Germany and the despair gripping young people between twenty and thirty.

August of that year found Percy Bartlett at the Regional Conference at Boissey in Switzerland, and three other F.o.R. members, André Trocmé, A. J. Muste and Vera Brittain, travelling in Germany. All three were oppressed by the dusty devastation of German cities, and embarrassed by the friendly readiness of the hungry, overcrowded people to share their meagre rations and living-space when the only alternative was the Allied luxury hotels where Germans could not go. André Trocmé's task was to seek former fellow workers in the British Zone, now overwhelmed by eleven million refugees from the East. In Cologne—which made the most terrible impression of the ruined cities owing to its former beauty—Vera Brittain talked with Frau Asta Brügelmann, now secretary of the Western-organized Versöhnungsbund of which Dr Siegmund-Schültze had become the chairman.

Two months later the Fellowship announced the death of one of its leading scholars, Dr C. J. Cadoux. This loss preceded by one year that of another distinguished early member, Leyton Richards, and in February came the death of Oliver Dryer, who had become General Secretary of the British F.o.R. in 1918, and visited every European country, including Russia.

At the June 1948 Council meeting at Le Chambon in Haute Loire, two Executive Committees were appointed for Europe and America. A third was set up for South America, where Fellowship groups existed in eight countries. National reports showed that a typical post-war lethargy had gripped Scandinavia, but in Britain the secretary, Clifford Macquire, reported 450 branches with growing support, and America, in spite of post-war depression, still had a paying membership of 12,500. An attempt to collect material for a book on the I.F.o.R. in the Second War had broken down, but the Japanese F.o.R. had been re-established.

This Conference discussed that autumn's meeting of the World Council of Churches at Amsterdam, and the need to urge its delegates to consider the Christian pacifist outlook as one of three Christian positions on war. The ultimate F.o.R. statement, first drafted by Canon Raven and Dr Siegmund-Schültze, was signed by leading churchmen from many countries.

At Bentveld, Holland, in 1949, Kaspar Mayr described the difficulties of the work in Austria, where he had gathered a study group mainly of Catholic young people. No organized movement yet existed there, though sixteen German peace organizations, Protestant and Catholic, had formed a *Friedens-kartell* of which he was secretary. [See Chapter 7 (ii).]

That winter occurred an event of unusual significance, when a World Pacifist Meeting gathered at Santiniketan and Sevagram in India to study Gandhi's non-violent philosophy. This conference had first been discussed by the F.o.R. at Cambridge in 1946, when Gandhi was still alive, and again at Le Chambon and Bentveld. Of the sixty-seven delegates who travelled to India, thirty-six belonged to the I.F.o.R.; they included Nevin and Kathleen Sayre, Magda Trocmé, Dietrich Lund of Norway, and A. C. Barrington of New Zealand. Muriel Lester, who had recently visited Australia, New Zealand and South Africa, was not present, but her previous visit to India had been sponsored by Gandhi himself.

After the Meeting it was generally agreed that no successor to Gandhi had emerged and no useful plan was achieved in the attempt to mediate between India and Pakistan, but the delegates who travelled round India for the fortnight which divided the two conferences carried home a vivid realization of India's problems.

The February 1950 European Committee meeting at Cologne had to report the deaths of three more F.o.R. pioneers, George Llewellyn Davies, Theodore Walser and Ethel Stevenson. By the time that the July I.F.o.R. Council met in Holland, war had broken out in Korea.

This war definitely established the Cold War pattern of East-West relations. An address to the I.F.o.R. Council by Dr G. H. C. Macgregor when the pointless conflict was ending summarized the tragedy: 'What a price has been paid in order merely, at the end, to arrive at the same division of Korea which existed before the war. Something like a million dead; uncounted millions homeless and displaced; the cities and industries of Korea in ruins. And no problem solved, no bitterness assuaged.'

Turning to a more constructive field, the American F.o.R. set up a Committee in 1950 for work in the Churches. From a conference held in Detroit came the Church Peace Mission, with A. J. Muste as a prominent missioner, to bring the pacifist position before the Christian Church in America and the World Council of Churches. Three years later the Mission distributed several thousand copies of its booklet, *The Christian Conscience and War*.

In July 1950 the International Council met at Woudschoeten in Holland, where nearly 200 attended and many young people asked for an international youth conference. At the end of the year Dr Iwao Ayusawa, Chairman of the Tokyo F.o.R., became a Vice-Chairman of the I.F.o.R. in addition to Pasteur Henri Roser, Dr Siegmund-Schültze, and Dr J. J. Buskes of Holland. The suggested youth conference, held at Elsinore in Denmark, followed a meeting of the European Committee near Copenhagen in August 1951. Forty young delegates, both Catholic and Protestant, attended the conference.

The following January the Committee, meeting at Versailles, had before it the resignation of the I.F.o.R. Treasurer, Barrow Cadbury, aged ninety. This great Treasurer, who had financed the missions organized by Embassies of Reconciliation, lived to be ninety-five and survived his successor, Dr J. F. Paton,

E

Moderator of the United Free Church of Scotland, who died in 1954.

The Zeist Council in August 1952 discussed Christian pacifist principles in relation to the problems of evil, especially those arising from the Cold War. The delegates faced the power conflict between Russia and the West; though co-operation for peace seemed almost impossible with Communists, a few members were shortly visiting Moscow. Nevin Sayre reported the condemnation of conscientious objection in East Germany, and described his tour of South Africa. The German delegate attributed a loss of members in West Germany to the confusion of peace workers with Communists. Another change discussed was the spread of the I.F.o.R. to countries where the majority subscribed to faiths other than Christianity, and it was decided not to exclude those willing to join a Fellowship rooted in Christian values.

At a widely-attended meeting at Dortmund in July 1953 the I.F.o.R. again considered East-West tension, concluding that Christian love and justice were not embodied in the economic systems of either West or East. While unwilling to send delegates to peace gatherings controlled by propagandists for the foreign policy of either side, the Council agreed that observers might sometimes attend such assemblies. More valuable would be reciprocal visits and cultural exchanges between East and West, and the drawing together of Eastern and Western churches.

The Council met in the new *Jugendwohlfahrteschule* of which Dr Siegmund-Schültze was Principal. Nevin Sayre reported an amnesty in the Philippines for over 100 Japanese 'war criminals' which gave new hope for Japanese-Filipino relations. A discussion also took place regarding the 1954 Assembly of the Churches at Evanston, USA, which was to consider Soviet and non-Soviet tension and the revolutionary changes in underdeveloped countries. The unified pacifist statement, 'Peace is the will of God', was sent to the international commission in Switzerland preparing the Evanston agenda.

At the October European Committee meeting in London, references were made to the new Italian Fellowship, and the death in Sweden was reported of Natanael Beskow, aged eighty-eight.

By 1954, the United States Fellowship had a national staff of nearly twenty in New York, and eight regional offices. Two new projects now dominated the American programme: an educational protest campaign on the H-bomb, and an endeavour to persuade the Government to make vast quantities of surplus food available to famine victims in China.

In Europe Kaspar Mayr's daughter Hildegard was preparing, by an international distribution of the publication *Der Christ in der Welt*, for a Catholic pacifist conference in Colmar. A Catholic study-conference at Namur, with sixty students from five countries, followed in 1955. In September occurred the death of Dr W. E. Orchard, an outstanding pacifist leader of the First War who later joined the Roman Catholic Church.

The I.F.o.R. office was now in Gray's Inn Road, London. At a Council meeting at Haverhill, England, in July, the delegates stressed two main handicaps to Christian pacifist work: German propaganda for the militarization of the country, and the rearmament of Japan, where it was proposed to change or abolish the post-war peace Constitution.

In October 1954 a small 'information conference' of leading F.o.R. members from Germany, France and the Saar, who included Pasteur Henri Roser and Dr Siegmund-Schültze, met at Saarbrücken to study the perennial problems of this area. Another member of the mission, Richard Ullmann, brought their conclusions the following year before a meeting of the European Committee at Arnhem, where Dr Macgregor presided. The Saarbrücken document pressed for a statute to regularize the Saar State. Reports were also given of the Evanston Assembly, where several resolutions proposed by the Bishop of Chichester had been adopted.

A recent article by Dr Macgregor, 'The Christian's Dilemma', discussing the apparent approval by Church dignitaries of Allied mass bombing, inquired whether the Christian was ever actually caught in the choice between two evils, since there was always an exit from this position by way of the Cross.

In February came accounts of the deputation to Moscow the previous year, led by Canon Raven at the invitation of the Metropolitan Nicolas. The travellers had included Dr Donald Soper and Ebenezer Cunningham, who subsequently commented: 'The Russia one leaves is not the Russia to which one came for it is the home of real people. The bogey-man is disclosed as a brother.'

That summer a group of I.F.o.R. leaders toured Germany to study problems of rearmament and conscription, and a series of conferences in Norway, Britain, Holland and Germany led up to the August 1955 International Conference at Vaumarcus in Switzerland, where 200 delegates from twenty countries discussed 'The Christian and Co-Existence'. The programme began with the problems of the Pacific and, passing to Europe, gave special thought to divided Germany. The chief speakers were Charles Raven, Martin Niemöller, G. H. C. Macgregor, F. Siegmund-Schültze and Hannes de Graaf. Lilian Stevenson, now aged eighty-five, also took part.

From 1945, when nuclear weapons took war into a new dimension of evil, their moral challenge dominated much F.o.R. thinking. In 1954—two years after a series of H-bomb tests in the Pacific had irradiated several hundred Marshall Islanders and a group of Japanese fishermen—*Fellowship* devoted a whole issue to a 'Report on the Bomb' in which Dr George MacLeod wrote: 'The H-bomb is the showdown for the Church'.

All over Europe and America, protest marches and vigils began. One vigil initiated by the American F.o.R. at Fort Detrick, Maryland, a germ warfare factory, lasted for two years (July 1959 - July 1961). In 1957 Albert Bigelow and Earle Reynolds deliberately took their yachts *Golden Rule* and *Phoenix* into the Pacific testing areas. Many F.o.R. members supported the American Campaign for a Sane Nuclear Policy and the British Campaign for Nuclear Disarmament.

By 1961 one breakaway section of the British Campaign, the Committee of 100, was practising widespread civil disobedience. During the same period A. J. Muste led an international protest march from San Francisco to Moscow. The decision to base American Polaris submarines in Britain brought new British demonstrations and more arrests. Pronouncements from such nuclear scientists as Edward Teller and Hermann Kahn inspired resistance in other scientists headed by Bertrand Russell and Linus Pauling. Throughout the literate world, millions of words embodied the determination of concerned Christians to repudiate nuclear warfare.

In *Reconciliation* for January 1962, D. Martin Dakin summed up this united witness: 'The question of nuclear weapons, involving as it does the possible extinction of mankind, is the most pressing moral problem of our day'. A British television discussion in February 1962, between the Archbishop of York and the singer Adam Faith, brought a frank admission from the Archbishop that the Church was divided on this vital issue.

More rewarding if less immediately urgent was the social service of the I.F.o.R. in this period, particularly the development of youth work. Before 1950 younger members in Europe had little mutual contact, but between 1951 and 1960 the work grew rapidly owing to a series of Youth Conferences and to the witness of newly-trained leaders in their own countries. Between 1957 and 1962 the form of international service now known as *Eirene* developed in areas where physical rather than verbal testimony to the Gospel was needed. These united teams, owing their original inspiration to Pierre Cérésole, worked especially in Algeria and Morocco. The Eirene group was first on the spot after the disastrous Agadir earthquake, and united a score of young volunteers from a dozen countries to help the victims. Other forms of practical service include a Youth Centre, a home for 100 small boys, help to peasant farmers, poultry raising, and community projects in co-operation with the Church of the Brethren and the Mennonites.

Yet another advance was the growing witness of the I.F.o.R. against racial hatred (to be more fully described in Chapters 6 and 10), especially in the American South and in South Africa. But Britain, owing to her large influx of West Indians, was not immune from this problem, and a Conference on 'Race Relations and Reconciliation' at I.F.o.R. headquarters in July 1961 faced its different aspects.

In 1956-7 the Rev. Ernest Best of Canada became General Secretary, and during this period the I.F.o.R. *Newsletter* acquired another title, *Christus Victor*. After one year's service, Mr Best returned to teaching and pastoral work in the United States and THE REV. PHILIP EASTMAN, a Congregational minister born in 1918 in Auckland, New Zealand, who received his theological training at New College, London, took his place.

In 1948 the new Secretary, who four years earlier had been ordained minister of Islington Chapel, set up the London office of the Churches' Commission on International Affairs with Sir Kenneth Grubb as Chairman, and served this body until 1957, when he became assistant secretary of the Free Church Federal Council in England. From 1952 to 1956 he was joint secretary of the international department of the British Council of Churches. His travels for these organizations and later for the I.F.o.R. carried him all round the world, and gave him close contacts with Church and missionary leaders. One of his recent journeys took him to the meeting of the World Council of the Churches in Delhi in December 1961. As a convinced Christian Pacifist from his youth, Philip Eastman brought both administrative skill and firm convictions to the service of reconciliation.

DR HOWARD SCHOMER, President of the Chicago Theological Seminary, became I.F.o.R. President in 1959. Dr Schomer, whose first memory was that of Armistice Day 1918, became a pacifist through the internationalist influence of his school and Church (his father, a Roman Catholic, belonged to the Drug Clerks' Union).

As a graduate student in 1937 in France and Germany, he learned that Nazism was the logical conclusion of militarism. In 1938 he travelled home on the *Bremen* where the ships' officers were Nazi propagandists, and organized a Protestant service on board to which they had to agree. He then joined the Chicago Seminary under Dr Albert Palmer, whose influence led him to the F.o.R. In 1940 he found that Roman Catholic priests were lobbying Congressmen to support the exemption of theological students from military service, and came to the conclusion that the exemption of ministers cut the nerve of Christian social action.

Thenceforth Dr Schomer took a double stand, both as a pre-ordained minister and as a conscientious objector, against Selective Service. As a result he was arrested, and had to go to court in October 1940 after discussing his problems throughout the previous night with Nevin Sayre, who had taken the same position in the First World War. After a brief imprisonment Howard Schomer went out on bail and continued his campaign against ministerial exemption.

He finally registered as a conscientious objector and, since his thinking had led him to accept alternative service, worked for nearly four years with the Civilian Public Service, chopping trees and doing other forms of strenuous work. He came however to believe that this Public Service was a form of exploitation, which tested the pacifist convictions of many workers who felt that their ability was being deliberately wasted. He and his colleagues had volunteered for work of 'national importance', but the majority were given unimportant tasks where they had no opportunity of exerting any influence. They were not allowed to go abroad, though some of them had offered themselves for dangerous service on the Burma Road.

Dr Schomer's post-war work took him back to the Continent, where he served both the World Council of Churches and the F.o.R. For nine years he lived in France, spending much of his time at the Collège Cévenol in close association with André Trocmé.

As President of the F.o.R., he saw an important future for it in three directions. First, he believed its task to be the development of a strong theological understanding and exposition of the uncomfortable pacifist element in the gospels.

Secondly, he desired to see the implications of Christian nonviolence translated into positive social and political action. Thirdly, he felt that the F.o.R. had a responsibility to preserve the spirit of nonconformity within the Churches and thus defend the right of all minorities, including Communists, to express their views. During the period of McCarthyism in the United States, the F.o.R. in fact protested against the suppression of Communists, and worked with the Civil Liberties Union, which under Roger Baldwin had similarly withstood antileft-wing hysteria during the First World War, to defend individuals whose liberties were violated.

In 1959 the I.F.o.R. acquired a new international headquarters in Finchley, North London. Generous friends made it possible to buy a large house known as 'The Grange' which provided the Fellowship with a much-needed Conference Centre. An international 'Reconciliation Library' was also founded there, and on September 17, 1960, the new centre was dedicated by Canon Raven in the handsome conference room overlooking a pleasant English garden.

Two years earlier one of the goodwill visits to Russia suggested at Dortmund had occurred in May and June, when Max Parker of the British Fellowship accompanied the representatives of other peace organizations. From the Vienna Centre Hildegard Goss-Mayr had meanwhile expanded her Catholic work as travelling secretary. In 1957 she spent three weeks in Ireland to promote better understanding between Catholics and Protestants. She visited Italy in 1958, and in 1960 invited national Fellowships to send her statements for transmission to the Vatican Council. During 1960 she and her husband worked with Roman Catholics in Yugoslavia.

Central Europe was also the scene of the I.F.o.R. Conference on 'Power for Peace'. This took place at Stainach in Austria, and was followed by a Council meeting at Bischofshofen.

In May 1960 the I.F.o.R. shared in the universal frustration caused by the failure of the Paris Summit Conference. Meetings had been arranged for the opening day, May 16th, and were held in fifteen cities round the world, including one at the Albert Hall, London, on the theme of 'Plan for Peace'. The following year the topic of 'Religion and Peace' proved more rewarding than politics. In April 1961 an invitation Conference on this subject brought nearly thirty representatives of the Christian, Jewish, Hindu, Muslim and Buddhist communities to All Souls' College, Oxford.

The I.F.o.R. Council met at Le Chambon-sur-Lignon that August during the Berlin crisis. This Conference examined a large advertisement, inserted in the *New York Times* by the American National Committee for a Sane Nuclear Policy and supported by the F.o.R., proposing an international Berlin Authority in an arms-free Germany for consideration by the United Nations. A statement sent to the press from Le Chambon similarly emphasized that the existing tension was not really a Berlin crisis, but 'a further manifestation of the plight of a world victimized by the struggle between two groups of nations'. Several suggestions followed for a peaceful solution, 'given the will'.

The I.F.o.R. Report for 1959-61, studied at Le Chambon, outlined future policy under five main headings, which included Inter-Church Relations, the problems raised by Communism, Race Relationships, Non-Christian Religions, and contacts with other peace organizations. An introductory paragraph emphasized the main task as 'that of rousing the various Christian communities to a recognition that the reconciling non-violent power of love is an integral part of the Christian faith'.

In December 1961 an article by Ethel Comber in *Reconciliation* estimated as follows the number of F.o.R. members in several countries other than the United States, Britain and France: Belgium 75, West Germany 1,400, Italy (a new centre) 29, the Netherlands 2,200, Norway 500, Sweden 130, Switzerland 150, India over 300, South Africa under 100, Canada 800, Australia 200. The main strength of the I.F.o.R. still lay in Britain and America, but in several smaller centres the F.o.R. inspiration extended far beyond the limited membership.

On the whole the influence of the British and American Fellowships has been differently exercised. While the Americans tend to distrust co-operation with the State, the British have sought quietly to influence the Government whenever possible. In the Second War, for instance, the so-called Cloister Group of pacifists and non-pacifists which met regularly at Canon Raven's home was able to arrange for new forms of alternative service for conscientious objectors. Dr Henry Carter, of the strong Methodist Pacifist Fellowship, succeeded through his personal friendship with Ernest Bevin, the Minister of Labour, in creating the Forestry Units which employed many C.O.s. But the British F.o.R. has always seen its first task as lying within the Church as a whole, and has consistently urged the full acceptance by all the Churches of Christ's creed of sacrificial love, which would make inevitable their repudiation of State-engineered international quarrels.

The American Fellowship is not only better financially endowed, but has a more executive conception of its functions. In consequence it can claim many noteworthy political achievements, though it failed immediately after Stalin's death to take advantage of an opportunity for creating better relations with Russia. It obtained the eventual release of all Japanese prisoners by the American Government after prolonged representations that these men were unjustly detained, and its revolutionary campaigns in the Southern States are rapidly substituting an attitude of freedom and independence among American Negroes for the old pattern of racial discrimination.

Part at least of the American Fellowship's record of political success is due to the fortunate accident that its long-time Chairman, the Rev. Nevin Sayre, is brother to Francis Sayre, President Wilson's son-in-law, and thus in the earlier years had easy access to the White House. Once he persuaded Mr Wilson to lift the Post Office ban on the circulation of *The World Tomorrow* and *The Nation*. Again, on the day before he left for the Versailles Peace Conference, the President received evidence from Mr Sayre that thirty conscientious objectors had been manacled standing for nine hours a day at Fort Leavenworth for five weeks. The President immediately said that this must stop, and a few days later the War Department abolished the practice in all military prisons.

Through fifty years some important psychological and intellectual changes can be seen in the development of the International Fellowship as a whole. The early movement, starting in England, had perhaps a moral rather than a theological influence on the majority of members, though Lucy Gardner's distinguished group in Pimlico shared a profound theological concern with the Cambridge scholars who, at the 1914 Conference and after, preached the way of the Cross as the only road to salvation. For its subsequent Biblical and theological tendencies, the Fellowship is indebted especially to the late Professor G. H. C. Macgregor and to Canon C. E. Raven.

In his *New Testament Basis of Christian Pacifism*, published in 1936, Dr Macgregor produced a Biblical classic which is still essential reading for all F.o.R. members. Through the writing and teaching of Charles Raven, who has made theology comprehensible to students with no theological training, the Fellowship has acquired a new intellectual quality. For Canon Raven, who came to the pacifist position after prolonged mental conflict, pacifism represents an inevitable outcome of Christian commitment. He has always emphasized the fundamental difference between the F.o.R. and such non-sectarian pacifist bodies as the Peace Pledge Union and the War Resisters' International.

Many peace workers who joined the pacifist movement between the wars had a political rather than a theological or even a moral attitude. Pacifists of this type never fully recognized that, from a worldly standpoint, Christianity was founded on a *failure*—the death of its leader on the Cross—and that politically the pacifist movement has never succeeded and (unless some basic transformation occurs in the character of modern politics) can probably never hope for success. This misunderstanding of the religious foundation of a Christian pacifist community accounted for many resignations during the Second World War. Those members who looked, like politicians, for executive triumphs inevitably felt too frustrated when war came to maintain their pacifism. Dr Maude Royden's much-criticized wartime vacillations may well be explained by the chance that as an Oxford student she read Modern History and not Theology (a school closed to Oxford women until 1935).

Within recent years the growing ecumenical movement in the Churches has appeared one of the most hopeful developments to all concerned Christians. The I.F.o.R. was an ecumenical movement from the start; even in 1915 its founders saw denominational differences as relatively trivial compared with the task of freeing the Christian Churches from their confused association with the evil of war. Hence all the British denominational pacifist Fellowships founded during the nineteen-thirties came under the F.o.R. aegis except that of the Anglicans, who were sometimes members of the Fellowship and sometimes outside it owing to the belief of their leaders that they could influence the Church of England better by dissociation from other denominations. The ecumenical emphasis of the nineteen-sixties may eventually cause this outlook to appear outdated, and suggests that the vision of the I.F.o.R. founders is at last coming close to realization.

'How extraordinarily different were our units . . . ritualist and Quaker, theologian and scientist, Celt and Saxon, Mary and Martha, Catholic and Protestant of every type and temper and temperament', wrote George Llewellyn Davies of the early days of the Fellowship in *Reconciliation* for May 1927. 'And what unity we reached as a whole over and over again in facing actual and urgent situations . . . More than once we found the jagged edges of our judgments that grated so hardly on cherished prejudices and antipathies, fit in at last like cogs which moved the wheels of both of us.'

Triumphantly he concluded with a judgment of prophetic quality fully justified by the progress of the Fellowship since his death: 'There has been spread through such witness . . . a new conception of discipleship which would seek to restore peace in the whole estate of the Catholic Church, in the family, in the congregation, in industry, in international life. Whether one thinks of the work of C. F. Andrews in South Africa or India, or of Henry Hodgkin in China, or of Siegmund-Schültze in Berlin, there emerges a unity of outlook or of method that brings a new conception to men of the relation of religion to life.'

Chapter 5

BRITISH WITNESSES

After the outbreak of the First World War, Henry Hodgkin and Richard Roberts were among the first to confront the profound contradiction between war and the way of Christ. A leading contemporary scholar, the Rev. John Skinner, Principal in the College of the English Presbyterian Church, had deeply influenced their thinking.

HENRY HODGKIN, belonging to an old Quaker family from Darlington, Yorkshire, was a medical missionary and student of international affairs. After his education at Bootham and Leighton Park Schools and King's College, Cambridge, he spent three years with the Student Christian Movement as Travelling Secretary. In 1905 he went to China under the Friends Foreign Mission Association (later the Friends Service Council) and worked at Chengtu, where he helped to found the West China Union University.

Five years later he returned to England to become Secretary of the Association. In 1914, aged thirty-seven, he was Clerk to the London Society of Friends, a man of dominating though genial presence and a persuasive speaker. He went to the Constance Conference in this capacity and later helped to found the F.o.R. When he was called up as a layman before the Military Service Tribunal, he was given absolute exemption.

In 1917 the F.o.R. office was raided, and everything removed except the chairs and typewriters. Immediately Dr Hodgkin went to Scotland Yard to ask what offence the Fellowship had committed which caused even the linoleum to be torn up in the search for incriminating documents. Leyton Richards, who was present, recalled long afterwards the embarrassment of the police officials when the inquiry was made by a commanding, unintimidated Friend who overtopped the tallest detective by several inches.

After the war, as Secretary of the Association, Dr Hodgkin visited India, Syria and Madagascar, but in 1920 he resigned his position for a lecture tour of Chinese universities. Between 1922 and 1929 he took his wife and three sons to China, where he became Joint Secretary of the National Christian Council—an important step towards the formation of an indigenous Chinese Christian Church. While on leave in England in 1925, he was the first Quaker to give a religious radio address.

When he died after an operation in 1933 at the relatively early age of fifty-five, Henry Hodgkin had been for over two years Director of Studies at Pendle Hill, the Pennsylvania Centre for American Friends. His had been a typical but all too short Quaker missionary's career, faithful, fearless and loyal. After his death a memorial fund of nearly £2,000 went to the West China University.

RICHARD ROBERTS, from whose initiative on the first Sunday of the 1914 War the Fellowship ultimately grew, became on Henry Hodgkin's invitation its second secretary at Red Lion Square. The first for a few months was LUCY GARDNER, the dominant Quaker Warden of the Collegium where the embryonic Fellowship first met.

She was a remarkable woman who subsequently created the body known as C.O.P.E.C., and formed its national groups by travelling incessantly. 'A slave-driver without ever forgetting that the individual she dealt with was a person', one judgment on her ran. She drove herself as well as others, and tended to create tension in those with whom she worked. An early editor of *Reconciliation*, who remarked that he liked her 'more than some did', stressed her belief that F.o.R. members should be ready to explain their 'extreme position' to any inquirer.

Richard Roberts was soon to write to Lilian Stevenson that looking after an office was not his job—'and no change of circumstances can make it my job. I must preach, and I must come to first-hand grips with people's souls.' Thanks to what has been called 'a well-schooled Celtic temperament', Dr Roberts had an extraordinary power as a preacher, and always struck the prophetic note. Later his great church in Canada was invariably crowded to capacity. At his best he had the reputation of giving the most outstanding sermons of a minister from any Canadian denomination, though some of his more conventional hearers were offended by his unorthodox outlook.

Dr Roberts was born in 1874 at Blaenau Ffestiniog, a Welsh slate-quarrying centre. Throughout his life he suffered from poor eyesight, which later spared him a battle over conscription, but he did well scholastically and entered the University College of Wales in 1891. There, conscious of a 'call' to the ministry, he left impetuously without graduating, and studied for two years at Bala Theological College.

He was asked to resign from his initial charge in a South Welsh village because he took the chair for Keir Hardie at a political meeting. In his first London ministry, at the Welsh Church in Willesden Green in 1900, the South African War caused him to adopt an anti-war position. His happiest assignment was that of St Paul's, Westbourne Grove, where his tolerant officials did not complain when he marched with the unemployed, and joined Bernard Shaw in publicly protesting against the living conditions of shop-girls.

In 1910 came the summons to Crouch Hill, a residential neighbourhood which his pacifist opinions obliged him to leave in 1915. As F.o.R. Secretary and first editor of *The Venturer*, he visited the United States in 1916, and there received a call to the beautiful historic Church of the Pilgrims in Brooklyn—'a very much greater responsibility than I dare refuse', he told Lilian Stevenson. He expected to find a new people free from inhibitions, but America's emotional entry into the war brought disillusionment. He found himself oppressed by the national emphasis on conformity, and in 1918 wrote Miss Stevenson that 'acute housekeeping difficulties' disturbed his wife and three daughters. He nevertheless believed that he had been 'guided' to America because 'the F.o.R. and what it stood for here would have been seriously handicapped had it not been that I was on the spot with the British experience to fall back on'. He also reported 'the subtle persecution of the F.o.R. through the Y.M. International Committee'.

After deciding to return to England in 1921 he was approached by the American Presbyterian Church in Montreal, which became the 'high spot' of his ministry. Here he helped to found the United Church of Canada in 1925, educated his

daughters at McGill University, and attracted a large congregation from all over Montreal. After five years he moved to the
Sherbourne Street United Church in Toronto, the most select of
the non-Anglican Churches though set in a deteriorating neighbourhood. In 1934 he was elected Moderator of the United
Church and travelled all over Canada. Two years later a major
operation, followed by difficulties with his official Board, brought
his resignation.

Much of Richard Roberts' rebel quality had been sacrificed to
his exacting administrative work; though he had burned himself
out by the Second World War, he was not widely known as a
pacifist crusader. But in 1939, when a group of United Church
ministers issued a manifesto repudiating war he signed it, not
wishing to suggest that he had abandoned his 1914 position.
The Church promptly disavowed the seventy-five signatories,
and 'being the most well known, he received all the brickbats',
his daughter Dorothy recalled long afterwards.

Perhaps an even greater challenge was Mr Sayre's request to
him in March 1944 to join the group of American ministers who
sponsored the booklet *Massacre by Bombing*, and to write the
Foreword. He complied, but remarked that this action would
probably prevent his return to England. In fact it was his health,
not his convictions, which frustrated him, and in April 1945 he
died.

Twelve years later Nevin Sayre travelled to Wales with his
ashes, which were scattered on the slopes of Cader Idris at a
service conducted by George Llewellyn Davies. In 1951 the
Erskine-American United Church in Montreal dedicated a tablet
to his memory.

In addition to Henry Hodgkin, Richard Roberts and Lucy
Gardner, the first F.o.R. Committee included W. E. Orchard,
Maude Royden and Lilian Stevenson. Among the earliest mem-
bers were Barrow Cadbury, Claud Coltman, Stephen Hobhouse,
Constance M. Todd, Marian E. Ellis, and F. W. and Emmeline
Pethick-Lawrence.

From the beginning until her death in January 1960, LILIAN
STEVENSON devoted her life to the F.o.R. and became its scribe.
For many years she was an active member of the I.F.o.R.
As a wealthy woman owning a large house in Buckingham-

shire she enjoyed entertaining, and gave the F.o.R. a generous share of her riches and a substantial last bequest.

She has alternatively been described as 'the *grand dame* of Christian pacifism' and 'an example of paternalism at its best', acting as a conscientious hostess to continental I.F.o.R. members. Born in 1871, she remained to the end of her long life a member of her Victorian generation, and probably did not even wish to adapt herself to a later epoch of which dignified behaviour was to be as little characteristic as gracious living.

Grand dames are out of date today. They belong to a vanishing era of class distinctions, but in a period when condescension from the old to the young, and the rich to the poor, was taken for granted, her objectives did her credit. At least she identified herself with an unpopular minority without social pretensions, and served it with the dedicated resolution of an austere personality.

The young society soon joined in the work of the Friends' Emergency Committee for the Assistance of Germans, Austrians and Hungarians in distress. Another early endeavour was a vaguely worded petition urging the Government to take 'the earliest possible opportunity' for discussing 'terms of settlement', which became known as 'the Memorial'. In July 1915 a 'Peace Caravan' sought to disseminate this message. At Hinckley near Nuneaton, where the population had suffered severely from war casualties, the twenty pilgrims, who included Reginald Sorensen, later a Member of Parliament, encountered disaster; their caravan was set alight and totally destroyed.

Shortly afterwards a series of press attacks followed the F.o.R's reproduction of the Pope's appeal for peace sent out on July 28th. With understandable trepidation after the Hinckley episode the pilgrims undertook further campaigns in Somerset, Lancashire and Cheshire, and found unexpected success. Additional encouragement came from the valuable support of George Lansbury, who joined the F.o.R. in September 1915, and remained a member throughout his life.

GEORGE LANSBURY, for many years Editor of the *Daily Herald*, had been elected M.P. for Poplar, one of the poorest boroughs in London's East End, in 1910, but two years later resigned his seat to fight as an Independent supporter of Woman Suffrage. Defeated, he remained for ten years out of Parliament, but had

F

been a Poor Law guardian since 1891 and a Borough Councillor since 1903. In 1919 he became Mayor of Poplar, and in 1922 was re-elected for this constituency which he represented till his death.

Born in 1859 and educated entirely at elementary day schools, George Lansbury was the father of twelve children, and from boyhood had been active in political life. As First Commissioner of Works, he became a member of the Labour Government of 1929-31.

Twice in prison for reasons of conscience before the First World War, he was a convinced Christian pacifist who held many important offices in pacifist organizations and belonged, unexpectedly, to the Church of England. In his youth he had seen international Socialism as the only remedy for war, but was later obliged to modify this view when he found such working-class States as Russia fighting as vehemently as any other nation.

Though he was a popular and effective speaker in continual demand for political and religious meetings, George Lansbury never tried to 'handle' an audience; he said exactly what he wished to say, and dominated it by the sheer weight of his uncompromising sincerity. In August 1938, after his vigorous leadership of Embassies of Reconciliation, America's *Christian Science Monitor* described him as 'Spokesman for Humanity'— a lover of his fellows who could see human beings only as human.

After he died on May 7, 1940—the day of the historic Parliamentary debate which followed the disastrous Norwegian campaign and decided that Winston Churchill should replace Neville Chamberlain — his fellow Socialists lined three miles of road to the garden where his ashes were taken before being scattered at sea, and the flag flew at half mast over Bow Conservative Club, the headquarters of his political opponents.

In November 1915 the F.o.R. acquired a new Assistant General Secretary in GEORGE LLEWELLYN DAVIES, an aristocratic Welshman born in 1880, with the normal restraints of his background. A very attractive personality, he was completely at home in Government circles, and his distinguished appearance suggested Membership of the House of Lords or Commons. He was in fact elected Christian Pacifist M.P. for the University of

Wales in 1923, but found Parliament too restrictive, and soon resigned.

When the First World War broke out, George Davies abandoned the traditional safeguards of his upbringing, resigned his Commission in the Territorial Army, became a conscientious objector, and was imprisoned in 1918. In April 1917 he had written ruefully to Richard Roberts of his own F.o.R. work, referring appreciatively to Dr Roberts' warm humanity 'which I often miss in the counsels of good Saxons'. Another letter, from Birmingham Prison, referred to the 'inner freedom' which had come from abandoning 'the struggle to be top dog according to the ethics of the dog-fight'. An early post-war letter described his astonishment when the Presidents selected for the Carnarvon Eisteddfod were Lloyd George, Marshal Foch and George Llewellyn-Davies.

In the F.o.R. office in Red Lion Square a sickle stood above the central fire-place, made from the transformed sword used by George Davis as a cavalry officer. After the war he devoted himself to bettering the condition of the unemployed in South Wales, and became known as a reconciler of industrial disputes and family quarrels. During the Irish troubles of that period he and Edith Ellis won the confidence of both Protestants and Catholics, and some of the credit for the settlement belonged to them. His technique was that of the personal approach, which he described as 'direct action'; he regarded this as the supreme method used by Christ. For much of his time he roamed the Welsh countryside, making friends with workers and peasants, and speaking at public meetings with a characteristic elusive charm. He was a profound lover of the country and of all wild life, believing that the higher animals could be converted to trust and affection through the elimination of fear.

As he grew older, George Davies's profile and expression came strangely to resemble those of John Stuart Mill as shown in the statue at the end of the small Embankment Garden beyond London's Temple Station. For three years (1946-49) he was Chairman of the Peace Pledge Union, and died suddenly soon after resigning his office.

By the end of 1915, the British Fellowship had fifty-five branches, including an Irish section, in places as far apart as Cardiff and Newcastle-upon-Tyne. A year later it appointed its

third secretary, LEYTON RICHARDS, after his return from a tour
of America. Dr Richards, a very tall man, carried himself
magnificently and spoke with authority. A fellow minister called
him 'the Colossus of Congregationalism'.

Born in Sheffield in 1879, Leyton Richards was the son of a
mother so strongly moved by Liberal and Noncomformist
enthusiasms that she died from excitement on the night of the
1906 Liberal victory. It was perhaps from her that he acquired
his gift for controversial preaching and love of public debate.

Through his University life in Glasgow and Oxford he met
his wife and subsequent biographer, who had gone up to
Somerville College in 1903; she has described him as a tall, fair,
eager-faced laughing young man whose youthful boisterousness
gradually mellowed into 'a cheerful buoyancy'. Four years after
his ordination in 1906, the Collins Street Independent Church
in Melbourne invited him to become their minister. There in
1912 he protested against Australia's 'boy conscription' (a form
of compulsory military training for boys still at school) and was
denounced as 'seditious' by the Minister of Defence. Though
not actually prosecuted he returned to England in 1913, and
became minister at Bowden Downs Congregational Church,
near Manchester. Here he startled his congregation after the
outbreak of the First World War by his outright pacifist witness,
which he thought an isolated view until Henry Hodkin summoned him to the Cambridge conference which founded the
F.o.R.

'He went a depressed and lonely man', Edith Richards has
written, 'and came back a few days later transfigured.'

His church gave him leave for the duration but insisted that
he remained their minister. In 1923 he received a call from
Carr's Lane Church, Birmingham—'one of the most commanding ecclesiastical positions in the British Empire'—with which
his outstanding reputation has always been identified. He
remained there till 1939, when he accepted a Fellowship at
Woodbrooke, Birmingham. Two years before his death from a
heart attack in 1948 he had joined the Society of Friends.

For several years Dr Richards was Chairman of BBC Religious
Broadcasting in the Midlands. His last broadcast, not yet
officially 'vetted' in 1940, had a strong pacifist emphasis, and
he was never asked to broadcast again. His talk caused three

eminent pacifist clergy, Charles Raven, Donald Soper, and Henry Carter, to be banned from the air throughout the Second World War. The ban on a fourth, Dr George MacLeod, could not be maintained (see p. 92).

With the ending of First War tensions the F.o.R. began its period of 'dispersion', carried out after the 1919 Bilthoven Conference by the appointment of travelling secretaries. Conspicuous among these was MURIEL LESTER, a young woman in her middle thirties who became the Fellowship's best-known woman evangelist for nearly forty years.

A gifted and eloquent preacher whose musical voice enhanced her message, Muriel with the help of her father and sister Doris founded an East End Settlement, Kingsley Hall, Bow, in memory of her brother Kingsley who died in 1914. Though she came from a well-endowed family and had many distinguished friends, Muriel habitually repudiated convention. As a Poplar Alderman when George Lansbury was Mayor, she espoused local human rights for half a decade. Her pacifism was bound up with her belief in the power of prayer, but like other pacifists she felt isolated after August 1914 until a leaflet reached her describing the newly founded F.o.R. Soon she was organising F.o.R. meetings in churches, halls, and at the dock gates. In a large East End dug-out during Zeppelin raids, her friend Cornelius Boeke, the Dutch pacifist, sustained the shelterers with his violin and, until he was deported to Holland, joined Muriel in protecting the victims of anti-German riots and marching through London in the 1917 demonstration supporting Lord Lansdowne's Peace Letter.

Also associated with Poplar as minister of Trinty Congregational Church was the REV. ALAN BALDING, later British F.o.R. Chairman for several years.

Immediately after the war, Muriel protested against the continuing blockade. At the editorial offices of *Punch*, she demanded a full-page cartoon to publicize the plight, reported by Henry Nevinson, of Europe's starving children. At an open-air service which she addressed near Marble Arch, a listening soldier commented: 'That girl's talking sense!'

In 1920 Muriel began to travel, and spoke all over Europe. Gandhi's non-violence programme was now acquiring momen-

tum in India, and she spent a month by invitation at his Sabar-
mati ashram. Her Indian audiences were astonished to hear of
a British movement which accepted his ideals. She next visited
Japan and China, where her meetings always included a prayer
for the forgiveness of Britain's nineteenth-century crimes against
the Chinese. Constant mentions of Russia by Asian colleagues
involved a visit there in 1934. After one meeting she learned
that the official Communist guide had remarked: 'I didn't know
Christianity was anything like that'.

Between 1934 and 1954 Muriel frequently preached in the
Far East and India, and in Central Europe, Palestine, Latin
America, Australia, New Zealand, South Africa, the Philippines, Ceylon, Greece, Pakistan, Beirut and Hong Kong. Her
many adventures included the discovery in 1934 of Japanese
drug-traffickers in China, and the presentation of her evidence
to the League of Nations Opium Committee; a month in Hitler's
Germany which revealed the spiritual strength of the underground resistance; and her internment in Trinidad in 1941. Her
South African tour in 1950 included a visit to Manilal and
Sushila Gandhi at Phoenix, Natal. A journey to Rangoon the
following year made possible an hour with Burma's Japanese
war-criminals, where the red-robed prisoners destined for execution entrusted her with their last letters to relatives in Japan.
Thanks to the support of her work by the American F.o.R., all
the surviving Japanese prisoners were ultimately transferred to
their own country.

In 1931 Kingsley Hall became famous as the temporary home
of Gandhi during the Round Table Conference. Seven years
later, at the Council's request, Muriel joined the I.F.o.R. staff.
After 1954, enriched by her memories and dreams, she left Bow
with her sister for Kingsley Cottage at Loughton in Essex.

During 1921 the Fellowship found homes for over 400 under-
nourished children from Central Europe. In November that year
T. C. FOLEY became Secretary in order to organize the provincial
work and to add a social and industrial significance to the F.o.R.
teaching. The next British Secretary, OLIVER DRYER, took charge
for six years and then became General Secretary of the I.F.o.R.

His work had always been potentially international, and in
two years of quiet, steady persistence he developed the Fellowship's external contacts beyond all expectation, visiting many

countries and forming F.o.R. groups. These include the Balkans, a virgin field which he saw as an appropriate region where young and tough members of the Fellowship might initiate the work of reconciliation. An attractive personality helped him to bring together people of different customs and languages, and he made the I.F.o.R. a potent force for peace in Europe.

A memorable contemporary of Dryer was HUBERT B. PARRIS, a colleague of Percy Bartlett in London's GPO. He joined the British Fellowship in 1915, and in 1917 went to prison as a declared conscientious objector. After the war he joined one of the first teams sent by the Friends' War Victims Relief Committee to undertake reconstruction work in the devastated areas of Northern France. In 1920 he was suggested as I.F.o.R. Secretary but preferred practical work, and with Pierre Cérésole toured the old Hindenburg Line in search of a site where a tiny 'wedge of active goodwill' could be driven home.

Hubert Parris subsequently joined the Baptist Missionary Society's team in the Belgian Congo, and for many years took charge at Stanleyville.

In December 1924 a Cambridge Conference celebrated the tenth anniversary of the Fellowship's foundation, recalling the initial sense of urgency. By this time the British Fellowship had 7,481 recorded members and 1,108 supporters. PERCY BARTLETT himself now became General Secretary and remained in this post till 1938, when he went on to the International Fellowship with part-time work for Embassies of Reconciliation.

Percy Bartlett had joined the Society of Friends in 1911 at the age of twenty-three, and the F.o.R. four years later. During the First War he was imprisoned as a conscientious objector, but afterwards seldom referred to this experience; 'he is too good at forgiving people', a colleague once commented. In 1920 he served as secretary of the World Conference of Young Friends at Jordans. Of this period he has said: The man who helped me most is gone now and practically forgotten. He was Isaac Goss.'

ISAAC GOSS, too valuable to be forgotten so easily, was then looking for assistance with 1,400 young war victims from Austria and Hungary. This work led Percy Bartlett to the Secretaryship of the Fellowship's London Union and thence to his later posts.

In the December 1956 issue of the I.F.o.R. *Newsletter*, Lilian

Stevenson referred to his understanding, without any theological training, of the complex trends of the religious thought of Europe, and his familiarity, through dogged hard work rather than linguistic gifts, with French and German. Like many Friends he had taken a prominent part in ecumenical discussions, and after the I.F.o.R. Conference at Sandwich in 1928 he organized, with the help of Dr G. K. Bell, later Bishop of Chichester, Canon Raven, H. R. L. Sheppard, and Leyton Richards, a Council of Christian Pacifist Groups. This body united peace workers from nearly all the churches, and on successive Armistice Days held large London meetings in the endeavour to prevent a second World War.

Towards the end of the nineteen-thirties the Embassies of Reconciliation, for which Percy Bartlett was largely responsible, took him all over Europe—including Spain in 1937 during the Civil War—to initiate international peace conversations as suggested by the Van Zeeland Report. He also visited India, with C. F. Andrews and Agatha Harrison, during the long period of tension which preceded Independence.

Spectacular though these efforts were, his ten years of quiet spade-work after the First World War had been equally rewarding, for it led many outstanding individuals such as Charles Raven, Henry Carter, and H. R. L. Sheppard, to dedicate themselves to Christian pacifism and give it new vitality. In 1937 Canon Raven said that to Percy Bartlett was due 'the extraordinary growth of the Christian pacifist influence and activity during recent years . . . and in general the bringing of our cause into a position of public importance'. Twelve years later, when a gathering of clergy, ministers, and lay Christians gave a party at Friends' House to celebrate Percy Bartlett's twenty-five years of active service for peace, Canon Raven added that he had been responsible for his own conversion to pacifism.

A self-effacing man whose potentialities have clearly exceeded their public recognition, Percy Bartlett has spent much time collecting material for books which by the date of his unwilling retirement in 1956 he had not written. He did however publish a small volume, Quakers and the Christian Church, in 1942, and in 1961 a biography of his colleague Barrow Cadbury, to whose treasureship the Embassies of Reconciliation were so much indebted.

Early in 1926, seventy-five British 'personalities' published a Press appeal, initiated by 100 French signatories the previous July, for the amendment of the Versailles Treaty. This followed a widely-publicized Peace Letter from Arthur Ponsonby to the Prime Minister in September 1925. Had these efforts succeeded, Hitler might never have arisen. The General Strike of May 1926 gave the F.o.R. opportunities for social reconciliation, and the Annual Labour Party Conference carried a unanimous but ultimately unreliable resolution pledging itself to resistance if war came.

The failure of a military Tattoo in Birmingham that year seemed a further tribute to recent peace witness, while the formation of two F.o.R. groups in Egypt showed that its effect was spreading far beyond Britain. A Cambridge University Union motion passed in March 1927 by 213 votes to 138: 'That lasting peace can only be secured by the people of England adopting an uncompromising attitude of pacifism', clearly arose from the growing influence of CHARLES EARLE RAVEN.

Since the death of George Lansbury, a totally different personality, Canon Raven D.D. has been almost the only British F.o.R. leader widely known outside pacifist circles. An outstanding scholar of his generation, he was Regius Professor of Divinity at Cambridge from 1932 to 1950, and in 1947-9 became University Vice-Chancellor. He holds many honorary degrees in Britain and the Commonwealth, is Chaplain to the Queen (as to her two predecessors), and has delivered special lectures in Dublin, Cambridge, Harvard, Glasgow, Oxford, Edinburgh, Liverpool, and Canada. His many books include not only studies of Theology and of international politics but also of Natural Science, since he is a naturalist who specialises in observing birds and flowers.

Contemporaries of Canon Raven, born in 1885, testify to his spectacular brilliance in youth. From the outset he has been an intellectual *prima donna*, reinforced by a handsome, commanding appearance, and always aware that his destiny made him a potential leader and public character. One long-time acquaintance emphasises his youthful arrogance, combined with 'complete intellectual honesty'. An important gift is that of making theology acceptable to the unacademic man-in-the-street, and his chief service to the I.F.o.R. has been the much-needed mental development of the whole movement.

In 1914 he saw no alternative for himself but military service and, though ordained in 1909, he applied for a combatant commission. Rejected on medical grounds, he became a Chaplain in 1916, and went through the 1917 campaign at Cambrai. An incident related of his experience at the front explains the gradual modification of his arrogance, now apparent only when he is confronted with persons of dubious sincerity. After being blown up by a shell, he found himself in a shell hole with a private soldier who started nervously whenever the guns went off. The young Chaplain commented adversely on this reaction, and then realized that, owing to their position in the crater, the private was deliberately sheltering him with his own body. Like a flood of light the realization came to him that this illiterate man had understood the meaning of total self-sacrifice.

After demobilization, the 'Hang the Kaiser' election shocked him into helping to run a Labour Candidate at Cambridge. In 1920 he resigned his work there (Dean and Lecturer in Divinity at Emmanuel College) for a parish in Southwark diocese, where he edited a weekly paper, 'The Challenge', and helped Lucy Gardner to organize the C.O.P.E.C. movement. He drafted Volume I of the preparatory Reports, and contributed to Volume VIII, Christians and War, part of its statement on the pacifist position. But he did not fully accept pacifism as a creed until the 'Christ and Peace' campaign of 1930. By that time his theological studies, combined with social and spiritual service, had brought conviction. He joined the F.o.R., and in 1932 became Chairman of the British Executive.

During the next ten years his main concerns were, first, to replace the negative war-resistance policies of such bodies as the War Resisters' International and the Peace Pledge Union with a positive emphasis on reconciliation; this led to the formation of Embassies of Reconciliation and George Lansbury's missions to Hitler. Secondly, he sought to unify the denominational Christian peace societies, and to keep closely in contact with such bodies as the League of Nations Union, Federal Union, and the Society of Friends. One consequence was the creation of the Christian Pacifist Groups Committee, and for him the membership of many different societies, in association with Percy Bartlett,

Henry Carter, George MacLeod and H. R. L. Sheppard. Thirdly, he endeavoured to formulate a more coherent and wide-ranging theology of Christian pacifism by both special lectures and books, such as the Halley Stewart Lectures, *Is War Obsolete?* 1934; *War and the Christian*, 1938; and *Is Christ Divided?* 1943.

In later life a certain sardonic quality has redeemed him from unmitigated sainthood, and made him a supremely attractive colleague for both old and young fellow-workers.

Canon Raven's concern for the development of theological pacifism has been reinforced by the work of two other distinguished scholars, PROFESSOR G. H. C. MACGREGOR D.D., and DR, GEORGE MACLEOD D.D.

Professor Macgregor (1892-1963) was the author of two famous pacifist classics, *The New Testament Basis of Pacifism* (omitted by *The Times* from his Obituary) and *The Relevance of the Impossible*. From 1933 he was Professor of Divinity and Biblical Criticism in Glasgow University and was also President of the Scottish F.o.R. As an eminent theologian he gave a Biblical bias to the F.o.R., and was its Chairman from the end of the Second War until 1958. He belonged to the front rank of trained theologians and was an impressive speaker, but not a passionate preacher. His share in the development of pacifist thought and action had little in common with that of such dominant natural orators as Leyton Richards.

In an address, 'Looking to Our Foundations', to the Council of the F.o.R. in 1953, he used significant words: 'We Christian pacifists have often been taunted by our "realist" friends that we cannot bring in the Kingdom of God by acting as if it were already here. Yet this is, I believe, precisely what Jesus did teach; if only men were prepared to take Jesus at His word, and to order their lives here and now by the laws of a heavenly kingdom, then the power of God would break in upon them and take them unawares!'

By contrast Dr George MacLeod, the founder of the Iona Community, is a magnificent colourful figure who has been associated with reformist, rather than devotional, movements in the Church. A member of an aristocratic family with a long line of Presbyterian ancestors, who is correctly described as 'the Very Rev. Sir George F. MacLeod', he went to school at

Marlborough, and won the Military Cross as an officer in the First World War. He feels that war, though in part redeemed by sublime moments of unselfish gallantry, has now had its day, and that nuclear warfare is no more than a form of scientific cowardice.

In 1957 Dr MacLeod was elected Moderator of the General Assembly of the Church of Scotland, though half his compatriots must have been opposed to his views which he proclaims in the spirit of a warrior 'going over the top'. During the Second World War he was one of four pacifist clergy who were banned from the air after Leyton Richards' broadcast, but the ban on him could not be maintained since he is the only Scottish preacher popular enough to fill an outsize church north of the Border. He became President of the I.F.o.R. in September 1963, succeeding Dr Howard Schomer.

A younger theologian from Northumberland, the REV. R. G. BELL, joined the F.o.R. in 1931, and now combines theology with politics. He believes that pacifism should be made politically relevant, and that modern pacifists have two main tasks to perform: to build up a community which does not lead to crime, and to find the right kind of spiritual deterrent.

During 1927 the Fellowship's perception of social tension as a form of violence found expression in a September Conference at Caerleon. A November campaign for industrial peace took George Davies, Percy Bartlett and Gilbert Porteous to Liverpool. Early in 1928 the distinguished economist, Sir George Paish, prophetically warned a Manchester assembly of the coming bankruptcy precipitated by post-war policies.

At this time AGATHA HARRISON, the Quaker interpreter of India and friend of Gandhi, worked closely with the F.o.R. Gandhi's teaching on non-violence showed her social and industrial reconciliation as part of the struggle against war, and she brought the Fellowship into growing contact with India. She co-operated with such pro-Independence pacifists as Carl Heath, and meetings of the India Conciliation Group took place in Percy Bartlett's office.

At her memorial meeting in 1954, Krishna Menon, then India's High Commissioner in Britain, commented: 'No flags were flown for her, but all over India people mourned her name'. What probably remains most clearly with those who gratefully remember her is the impressive quality of her grave, deep voice. When the Second World War approached, the increasing concern of the British Fellowship for world poverty and industrial strife gave way to protests against the Government's rearmament policy as embodied in the White Paper of 1935. At the Central Hall, Westminster, a respected Presbyterian Minister, the REV. HERBERT GRAY, helped Percy Bartlett to organize a series of Christian Pacifist Group mass meetings on the Christian attitude to war. Also associated with this protest was Canon H. R. L. ('Dick') Sheppard, who that year published the letter calling for individual war renunciation which led to the formation of the Peace Pledge Union.

In 1935 the Editorial Board of *Reconciliation* included Canon Raven (Chairman), Henry Carter, Ruth Fry, Herbert Gray, and the Editor, Lewis Maclachlan. The magazine vigorously supported George Lansbury's letter to *The Times* on August 19th, appealing to the Pope and the Archbishops to give a lead for peace in a world preparing for war. One of these was not a sympathizer; in a broadcast on September 7th Archbishop Temple of York (and later of Canterbury) took the view that in a sub-Christian world, armies and navies must be accepted by the Church. The remarkable development of the British F.o.R. in the nineteen-thirties nevertheless continued up to the outbreak of war.

From 1936-46 the General Secretary was the REV. LESLIE ARTINGSTALL, who had a gift for organization and appointed Regional Secretaries to be responsible for different areas of Britain. They kept closely in touch with him, and though they included clergy and laity of many denominations, his skill welded them into an effective team. A large increase in membership and activity resulted.

A militant Quaker, BEATRICE BROWN, who became Secretary of the London Union (then the spearhead of the Movement) in 1938, valuably assisted him. A small woman aged sixty-four, with rosy cheeks and a halo of white hair, she obtained her own way by sitting quietly with folded hands. She died in 1955, aged eighty-one.

Another leader responsible for the remarkable strength of the F.o.R. at the outbreak of war was Dr HENRY CARTER, the stern father-figure who since 1911 had been General Secretary of the

Social Welfare Department of the Methodist Church in Britain. His chief service to the pacifist movement, in addition to his work with Embassies of Reconciliation, was probably the creation of the Christian Pacifist Forestry and Land Units which offered a new form of alternative service to Britain's 55,111 registered conscientious objectors. Of the 10,836 allowed non-combatant service, many found this forestry work a solution to their problem. Dr Carter's commemoration service in June 1951 crowded the Central Hall, Westminster.

When pacifists found themselves deeply concerned by the combined Second War inhumanities of blockade and bombing, imposed by their own Government upon the most helpless members of the 'enemy' population, an intrepid Quaker member of the F.o.R., CORDER CATCHPOOL, formed a Bombing Restriction Committee which publicized, as widely as its resources permitted, pamphlets giving uncompromising details of the crimes committed in the name of the British people.

Corder, a white-haired, mild-mannered Friend, never accepted the existence of defeat. After three years' imprisonment as a First War conscientious objector, he and his wife Gwen dedicated themselves to relief work in Germany, and remained there, though hampered by the Gestapo, until 1936. During the air raids, Corder cycled through the bombs from his Hampstead home to serve in East End shelters. A dedicated mountaineer, he characteristically died while climbing Monte Rosa in 1952 at the age of sixty-nine.

In 1947 the Rev. CLIFFORD MACQUIRE became British Secretary after a year of shared responsibility by DORIS NICHOLLS and the Rev. HAMPDEN HORNE. His pacifism dated from a conversion to Christianity at twenty-five, after some years as a speaker who espoused free-thinking in reaction against Sunday School teaching. The acute experience which transformed his life came in 1931, when a Christian mission visited his home church at Norwich. Later he was shocked to find that most Christians were not pacifists.

An effective, fiery speaker, Clifford Macquire left the Secretaryship in 1957 for a church of his own, and MAX PARKER took his place.

From 1915 to the present day the British F.o.R. has always published a magazine, though its name has varied from *The*

Venturer, the F.o.R. *News-Sheet, Reconciliation, The Christian Pacifist,* and back to *Reconciliation.* The successive editors have been Richard Roberts, Lewis Maclachlan, Percy Bartlett, Paul Gliddon, again Lewis Maclachlan, Glyn Lloyd Phelps, Leonard Hurst, and Clifford Macquire.

It is all too easy from a professional standpoint to criticise this magazine, which has suffered from insufficient funds, half-trained voluntary contributors, and other characteristic problems of idealist publications. Its editors have all been dedicated, self-sacrificing men, and one especially deserves commemoration.

The Rev. LEWIS MACLACHLAN, a mildly satirical Scot with a penetrating intelligence and a fine sense of humour, edited the F.o.R. *News Sheet* from 1919 to 1923, and *Reconciliation* from 1942 to 1954. He joined the F.o.R. at the outset, beginning as personal secretary to Richard Roberts. The movement owes him an incalculable debt for his clear, balanced, unsentimental interpretation of its message.

Formative influences in the early British Fellowship came from C. J. Cadoux, Halliday Orchard, Joe Rorke (editor of *The Venturer*), H. C. Carter, Hugh Martin and E. Cunningham. Other prominent persons who have served and spoken for it include Dr Alex Wood, the Rev. Alan Knott, Dr Donald Soper, Professor John Ferguson, and the Rev. Michael Scott. Each would deserve a full account of his work for the F.o.R. if space permitted.

Chapter 6

THE AMERICAN TESTIMONY

I. FIFTY YEARS' WORK

The American Fellowship, like the British which it succeeded in less than a year, was born from the travail of the First World War. It was founded on November 11, 1915, after Henry Hodgkin had met sixty-eight men and women of like convictions in Long Island, New York. Gilbert A. Beaver, Edward W. Evans, and Charles J. Rhoads were respectively the first Chairman, Secretary and Treasurer. In 1917 Norman Thomas joined as co-secretary and in 1919 Bishop Paul Jones, removed from the Diocese of Utah for his pacifist creed, became Secretary for ten years. When the US entered the war, the Fellowship had already 300 members.

Before 1917, the work was directed towards ending the fighting and helping conscientious objectors, for whom legal aid was arranged after America joined the Allies. They suffered much early persecution, but after the Rev. J. N. Sayre and others had interceded with President Wilson their treatment was modified, and in 1933 President Roosevelt finally granted an amnesty to all conscientious objectors still in prison. In 1938 he also received two delegations led by Mr Sayre, who was President of the National Peace Conference for three years preceding the Second World War.

When the War ended, work began wherever reconciliation appeared to be most needed. In the field of labour relations A. J. Muste, Evan Thomas and Charles Webber personally intervened in strikes with fruitful results. Other spheres included work for racial brotherhood and for reconciliation in the South, to which a section is given later in this chapter. Continuous peace education went on through such publications as *The World Tomorrow*, which in January 1918 replaced the

British magazine *The Venturer*, and was itself replaced in 1934 by the monthly *Fellowship*, which has continued under the successive editorships of Harold Fey, five years Executive Secretary of the F.o.R., and later Executive Editor of *The Christian Century*; John Nevin Sayre; and Alfred Hassler (from 1946). The publication programme expanded greatly after the Second World War, and by 1954 was using the full-time work of eight persons with a budget of $55,000.

The nineteen-thirties saw a period of great activity, which involved attendance at many international conferences, and prolonged goodwill tours, especially by Nevin and Kathleen Sayre, to Fellowship centres in Europe. These tours extended to the Far East as soon as the Japanese invasion of Manchuria brought a crisis in Sino-Japanese relations, and to Latin America (on which a special report follows this section).

In 1931, as reported by *The World Tomorrow* for May, Dr Kirby Page arranged the circularisation of 53,000 US clergymen with fifteen controversial questions, and obtained over 19,500 replies of which 12,000 expressed the opinion that American churches should no longer sanction war. In this period the Fellowship weathered a serious crisis when an attempt was made to modify its opposition to all war by endorsing the concept of the 'class war'. This was emphatically rejected by the membership. At about the same time the Fellowship's Statement of Purpose was re-drafted, specifying the relevance of pacifism to the total organization of society, and while retaining its essential Christian basis, providing for full membership by non-Christian religious pacifists.

By the outbreak of the Second World War, the Fellowship's educational work and that of other pacifist bodies was showing definite results (see Appendix, p. 226). Most major religious denominations had gone on record as officially supporting conscientious objectors, and in 1940 Congress incorporated some relatively generous provisions in the Selective Service Act. Thousands of young men, as the Act permitted, chose non-combatant service in the medical and other branches of the armed forces, and over 16,000 others chose 'work of national importance' in Civilian Public Service Camps and, later, in mental hospitals. But many weaknesses developed in the Selective Service law, and 6,000 conscientious objectors who could not

G

accept its terms, including five F.o.R. secretaries, had gone to prison before the war ended.

Attempts initiated during the First War to end the fighting and lay foundations of a peace based on justice were repeated in the Second. In Switzerland eleven members of the Fellowship acted as intermediaries between groups of British and German Churchmen seeking a basis for ending the war. Contemporary passions defeated these experiments, but they bore fruit later in the relatively swift termination of hatred between combatants who found possible a new fellowship based on mutual suffering. Continuous attempts were also made to keep the real nature of war before the peoples taking part, and to help refugees. Strenuous efforts went into opposition to the evacuation of Japanese Americans from the West Coast and in helping them to relocate in other parts of the country. (See the section on Japan in Chapter 11).

Constant F.o.R. conferences took place in the United States themselves during the war years, and soon after it ended new world tours began; one by Nevin and Kathleen Sayre in 1950 took them to India, Pakistan, Japan, Hawaii, the Philippines, Hong Kong, and Thailand. They returned via the Near East and Europe, crossing from England in one night after a journey which had abundantly demonstrated the now global character of the I.F.o.R.

In a *Fellowship* article published in 1955, Alfred Hassler summarized the work of the American Fellowship under three headings: (1) The overall educational and 'project programme' directed by the national office in New York; (2) The regional programmes, consisting partly of an extension of the national projects and partly of specific local programmes; (3) The activities of the 300-odd local groups and 12,000 active members who made up the 'grass roots' of the Fellowship. By this time the work was organized from nine Regional Offices, in the Far West, New England, the South-east, the Midwest, the South-west, the Middle Atlantic, the region of the Great Lakes, the Mid-South (the newest Region with headquarters in Nashville, Tennessee), and New York, where the national office staff numbered twenty persons.

Between 1950 and 1957 the Fellowship, in addition to its regular activities, vigorously opposed a renewed effort to impose

Universal Military Training on the country; inaugurated a Food for China campaign under the biblical injunction 'When Thine Enemy Hungers, Feed Him;' and established a 'Committee to Aid the Bombed Christians of the South' to raise funds to rebuild churches bombed in the struggle over racial segregation.

Shortly afterwards the Fellowship began its recent policy of education by displayed advertisements, starting in 1960 with a large notice advocating a more mature attitude towards political questions in the UN Assembly; a policy of total world disarmament; the end of 'tit-for-tat' diplomacy; a new policy towards the Caribbean; and a programme of massive aid for handicapped countries. The next large advertisement, 'If Thine Enemy Hunger', coincided with a statement adopted by the Fellowship's Executive Committee which expressed concern regarding the Government's attitude towards China. On April 23rd, 1961 another outsize advertisement in the New York Times, entitled 'We Cannot Condone This Act', was signed by thirty-four key individuals condemning the US invasion of Cuba.

On October 29, 1961, another advertisement, entitled 'A Time to Speak', was supported by fifty-one important signatories who deplored the 'moral atrocity' of atmospheric testing whether by the Soviet Union or by the United Sates. These widely circulated statements helped to create the public opionion which in 1963 resulted in the Test Ban Treaty signed by the USA, USSR, and the UK.

In five decades of dedicated work the F.o.R. in the United States has left few areas of American life unaffected by its influence. Though anti-militarism, peace, and international reconciliation have always been its major interests, it has worked in many other areas where Christian pacifist insight had significance. From its concern have grown such diverse organisations as the National Conference of Christians and Jews, the American Civil Liberties Union, the Religion and Labor Foundation, the Workers' Defence League, the Committee on Militarism in Education, the Congress on Racial Equality, the National Council against Conscription, the Society for Social Responsibility in Science, the Church Peace Mission, and, more recently, the American Committee on Africa. The chronology of its interests coincides with the areas of tension which have stirred America in the past half-century.

The work of the Fellowship was appropriately summed up in a statement made by John Haynes Holmes on its thirtieth anniversary: 'More truly than any traditional church of which I know, the Fellowship preaches and practices that principle of spiritual good will, that ideal of love so alien to all force and violence, which lies at the core of the great religions of history.'

II. WORK IN LATIN AMERICA

In 1919 propaganda for military intervention in Mexico spread throughout the United States. On December 4th Norman Thomas, then Secretary of the American F.o.R., sent a letter to its members urging them to oppose war with Mexico. In the next two years the F.o.R. contributed substantially to the development of a public opinion which finally induced President Coolidge to decide on peace.

The F.o.R. was subsequently responsible for similar protests against U.S. intervention in Haiti and Nicaragua. In 1927 a joint mission of four persons, which included J. N. Sayre and Carolena Wood, went from the American Friends Service Committee and the F.o.R. on a goodwill mission to the five Central American republics.

From that time to the present, reconciliation work in Latin America has continued. In 1929 the F.o.R. sent CHARLES A. THOMSEN to Costa Rica to be its travelling Secretary for three years in Central America and the Caribbean. When his noteworthy task of interpretation ended, the current economic depression and the F.o.R.'s own 1934 internal crisis cut out further early work in this area, but by that time the US had withdrawn its marines from Nicaragua and President Roosevelt's Good Neighbour policy for Latin America had started.

When the Second War began Nevin Sayre asked Muriel Lester, who was in America at its outbreak, to undertake a South American tour with Margaret Campbell of the US Fellowship. Their work was responsible for the foundation of F.o.R. groups in Montevideo and Buenos Aires, but in August 1941 Muriel was interned at Trinidad for four months by order of the British Government. She was then deported to Britain, to spend several days in Holloway Gaol, three weeks before the Japanese attacked Pearl Harbour.

During the urgent national problems of the next three years Latin America was not forgotten, and an F.o.R. centre was set up in Mexico thanks mainly to DEVERE ALLEN, a conscientious objector of 1917 and a former editor of *The World Tomorrow* who went to live in Mexico while building up connections for his Nofrontier News Service and its successor, *The Worldover Press*. Before his death in 1955 Devere Allen was supplying material to over 700 publications, including 210 in Latin America. He was also the American editor of the international symposium, *Above All Nations*. His extensive writings are now collected in the Peace Library at Swarthmore College.

Visits to Central America by Professor Alfred Fisk of San Francisco and Roger W. Axford, followed by a short tour by Mr Sayre in 1944, led to the formation of F.o.R. groups in Mexico. Here the problem—which still continues despite visits to Latin America by Hildegard and Jean Goss-Mayr in 1962 to reconcile its political 'left' and 'right'—has been the scarcity of Roman Catholic pacifists. The revolutionary ferment of Brazil presents a continuous challenge to the F.o.R.

In 1945-6 Mr Sayre, visiting Mexico, Cuba, Puerto Rico and the Virgin Islands, arranged for part-time work in Mexico by a religious pacifist from Monterray, FRANCISCO ESTRELLO, who founded a two-monthly magazine, *Fraternidad*. By that time functioning groups in Monterrey, Saltillo, Torreon, San Luis Potosi, Mexico City and Puebla had reached a combined membership of 285. In 1946 the US Fellowship was represented by Herman Will and the Rev. EARL SMITH at two Christian Youth Conferences in Cuba, which is not however a fruitful field for F.o.R. work today.

In Puerto Rico pacifism was introduced by the wartime Civilian Public Service camps for conscientious objectors of the Mennonites and Church of the Brethren, and Nevin Sayre returned from his visit convinced that the US should not continue to hold Puerto Rico as a colony. He visited the country twice after 1945, working in cooperation with Roger Baldwin, Chairman of the International League for the Rights of Man and an I.F.o.R. Committee member, on Puerto Rican civil liberties. The group here has continued but the F.o.R. message has not readily taken root in the native soil, and most members are North Americans.

In 1945 ANTONIO LOUREIRO, an associate of Earl Smith in Montevideo, was established as half-time Fellowship Secretary. As a leader of three youth camps, he spoke all over the River Plate area and produced Spanish translations of F.o.R. classics with the help of Luis Odell, first Chairman of the South American Committee, and Jorge Bullrich, a layman converted to pacifism by the writings of Richard Gregg.

During 1946, invited by the now established *Fraternidad de Reconciliation y Paz*, Nevin and Kathleen Sayre, accompanied part-time by Francisco Estrello and Antonio Loureiro, made a 14,000 miles tour of fifteen Central and South American countries. On his return Mr Sayre filed a protest against the US programme of multiplying and standardizing Latin American armaments and military training.

In April 1951 the F.o.R. sent Pasteur Henri Roser to Uruguay, Argentina and Brazil in response to the desire of South American members for a Latin visitor from Europe. He was followed by Herrick Young of the North American Committee, who reported seeing evidence of F.o.R. work. Two years later the Methodist Bishop SANTE U. BARBIERI of Buenos Aires attended the I.F.o.R. Council at Dortmund, Germany, but his request for another intervisitation tour by a F.o.R. leader could not be financed until the Sayres made a second extensive tour in 1958. This was unfortunate because economic austerity and the evil influence of Peron and other dictators undermined the Fellowship's work.

Nevin Sayre made a fresh start in Mexico in 1954 with the help of a devoted young Methodist layman, Pedro de Koster Fuentes. But the resignation of Antonio Loureiro in 1956 owing to the claims of other work caused the Sayres to decide on yet a further tour, which revitalized the Argentina centre, in co-operation with D. D. LURA-VILLANUEVA, a lawyer prominent in many Protestant church organisations who joined the F.o.R. in 1942 and is now Chairman of the South American Committee. Between April 10th and May 29th 1958 they visited Puerto Rico, Brazil, Chile, Bolivia, Peru, Panama, Costa Rica and Mexico in addition to Argentina, and came back with the conviction that the Latin American countries, with their harsh laws against conscientious objectors, represented a grave responsibility which the I.F.o.R. should permanently assume.

The developing crisis in relations with Cuba, following the Castro revolution in 1958, prompted new efforts by the American F.o.R. A proposal to send a nine-person 'reconciliation team' to Cuba in early 1961 was frustrated by the State Department's restrictions on travel, but the resulting discussions brought the Fellowship's concern strongly to the attention of both the US and Cuban governments.

Successive conferences in Cuba and Latin America since then have resulted in an ambitious programme of contact with democratic revolutionary leaders throughout Latin America, with plans for conferences and training sessions on non-violence, establishment of a US Committee on Latin America, and other appropriate actions.

III. THE RACIAL STRUGGLE

Since the first Negro slaves landed in the United States in 1619, some of the worst tragedies in America's turbulent history have arisen from the racial struggle in the South. It was the basis of the Civil War (1861-65); the direct reason for the assassination of Abraham Lincoln, whose death left the breach between North and South unhealed to this day; and the indirect cause of the assassination of President Kennedy, which many believe owed its pointless ferocity largely to the atmosphere of hatred and violence which the last-ditch fight against integration engenders.

The F.o.R. has been deeply involved in the revolution by which more than twenty million Americans are struggling to throw off the status of 'second-class citizenship'. If the Fellowship were an immense organization with millions of dollars to spend, it might provide a lasting solution for this chronic problem. Understaffed and under-financed as it is, it can only do sporadic pioneer work, and hope that other bodies with greater resources may follow where it leads. Its initiative has taken the direction of non-violent action, including civil disobedience where necessary, which involves a follower of this creed in openly committing illegal or socially disapproved acts with unquestioning readiness to accept the consequences.

Most of the direct action organized by equality-seeking

Negroes and their white supporters in the South has followed this pattern, originated by Gandhi in South Africa and India, and widely publicised by the F.o.R. though much of the initiative has been taken by the Negroes themselves. F.o.R. members, including those on the organization's staff, have been conspicuous in this work; among them are the present Associate Secretary Glenn Smiley, and former Race Relations Secretaries Bayard Rustin, George Houser, James Farmer, and James Lawson, and, of course, Advisory Council member Martin Luther King, Jr. Of these Rustin, Farmer, Lawson and King are themselves Negroes.

Others involved have been George Collins (F.o.R. Travelling Student Secretary 1923-28); Howard Kester, a Southerner who was F.o.R. secretary at Nashville from 1929 to 1933; Constance Rumbough (author of *The Ancient World*); Claud Nelson, F.o.R. Atlanta Secretary 1934-38; Howard Thurman (poet and Chaplain); and Shelton Hale Bishop.

JAMES FARMER, who joined the F.o.R. in 1939, was Race Relations Secretary from 1941 to 1945, and is now National Director of CORE (The Congress of Race Equality). He led the first CORE freedom ride that ended in Jackson, Mississippi, on May 24, 1961, and brought him forty days in jail.

The Fellowship's work in this field began in 1920, when *The World Tomorrow* carried articles on Gandhi's non-violent campaigns. By 1935 the F.o.R. had established a strong branch at Nashville, Tennessee, which effectively intervened where excessive penalties had been imposed on Negroes. In 1942 the Fellowship organized non-violent sit-in campaigns in northern cities to remove racial restrictions in restaurants and other public places. An F.o.R. 'Journey of Reconciliation', often called the first of the 'freedom rides', took place in 1946, when an interracial group toured the South urging Christian love of neighbours rather than un-Christian segregation.

In 1954 the historic Supreme Court decision to desegregate schools newly galvanized both the rebels and their intransigent opponents, since it was followed by desegregation in countless other institutions. An early struggle occurred in November 1955 at Orangeburg, North Carolina, where a request by Negro parents for token integration in the segregated schools brought mass boycotts of Negroes by shops and banks, and a counter-boycott against 15 white shopkeepers led by Matthew McCollum, Negro Pastor of Trinity Methodist Church. He wrote later: 'If it had not been for the great unpublicized work of the F.o.R. in the South these past three years, that section of our country might well be engulfed in violence and bloodshed today.'

On December 5, 1955 began the now famous bus boycott conducted by Martin Luther King in Montgomery, Alabama, when 50,000 Negroes 'walked for freedom' for 381 days. They avoided using the buses until December 21, 1956, when the boycott was called off as completely successful. F.o.R. secretary Glenn Smiley spent much time with the Negro leadership during this period, and rode with Dr King and Ralph Abernathy on the first desegregated bus. In September 1957 came the struggle for school integration at Little Rock, Arkansas, in which Governor Faubus opposed the Federal decision to integrate nine Negro students at the Central High School. Later Glenn Smiley, present for six days of the contest, organized a workshop on non-violence in the city.

In Greensboro, North Carolina, in February 1960, four Negro students read a popular illustrated F.o.R. 'comic' called 'Martin Luther King and the Montgomery story'. At once they decided to 'sit-in' at a local segregated lunch-counter. Though sit-ins had been used for eighteen years in the North, this was the beginning in the South. The experiment caught on like a prairie fire; the sit-ins were followed by wade-ins (at segregated swimming pools), kneel-ins (at segregated churches), and stand-ins (in white theatre queues).

These forms of protest by rebels well-trained in non-violence have continued ever since; in the first six months nearly 1,000 lunch-counters were desegregated, more than 10,000 young Negroes took part, and about 2,000, with some white supporters, had been arrested. In May 1961 began the protests of the freedom-riders, organized by the Congress of Racial Equality which the F.o.R. had started in 1942. This involved the deliberate use of white bus services and stations by Negroes who accepted without complaint or resistance the arrests and beatings-up which frequently followed.

Sooner or later the South will have to come into the twentieth century, and progressively helpful civil rights legislation will be passed by Congress. Meanwhile hundreds of Negro leaders have received a training, both theoretical and practical, in non-violent resistance, and Southern whites and Negroes are acquiring a new image of one another. Much of the work initiated by the Fellowship has now been taken over by CORE, the Southern Christian Leadership Conference, and the Student Non-Violent Coordinating Committee.

The Rev. GLENN E. SMILEY, in whose hands F.o.R. participation in this great liberation movement has lain since 1955, joined the Fellowship in 1942, and was Southwest Regional Secretary from 1942 to 1954. A Texan by birth, he had spent fifteen years as a Methodist minister in Texas, Arizona and California. From July 1944 to October 1945 he was imprisoned on McNeil Island in Washington State for refusing to cooperate with the Selective Service system. He then worked for ten years in the Los Angeles F.o.R. office organizing work camps on Indian reservations, but periodically travelled through the Deep South where he developed a profound concern for Negro aspirations. Now located in the F.o.R.'s national office, he has led in training the rebels in the techniques of non-violence, and in 1963 held six workshops from Boston to Seattle.

BAYARD RUSTIN, a Negro Quaker on the F.o.R. staff from 1941 to 1953, served twenty-eight months in prison as a conscientious objector during World War II. He is a graduate of the College of the City of New York and of Wilberforce University, and has worked with the American Friends Service Committee in the USA, Mexico, and Puerto Rico, striving for the reduction of human tensions especially in race relations. After serving with the road gangs of a North Carolina prison camp for disregarding segregation rules on an interstate bus, he published through the F.o.R. a report entitled 'Twenty-two days on the Chain gang at Roxboro, N.C.' A group of professors at the University of North Carolina directed the Governor's attention to this publication. Just before his work with the chain gang he visited India by invitation of Devadas Gandhi, son of the Mahatma, and in 1948 was one of nine citizens chosen by ballot to receive a Thomas Jefferson Award for the Advancement of Democracy from the Council Against Intolerance in America.

At the age of fifty-three Mr Rustin, now executive secretary of the American War Resisters' League and an editor of the monthly magazine *Liberation*, has been imprisoned twenty-two times during the integration struggle. In August 1963 he was deputy Director of the Washington Civil Rights March, which brought a quarter of a million people to the Lincoln Memorial.

MARTIN LUTHER KING, the young co-pastor of Ebenezer Baptist Church in Atlanta, Georgia, has been known to all the civilized world since he led the year-long non-violent protest against segregated buses in Montgomery, Alabama. During that year he served as pastor of the Dexter Avenue Baptist Church, Montgomery, and has since vividly described the protest movement—which caused his house to be bombed—in his widely circulated book, *Stride Towards Freedom*. He joined the F.o.R. in 1958, and received a message of support and appreciation from its National Council during the civil rights struggle in Birmingham, Alabama, in the spring of 1963, when he was imprisoned in Birmingham City Jail for 'parading without a permit'. On January 3rd, 1964, America's *Time* Newsmagazine named Martin Luther King 'Man of the Year'.

Today Dr King means as much to the American Negroes seeking liberation as Gandhi meant to the Indian people similarly struggling before 1947. In a recent (1960) issue of *The Christian Century*, Chicago, he wrote: 'The choice today is no longer between violence and non-violence. It is either non-violence or non-existence."

IV. CREATORS OF THE AMERICAN FELLOWSHIP AND THEIR COLLEAGUES

In attempting to estimate the chief personalities in the American movement, first place must be given to JOHN NEVIN SAYRE, for half a century the dynamic, indefatigable St Paul of the I.F.o.R., perpetually travelling and preaching all over the world. He has been consistently undaunted by the toughest problems, such as that of starting Fellowship groups in Catholic South America, and of negotiating the release of Japanese prisoners with those who had suffered at the hands of their military leaders (see chapter 11).

The fiftieth anniversary year of the F.o.R. coincides with his fulfilment of eighty abundant years. He was born on February 4, 1884, to Protestant Episcopal parents living in South Bethlehem, Pennsylvania—a city which is incongruously the site of a big armament-making steel company. They sent him to Princeton Union Theological Seminary and The Episcopal Theological School where he studied for the ministry.

His conventional, patriotic Republican forbears included no pacifists, but they succeeded in raising a family which acquired a political stake in the country and the large perspective that such a position brings. Nevin's brother Francis B. Sayre married a daughter of President Wilson in 1913, and by 1939 was the American High Commissioner (in effect Governor) in the Philippines. He escaped from Corregidor by submarine in 1943. More than once Nevin was able to use his White House contacts for the benefit of the F.o.R., which he joined in December 1915. He edited *The World Tomorrow* from 1922-24, acted as Chairman of the Fellowship from 1935-40, and thereafter at different times filled the positions of co-secretary, Chairman of the I.F.o.R., President of the National Peace Conference, and Editor of *Fellowship*. He has twice circled the globe and visited Europe twenty-five times and Russia three times, besides touring Japan, the Philippines, India, South Africa, South America, Mexico, Canada, and of course the United States. He was present at the 1948 Amsterdam and 1954 Evanston Assembly of the World Council of Churches as a representative of *Fellowship* magazine.

The basis for Nevin's conversion to pacifism lay in an intensive study of the Synoptic Gospels after the First War had begun. This work convinced him that Jesus called his disciples to commit themselves to the way of redemptive love as a basic requirement of the Christian's vocation. Norman Angell's book, *The Great Illusion*, read on a trip round the world from 1912-14, also persuaded him that no modern war could be an instrument of justice. In July 1915, after William Jennings Bryan had resigned as Secretary of State when he saw that President Wilson's policies were leading America towards war, Nevin publicly declared his pacifism in an early sermon during his first ministry at Suffern, N.Y. His parish loyally supported him, but he gave up his position in 1919 to become an evangelist of pacifism to youth and to many Churches.

During the Second World War Mr Sayre managed to send vital monetary assistance to Fellowship leaders in France and Germany, to keep in touch with Percy Bartlett at the London office, and to maintain intact the I.F.o.R. organization. It has had the best years of his working life and will eventually provide him with a lasting monument. He sees it as a lighthouse of Christian pacifism so long as military thinking darkens the minds of leaders in Church and State.

A happy family life has provided Nevin Sayre with a valuable background. Eleven years after the tragic death of his first wife after a year of marriage, he married Kathleen Whitaker, who has accompanied him on most of his travels, and shares with him two daughters and a son.

A. J. MUSTE, the second great stalwart of America's F.o.R., was seventy-two when in 1957 he began his autobiography *Not So Long Ago*, which first appeared as a series of instalments in *Liberation* magazine. At seventy-nine this formidable veteran is still to be found climbing over fences into missile bases, marching to Moscow, and trying to invade French or American nuclear testing grounds.

His tough Dutch family emigrated to USA in 1891 and settled in Grand Rapids, Michigan, where his father worked (at $6 a week) for a furniture factory. The eldest of five children, with the 'sonorous name' of Abraham Johannes, A.J. became a minister of Central Congregational Church, Newton, Mass., in 1915. Each day showed that the US would be involved in the European war, and he decided that he could not reconcile participation with the Gospel which he had been preaching. When America became a belligerent his pastorate ended and he faced the problematical future with a young wife and child.

In 1916 he had joined the newly-formed F.o.R., and now began work with the American Civil Liberties Union directed by Roger Baldwin. He also enrolled as a minister with the Society of Friends at Providence, R.I. His autobiography describes his early involvement in Labour affairs and his leadership of the 1919 textile strike at Lawrence, Mass. Twelve years followed of 'continuously exciting pioneering' as Educational Director of Brookwood Labour College, N.Y. Then for a time he acted as general secretary of the Trotskyist Workers' Party of USA, and during the early thirties became a convinced Marxist-Leninist.

The middle thirties saw his reconversion to Christian pacifism; 'what came back to me on a day late in July 1936 in Paris was the awareness that I belonged in the Christian fellowship', he wrote in the 25th anniversary issue of *Fellowship* in 1960. At that period Francis Thompson's poem *The Hound of Heaven*, with its reference to 'the trumpet that sounds from the hid battlements of eternity', echoed continuously through his mind. He returned home from Europe, 'and there was the Fellowship waiting to welcome me.' He attended its Annual Conference in September and made his new confession of faith. Since then his uncompromising witness, inspired by 'the inner commandment of compassion' implicit in *The Iliad* and other great literature, has changed the lives of many people all over the world.

Gaunt, fierce-eyed and impressive, NORMAN THOMAS, who ran six times for President on the Socialist ticket, has now completed eighty years. His staunch campaigning in America's lost cause has brought him nation-wide respect and admiration.

Settlement worker, preacher, reformer and journalist, Mr Thomas was a First War pacifist who joined the F.o.R. on December 2nd 1916, when as a minister of a mixed languages church in East Harlem he perceived 'an irreconcilable gulf between Christian ethics and participation in war.' His pacifism compelled him to leave his parish, and in 1917 he became Executive Secretary of the F.o.R., and in January 1918, for four years, the first editor of *The World Tomorrow*, which battled continuously for freedom of speech. He was also active in the Civil Liberties Union. Nevin Sayre wrote years later: 'He was, I think, the greatest orator which the F.o.R. has ever had.'

While steering the Fellowship through the war he carried a heavy emotional load, for one of his brothers fought in France, and another, Evan, was a conscientious objector who suffered severely in Leavenworth Prison. In 1921 he gave up his official duties with the F.o.R., and in 1940, owing to a change in his religious thinking, he withdrew from it in sorrow. His pacifism, he felt, had been naïve. 'I could not keep it in our troubled world as nearly absolute as it had been', he wrote in October 1961, but added: 'I have been delighted in specific instances to cooperate with the F.o.R. and deeply respected those of you who have kept it going.' At present Norman Thomas is national co-chairman of the coordinated effort called Turn Toward Peace, with which the Fellowship is affiliated.

On his seventy-fifth birthday in 1959 the *Washington Post* said in an editorial: 'Above all else he has been a conscience of the American people . . . among the most influential individuals in twentieth century politics.'

The influence of JANE ADDAMS, like that of Norman Thomas, extended far beyond the F.o.R. She joined it in 1917, remained a steadfast pacifist throughout the war, and was a member of the Fellowship Council until 1933, but her two major undertakings were the foundation of Hull House, and the Women's International League for Peace and Freedom. Of this she was International President for twenty years. From the establishment of America's first settlement in a sordid Chicago area in 1889 until her death at seventy-five in 1935, she was associated with practically every good cause in the United States.

Jane Addams combined deep compassion and great practical ability with an intellect keenly conscious of the evils of contemporary industrial society. After a profound religious struggle, she created a system of ethics expressed in active work. At Hull House she concerned herself with four overriding purposes—the elimination of corruption, the establishment of humane municipal government, the absorption of America's immigrant population with one law for all, and education for industrial citizenship.

She believed that violence even in a just cause 'has set forth on a dangerous journey', and in 1915, in spite of disabling illness, organized the Women's Peace Party with Carrie Chapman Catt and Emmeline Pethick-Lawrence. In 1931, with Nicholas Murray Butler, she was awarded the Nobel Prize.

When Gandhi was assassinated JOHN HAYNES HOLMES, minister of New York's Community Church from 1907 to 1949 and thenceforth minister Emeritus, called him, 'the greatest man since Jesus Christ'. Dr Holmes had been the leading interpreter of Gandhi and non-violence in the United States. At the outbreak of both wars, backed by his Church, he made front page news by boldly declaring his non-support.

Born in 1879, he joined the F.o.R. on December 19th 1915. He first became known to its personnel through his book *New Wars for Old*, which 'was my pacifist Bible,' wrote Nevin Sayre. Through two World Wars, Dr Holmes continued to preach and practice pacifism even when for most of his fellow ministers the First War had become a holy crusade. 'The loneliness of those days was killing', he once said, but he continued to preach that war was 'an open and utter violation of Christianity'. If war was right, then 'Christianity is wrong, a fake, a lie'.

He and his congregation were outstanding for many years in the practice of inter-racial and inter-credal unity. For a long period he worked on the Editorial Boards of F.o.R. publications, contributing a commentary to *Fellowship* throughout the Second World War. His leavening work in both preaching and writing contributed to the greater tolerance of pacifism during the Second War, though America risked and suffered more than in the First.

His latest book, an Autobiography called *I Speak for Myself*, appeared in his eightieth year. He contemplated death without fear, for he belonged to the succession of prophets for whom God's promises come true. He died on April 3, 1964.

The First War loneliness of Dr Holmes was revealed in an article he wrote for *The Christian Century* after the death of BISHOP PAUL JONES in 1941. Bishop Jones of Utah took the Commandments seriously and resolved to live by them, though he realised the probable consequences which he accepted without bitterness.

The youngest Bishop at thirty-four in the Protestant Episcopal Church, he gave up his diocese rather than compromise with war. Dr Ray H. Abrams, author of *Preachers Present Arms*, states that only six other Episcopal clergymen took the pacifist stand in 1917, and he alone was a Bishop. From the time of his election in 1914 his socialist philosophy caused criticism, but his supreme crisis came three years later when endeavours were made to have him removed from further episcopal duties. Eventually Paul Jones himself sent his resignation to the House of Bishops, which never chose him again. His successor in Utah, Bishop Touret, commented after the war: 'What a sad story for the Church to have to record'.

Paul Jones had joined the F.o.R. in 1915 and in 1919 he became its General Secretary for ten years. Then he accepted a chaplaincy at Antioch College in Yellow Springs, Ohio, where he died from multiple myeloma. In *The Christian Century* John Haynes Holmes wrote of their wartime association: 'No name shone more brightly in the dark than that of Paul Jones . . . He

HENRI ROSER

PHILIPPE VERNIER

ANDRE TROCME

PHILIP EASTMAN

Plate 5

KIRBY PAGE

A. J. MUSTE

JAMES FARMER

ALFRED HASSLER

Plate 6

lives with me still . . . that straight, spare figure, that kindly voice, that radiant smile, those gentle and tender ways, that heart brave to meet any trial'. Such a comrade, he said, had made his own solitary witness 'not only bearable but beautiful'.

Of KIRBY PAGE, a Texan born in 1890 who worked his way through Drake University and joined the F.o.R. on November 6th 1916, it is said that he 'probably converted more Americans to pacifism than any other person . . . between World Wars I and II'. His popular pamphlets conveyed the facts of contemporary situations to many readers who would not have tolerated extracting them from learned publications. He produced more than thirty works on peace and religion which sold over a million copies. An autobiography left in type at his death in 1957 has never been published.

Though ordained a minister of the Disciples of Christ, Dr Page was an itinerant social evangelist rather than a pastor. From 1916-17 he worked with the YMCA in France and in Britain, edited *The World Tomorrow* from 1926-34, and in 1939 became a leader of the Emergency Peace Campaign which slowed down American participation in the Second World War. He travelled, as he wrote, on the grand scale, speaking in 2,000 churches, 400 colleges, and on innumerable lecture platforms, covering over a million miles in forty-five countries and all the American States. Much of this work, extending over forty-six years, was financed by Sherwood Eddy, whose secretary he had been. His first tour with Dr Eddy convinced him that pacifism was an essential part of Christianity. After both wars he was vilified by opponents who made him into a controversial figure. He never retaliated but, supported by a happy home, strove always 'to open windows to the invisible world of the spirit'.

Professor MARY ELY LYMAN, born in Vermont in 1887, is one of the Fellowship's more scholarly exponents. Her education began at Mount Holyoke College in 1911, and extended through Union Theological Seminary and the University of Chicago to Cambridge, England (1919-20). She is an Hon.Litt.D. of Roanoke and Hood Colleges and of Western College for Women, and an Hon.D.D. of Colby College (1957). In 1926 she married Professor Eugene W. Lyman (who died in 1948) and adopted a daughter and a son. She has taught in Rockville (Conn.) High School and was Frederick Weyerhäuser Professor of Religion at

H

Vassar from 1921-26. Later assignments have taken her to
Barnard College as Associate Professor in Religion and back to
Union Theological Seminary as Morris K. Jesup Professor of the
English Bible.

She has been a visiting lecturer at many other institutions
both at home and abroad, and is the author of six books which
include *The Knowledge of God in Johannine Thought* (1924)
and *The Christian Epic* (1936). Professor Lyman's career is a
comprehensive reply to those critics of pacifism who regard it
as a limboland inhabited only by sentimentalists, visionaries,
and superficial thinkers.

Dr ALLAN ARMSTRONG HUNTER has been the pastor since 1926
of Mount Hollywood Congregational Church, a small but potent
spiritual power-house in Los Angeles, California. He joined the
F.o.R. in 1925, was its West Coast chairman in 1935 and from
1939-41, and became a national vice-chairman in 1955.

Born in 1893 in Toronto, and an American citizen since 1901,
Dr Hunter was a student at Union Theological Seminary
(1920-25) after a year of service in Palestine with the American
Red Cross. Here a strange vision of Christ came to him,
'standing by the dirt road between Jericho and the Dead Sea',
after he had witnessed the capture of some Turkish prisoners.
He has degrees from Princeton (where Nevin Sayre was
temporarily a professor) and Columbia Universities. His early
years as a pastor also gave him the experiences of a church in
New Jersey and a year's teaching in China. Of his religious
education he has written: 'I went to the Church studying for
one single reason: since Jesus was the only one who had not
let us down . . . it was Jesus a man must somehow try to follow
and work for.' During the Second War his church prayed
regularly for the Japanese and the Germans.

Dr Hunter has served the F.o.R. in a fashion comparable to
that of Kirby Page by writing biographical sketches of pacifist
leaders. Their titles are *White Corpuscles in Europe* (1939),
Courage in Both Hands (1951), and *Christians in the Arena*
(1958).

A F.o.R. secretary for twenty-one years, JOHN SWOMLEY is
now Associate Professor of Social Ethics at St. Paul's School of
Theology in Kansas City, Missouri. Born in Harrisburg,
Pennsylvania, he graduated at Dickinson College, and has an

M.A. from Boston University and a Ph.D. in Political Science from the University of Colorado. He is also a Methodist minister. In 1944 he persuaded Professor Albert Einstein and other educators to sign the Introductions to some of his pamphlets. With their help he organized a campaign against universal military training as Director for eight years of the National Committee Against Conscription. He divided his time between its office in Washington and the F.o.R. office in New York, where he succeeded A. J. Muste as Executive Secretary. Later he shared this work with Alfred Hassler.

In the opinion of a colleague, John Swomley's contributions to American college thinking represent one of his best achievements. An outgoing personality and a cultivated debating technique account for his popularity in lectures and radio talks. Like Kirby Page he is a prodigious worker who can quickly absorb and re-present the factual material with which he has educated two generations of college students. In small institutions his analyses of world events have so far converted the parochial mind as to cause mass movements to the Political Science Department.

He has travelled widely in Europe, South-East Asia, the Near East, North Africa and Central America. His publications include four major political works, many small pamphlets, and several magazine articles. His newest work is the book *Our Military Establishment*, published in December 1963.

ALFRED HASSLER joined the F.o.R. in 1942. He has served as Editor of *Fellowship* since 1946, and in 1960 succeeded John Swomley as Executive Secretary. An editor from 1937 of Youth Publications for the American Baptist Publication Society, he left it directly it showed signs of evading the war issue. He became a pacifist as a student in 1932, when his work as a columnist for a Long Island newspaper caused him to collide with the American Legion in its pre-McCarthy phase.

As a conscientious objector who had registered in 1940, he was called up in 1944 and, when he refused to accept alternative service, was sentenced to three years' imprisonment. From 1944-45 he was a prisoner in the Federal Penitentiary at Lewisburg, Pennsylvania, a supposedly 'model' institution. After his release he wrote his *Diary of a Self-Made Convict*, published by the Henry Regnery Company in USA, and in

England by Victor Gollancz Ltd., in 1955. In a Foreword to this book Professor Harry Elmer Barnes, who called it 'the best book on prisons ever written', says: 'His diary is free of any attempt to glorify the role of the conscientious objectors, and of any effort to condemn the prison administrators for a situation they did not wish or relish. His main interest is to tell just how prison life affects sensitive, perceptive and educated men.' Professor Barnes concluded that there is no such thing as a 'good' prison for criminals, who can only be reformed outside prison walls.

After his release from prison Alfred Hassler was the principal organizer of Skyview Acres, a 45-family, inter-racial co-operative community, and served as its first president. His concern for the peace movement today is to get beyond protest to practical means of reconciliation in such areas as Cuba, and to translate intellectual witness into non-violent action based on compassion —the 'rebel passion' to which this book pays tribute. He serves now as national vice-chairman of Turn Toward Peace and of the Consultative Peace Council, as well as on the executive of the International Confederation for Disarmament and Peace.

SOME LEADING FELLOWSHIP SUPPORTERS

ROGER N. BALDWIN, born 1884 at Wellesley, Mass., and a long-time member of the F.o.R., began his career as an instructor in Sociology at Washington University, St. Louis, and then moved to New York to organize the National Civil Liberties Bureau. From 1917 to 1950 he was Director of its successor, the American Civil Liberties Union, to which many F.o.R. supporters belonged. This Union, which played an important part in the resistance to McCarthyism during the nineteen-fifties, illustrates the influence of the F.o.R. in starting and helping to maintain other organizations.

After the Second World War, General MacArthur invited Roger Baldwin to set up a civil liberties organization in Japan. He carries on today as Chairman of the International League for the Rights of Man, a consultant agency with the U.N.

ALLAN K. CHALMERS, born in 1897, a graduate of Johns Hopkins University, was minister at Broadway Tabernacle Congregational Church from 1930 to 1948, when he joined Boston University School of Theology in which he is now

Emeritus Professor. Experiences as a First War soldier combined with a Christian background to convert him to pacifism, and Broadway Tabernacle became an important influence in the creation of pacifist witnesses. When the Second War approached, he organized a body of leading New York ministers who agreed not to sanction the war. Known as 'the Ministers' Covenant Group', they included several Protestant denominations and one or two Jewish Rabbis, though no Roman Catholics. Their membership reached between 2,700 and 2,800. Not more than twenty would have taken such a position in the First War.

GEORGE L. COLLINS, affectionately known as 'Shorty' owing to his height of 6 feet 4 inches, was like Allan Chalmers a First War soldier who came to pacifism through personal experience of militarism. He was the first Field Secretary of the American F.o.R., serving under Bishop Jones from 1923 to 1928. He set a record for 'field work' probably equalled only by Muriel Lester. His distinctive contribution was made in colleges throughout the South, where he was the first speaker directed to both white and Negro institutions by YMCA and YWCA organizers on the same tour. After leaving his F.o.R. service he became Baptist Student Pastor at the University of Wisconsin, and subseqently at San Jose State College in California.

Dr HENRY HITT CRANE, born 1890 and for some years a member of the F.o.R. Advisory Council, served with the YMCA in England and France in 1917, when he was one of the first Americans to go overseas. After long periods as a pastor in Malden, Massachusetts, and Scranton, Pennsylvania, he made a great reputation as minister at the Central Methodist Church in Detroit, and as a speaker at colleges. Of the F.o.R. he once wrote: 'It has maintained an unequivocal witness to its sovereign allegiance to Jesus Christ . . . thus moving far beyond the area of mere negative protest into the realm of positive affirmation and example.'

PHILLIPS P. ELLIOTT, born 1901, joined the F.o.R. in 1938 and was Chairman from 1943-46. He became minister of the influential First Presbyterian Church in Brooklyn in 1932, but belonged to the dedicated group of important New York churchmen led by Harry Emerson Fosdick and Allan Chalmers who, though 'respectable citizens', never compromised with their convictions or tried to cover up their pacifism. Fully realizing the furore that it might evoke, he signed the 'Massacre By Bombing' pamphlet in 1944. His death from cancer in the USA in 1961 coincided with the F.o.R. Council meeting at Le Chambon, where Nevin Sayre spoke of his courageous and devoted life.

Dr HARRY EMERSON FOSDICK, born 1878, is the celebrated minister Emeritus of Riverside Church in New York, and a member of the F.o.R. Advisory Council. For many years he conducted National Vespers on the Radio. He has written many books which have provided spiritual guidance for millions, and is the author of the famous 'Apology to the Unknown Soldier', first given as a sermon in Broadway Tabernacle in the nineteen-thirties, which begins: 'O Militarism, I hate you for this, that you do lay your hands on the noblest elements in human character, with which we might make a heaven on earth, and you use them to make a hell on earth instead.'

RICHARD GREGG, a Fellowship member from the beginning, wrote a well-known pacifist classic, *The Power of Non-Violence,* which he brought from India after living for years under Gandhi's influence. Dr Rufus M. Jones provided an Introduction, and persuaded the American firm of Lippincott to publish the book in 1935. Since then the F.o.R. has taken over the publishing rights; its most recent edition includes references to the civil rights movement and has a Foreword by Martin Luther King Jr. Sales up to date have reached 10,000, a large figure for a work of this kind. Many copies have been bought in England, and the book, which has been translated into Spanish, French and German, is now selling among Negroes in the Deep South. Several pacifist leaders have responded to its influence, including Chief Albert Luthuli in South Africa and Jorge Bullrich in Uruguay. An abridged edition has sold widely in Northern Rhodesia.

GEORGIA ELMA HARKNESS, an early member of the F.o.R. who rejoined in 1941, was ordained a Methodist minister in 1926. She became Associate Professor of Religion at Mount Holyoke College from 1937-39, and Professor of Applied Theology at the Pacific School of Religion in Berkeley, California, where she is now Professor Emeritus. In 1941 she received the Scroll of Honour for pioneer work in religion from the General Federation of Women's Clubs, and in 1950 the award of Churchwoman of the Year from Religious Heritage of America, Inc. Her numerous books include *Understanding the Christian Faith* (1947), *Towards Understanding the Bible* (1952), and the most recent, *The Bible Speaks to Daily Needs*.

JESSIE WALLACE HUGHAN (1876-1955), educator, pacifist, socialist, was born in Brooklyn and graduated from Barnard College in 1898. In 1915 she helped to establish the Anti-Enlistment League (the first American organization to enrol war resisters) and in the same year joined the newly-formed F.o.R. In 1923, feeling the need for a wider pacifist organization, she founded the War Resisters League and worked for it throughout her life. During the Second War she worked strenuously against injustices laid on conscientious objectors. She taught for thirty years in New York public schools, and in 1940 founded the Teachers' Pacifist League.

CHARLES RADFORD LAWRENCE, a Negro born in Massachusetts and reared in Mississippi, and a Ph.D. of Columbia University, was National Chairman of the F.o.R. from 1955 to 1963, and is a former Chairman of the Southern Fellowship. He works in the Department of Sociology and Anthropology at Brooklyn College. He is also a Director of the National Council of Religion in Higher Education and former President of Skyview Acres, the forty-five-family inter-racial co-operative community near New York. His wife MARGARET, also a long-time F.o.R. member, is a practising psycho-analyst and child psychiatrist and a Licentiate of the American Board of Pediatrics. She is consulting psychiatrist for two children's associations and an instructor in psychiatry at the College of Physicians and Surgeons, Columbia University.

FREDERICK J. LIBBY, a Quaker born in 1874 and known as the 'down-East' idealist, cooperated for many years with the F.o.R. as Executive Secretary from 1921 of the National Council for the Prevention of War. In 1918-19 he joined the Society of Friends in reconstruction and relief work in France. Just before the Second World War he organized an active campaign to retain the arms embargo, and prompted an educational movement against war throughout America. On his eightieth birthday in November 1954 he retired from the Executive Secretaryship of the NCPW after thirty-three years of service.

WALTER GEORGE MUELDER, born in 1907, Dean of the School

of Theology in Boston University, came into the F.o.R. through the group in South California. He belongs to the 'middle generation' of Fellowship members, and is influential in the World Council of Churches and the whole ecumenical movement. His acquaintances credit him with a mind similar in its working to that of Reinhold Niebuhr, but unlike Niebuhr he has not turned away from the pacifist creed, and his many books on Christian responsibility reflect its influence.

JOHN OLIVER NELSON, a Presbyterian, Professor of Christian Vocation at Yale Divinity School, and Treasurer of the Robert Treat Paine Peace Foundation (now closed), was Chairman of the Fellowship from 1950 to 1955. His special concern has been that of Peace Training Units, which he organized for several summers during the nineteen-fifties. He is the founder of Kirkridge, a retreat centre in Pennsylvania comparable to the Iona Community founded by George MacLeod, and recently resigned his appointment as Dean of Students at Yale Divinity School to concentrate on working for it.

Dr ALBERT W. PALMER, born in 1879, was President of Chicago Theological Seminary, and died when nearing eighty in the nineteen-fifties. He never actually joined the Fellowship because he did not want to be 'labelled' in his conspicuous position, but he brought many students to pacifism. One of the most notable was Howard Schomer, a later President of the Seminary, and I.F.o.R. President from 1959 to 1963.

EDITH LOVEJOY PIERCE has been for many years the poet of the American pacifist movement. Her work appears frequently in The Christian Century, Fellowship, and other religious magazines.

DOUGLAS VANN STEERE, a Quaker born in 1901, succeeded Dr Rufus Jones in 1941 as Professor of Philosophy at Haverford College after a brilliant academic career. He is an A.M. and Ph.D. of Harvard University and a Rhodes Scholar who graduated at Oxford in 1927 and took his M.A. in 1953. He has been appointed to many important lectureships both at home and abroad, and has conducted summer schools at such well-known institutions as Pendle Hill School of Religion and Social Studies, and Union Theological Seminary. He translated in 1938 Søren Kierkegaard's most important book, Purity of Heart Is To Will One Thing, and contributed a valuable introduction which pointed out that the note sounded by Kierkegaard 'is alien to the modern ears which are tuned to collective thinking'.

Dr Steere joined the F.o.R. in 1937, was for a time Vice-Chairman, and is still Chairman of the I.F.o.R. North American Committee. He has travelled all over the world, and is certainly one of the Fellowship's most distinguished members. He was an official observer at the Vatican Council in 1963.

OSWALD GARRISON VILLARD, born in 1872, was the famous owner and editor successively of the American magazine *Nation* and the New York *Daily Post*. He was a grandson of William Lloyd Garrison, the abolitionist. Though nearing seventy when the Second World War broke out, he travelled straight to Germany and came back with the manuscript of a short book, *Inside Germany*, which was widely read in both America and England. The war weighed heavily on his later years and was probably the origin of the paralytic stroke from which he suffered soon after it ended, but he never flinched from the pacifist position in spite of criticism and abuse by journalistic colleagues. He was a signatory of the F.o.R. pamphlet, *Massacre By Bombing*.

Other friends and colleagues to whom the American Fellowship owes gratitude include Edmund B. Chaffee, Chairman 1933-34 and a key figure in the 1933 Referendum Meeting, who died in 1936 while delivering a speech at St. Paul, Minnesota; Edward W. Evans, Executive Secretary 1916-19; Walter G. Fuller; Harold Hatch, probably the most generous donor to the international work of the Fellowship; George Houser, Race Relations Secretary from 1949-55 and now Director of the USA 'Committee on Africa'; Charles W. Iglehart (Chairman 1946-50); Rufus M. Jones; Arthur L. Swift Jnr., a Professor at Union Theological Seminary and Chairman 1940-43; L. Hollingworth Wood; George Lyman Paine, founder of the Robert Treat Paine Peace Foundation, an Episcopal clergyman and descendant of one of the signers of the Declaration of Independence, and a leader of liberal and radical causes in Boston for many years; and Bishop William Appleton Lawrence, who joined the F.o.R. in 1934 and helped to found the Episcopal Pacifist Fellowship in 1939.

At the present time the executive directors of almost every major peace organization in the United States are F.o.R.

members, such as A. J. Muste, Committee for Non-Violent Action; Robert Gilmore, Turn Toward Peace; Homer Jack, Committee for a Sane Nuclear Policy (SANE); Bayard Rustin, War Resisters' League; Mildred Scott Olmsted, Women's International League for Peace and Freedom; Stewart Meacham, Peace Section of the American Friends Service Committee; Kenneth Maxwell, Commission on International Affairs of the National Council of Churches; Herman Will, Methodist Board of World Peace; Paul Peachey, Church Peace Mission; and Emily Parker Simon, Committee for World Disarmament and World Development.

Chapter 7

FELLOWSHIPS IN CENTRAL EUROPE

I. GERMANY

Fifty Momentous Years

Contrary to a widespread impression, conscientious objectors existed in Germany both before and during the First World War. A pamphlet called *Kriegsdienstverweigerer in Deutschland und Osterreich*, published in the nineteen-twenties by Marthe Skinike, Helene Stoecker and Olga Misar, describes this movement.

Conscientious objection became illegal early in the eighteenth century with the introduction of standing armies, and members of anti-war religious sects left for America. During the 1914 war there were three groups of conscientious objectors—the Syndicalists, a working class movement about 5,000 strong whose members evaded rather than resisted; a minority group composed of Christian sects such as the Seventh Day Adventists, who were imprisoned but not shot or ill-treated; and a still smaller body of 'intellectuals' who were sent to asylums or nursing homes. (The author possesses interesting personal letters from Marthe Skinike and a First War resister, G. Wilhelm Meyer, who mentions the name of a fellow conscientious objector, and also refers to another, Heinrich Vogeler. Limitations of space unfortunately prevent the quotation of these unique documents, obtained through the War Resisters' International.)

After the First War military conscription was forbidden to Germany by the Treaty of Versailles; hence there was no refusal of training. F.o.R. members appear to have existed but were relatively quiescent, though a number of other peace organizations were formed, such as *Der Bund des Kriegsdienstgegner* and the *Deutsche Friedensgesellschaft*. In 1932 the F.o.R. held its first Conference for several years at Herrenalb in the Black Forest, and Wilhelm Mensching became German secretary. The following year Hitler came to power, and in November 1933 the Fellowship dissolved itself though its members remained closely united. Thereafter the whole pacifist movement turned to anti-Nazi resistance. A Fontana publication, *Dying We Live*, contains a collection of letters and speeches by resisters, whether religious or secular, about to be executed. In 1943-44 more than 25,000 members of this 'Inner Front' were executed in Berlin, Dresden and Stuttgart, and Annedore Leber, in *Conscience in Revolt* (Valentine Mitchell), tells the stories of sixty-four.

During the earlier years which followed the Second World War, the Fellowship struggled against the downward spiral of suffering, starvation and frustration in which most of Central Europe was caught. The Germans were confronted with enormous practical problems, such as the rebuilding of the destroyed cities, and the absorption of millions of refugees and expellees from the East. But the anti-war feeling was very strong, and during this period new international contacts were made. Gift parcels from former enemies saved the lives of thousands, and revived confidence in the reality of reconciliation.

The picture changed abruptly in 1950 with the Korean War, in which American policy put Germans into uniform again after the currency reforms of 1948 had brought a new wave of materialism to Western Germany. Nevertheless Dr Siegmund-Schültze succeeded, during this unpromising period, in rebuilding the F.o.R. New members such as Professor Hans Iwand, a leader of the Confessional Church in its struggle against Hitler, joined long-standing supporters such as Rudi Daur (Stüttgart), Hans Wirtz (Freiburg), Irma Schuchardt (Berlin) and Hermann Hoffman (Breslau). Subsequently two more Presidents of Protestant Churches became members, Präses D. Beckmann of Düsseldorf and Präses D. Wilm of Bielefeld.

At first the Fellowship was recognized only in the British and American Zones, but in 1948 Wilhelm Mensching successfully established his *Freundschaftsheim* at Bückeburg, and F.o.R. conferences were subsequently held almost annually in different cities. Martin Niemöller and Heinz Kloppenburg became members at Evanston in 1954, and in 1955 an international team consisting of Clifford Macquire, A. J. Muste and

André Trocmé visited several German cities. In 1956 at the annual meeting in Cologne, the new structure was established, with Dr Siegmund-Schültze as Fellowship President and Dr Kloppenburg as Chairman. In spite of the new problems raised by the division of Germany into two states and the rearmament of Western Germany, the Fellowship has about 1,500 members and its leaders are greatly in demand by other organizations.

After conscription had been accepted by the Bonn Parliament, Dr Siegmund-Schültze as Chairman of a Federation of peace organizations (Arbeitsgemeinschaft Deutscher Friedensverbande) became concerned to safeguard the right of conscientious objectors guaranteed by the Constitution. Eventually some reasonable legislation on Alternative Service was accepted and Dr Kloppenburg became Secretary of the Central Board for the Protection of Conscientious Objectors. Though many young C.O.'s would like to serve in 'Eirene', Alternative Service is not yet allowed in countries abroad. The German law gives priority to Alternative Service in hospitals, where the need for personnel is great. The Fellowship recognizes this necessity, but continues to press upon the Government the importance of international workers building bridges of understanding between the nations.

The German Fellowship now develops programmes of special aid to areas in need, and decides at its annual meeting which projects should be supported in the current year. These projects have recently included aid for Tullio Vinay's work in Sicily, and the gift of a cobalt bomb for cancer treatment at an Indian hospital.

When the border between the two Germanies was closed, many Fellowship members were separated. Within the Democratic Republic the Fellowship could not continue as an organization, but personal contacts have been maintained, and the DDR authorities usually grant exit visits for F.o.R. members to attend the annual conference. The co-operation of Fellowship members within the Christian Peace Conference (of which Heinz Kloppenburg is a Vice-President) has caused the F.o.R. to be viewed with new attention and appreciation.

The German Fellowship is a partner in the Puidoux Conferences established since 1957 as a platform for theological discussion between the continental churches and the Historic Peace Churches. The first East-West encounters in Germany occurred in the *Freundschaftsheim* with representatives of the Orthodox Baptist and Lutheran Churches from the Soviet Union.

The Nyborg Conference of European Churches, another meeting place between East and West, originated in the Liselund Conference which, under the authority of Präses Wilm and Dr Emmen of the Reformed Church of the Netherlands, had been practically organized by the German F.o.R. Chairman. The German Fellowship officially supports the Easter Marches against nuclear weapons. Inside Germany it upholds protest movements against the new Emergency Laws to be brought for approval into the Parliament of the Federal Republic. It also publishes four times a year a periodical, *Versöhnung und Friede*, edited by Dr Hans Gressel.

The continued activity of German conscientious objectors was hopefully illustrated at Christmas 1963 by a movement throughout West German towns called 'Disarmament on a tiny scale for the tinies'. In consequence hundreds of German children exchanged their military playthings for 'peaceable' toys, such as bricks and trains.

Fellowship Leaders in Germany

DR. F. SIEGMUND-SCHÜLTZE, born 1885, is a great European figure whose work and outlook helped to start the F.o.R. Before the First War he was Chaplain to the Kaiser and in personal touch with most leading figures in Germany from 1911 to June 1933, when the Nazis expelled him on pain of death. In Switzerland between 1933 and 1946 he worked incessantly for refugees, and tried to end the war. His return to Germany was followed by the remarkable resurrection of his social work amid the ruins of Dortmund, and eventually (1959) by his removal to Soest (Westphalia) with his huge collection of archives.

Friedrich Wilhelm Siegmund-Schültze grew up in the housefather tradition, with an autocratic outlook which impedes a sympathetic understanding of him by younger Germans. His work has been twofold: first, for the F.o.R.; secondly, welfare work at his *Soziale Arbeitsgemeinshaft* in the workers' quarter of East Berlin. The East German Government still maintains this settlement under another name.

In his book *How I Became a Pacifist* (1939), Dr Siegmund-Schültze explains that a physical defect which prevented military service much distressed him in youth, but 'the picture of Jesus in the Gospels and Epistles' converted him to pacifist ideals. As early as 1908 he visited England for the World Alliance for International Friendship through the Churches, met many Quakers, and became friendly with J. Allen Baker (the father of Philip Noel-Baker). In 1909 the Kaiser summoned him to the pastorate of the Peace Church in Potsdam. Three years later he visited Jane Addams in Chicago, studied her social experience, and exchanged books and letters with her to the end of her life.

His attendance at the Constance Peace Conference (cf. Chap. 2, pp. 29-30) arose from his work in the ecumenical Weltbund between England and Germany. The draft document subsequently issued as a leaflet by the Society of Friends and sent by him to German Church leaders led to his appearance before a court martial, apparently on a capital charge. When he produced a letter from the Kaiser's secretary acknowledging in friendly terms this very document, 'the effect on the court was electric', he told Kathleen Sayre in 1959, and he was immediately released.

In 1917 Allen Baker invited him to a Conference in Sweden, but his attendance was prevented by the military authorities, who in spite of his unfitness called him up for Army service. His obligation to refuse was now finally clear to him, and he became closer to the F.o.R. After the war ended he devoted himself to social service, but in 1933 he was allowed only three days to leave Berlin for Zürich. Here until 1946 he maintained a F.o.R. office, and initiated several plans for peace between the belligerents. One attempt to communicate with Archbishop Eidem of Sweden led to the death of Elizabeth von Thadden (see pp. 136-7). During these years he kept in touch with Percy Bartlett through Portugal, and intermittently received copies of *The Friend* and *The Christian Pacifist*. Letters also reached him from Finland, Sweden, Denmark, Holland and France.

He attended the first post-war I.F.o.R. Conference at Stockholm in 1946, and wrote to friends in London: 'The service set before me during the coming years is to help to overcome hate in my own homeland . . . This work will completely occupy all our German members.' Permitted at last to return from Switzerland, he found the site of his social work in East Berlin completely destroyed. The following year he accepted a Professorship at the University of Muenster, and resided in Dortmund where he founded a Seminar in Social Education, a 'Folk High School' or Labour College, and a Social Research Centre.

After thirteen years he resigned to establish the *Oekumenisches Archiv* in Soest (Jakobistrasse 13), where his massive assembly of papers, including four cabinets devoted exclusively to F.o.R. correspondence from 1919 to 1960, were examined by M. C. and Elizabeth Morris in 1961. It is to be hoped that a Fellowship research worker will some day be able to devote the many months which their thorough investigation would require.

DR. HERMANN HOFFMAN, who celebrated his eightieth birthday in 1958, was a Jesuit Professor at the University of Breslau and the head of a convent there after the First World War, when he joined the F.o.R. Council. He was also a foundation member of the Peace Union of German Catholics, and the one Roman Catholic priest associated with Archbishop Soderblom in calling the first World Council of the Churches in 1925. One of Professor Hoffmann's major concerns was work for German-Polish understanding.

During the period of Nazi domination his telephone and mail were watched, but *Fellowship* reached him safely and he put it in the public library. Between 1936 and 1938 a visit by Nevin Sayre led to a secret meeting at night in the convent garden, where friends arrived one by one and sat quietly round a small table. The Germans were then permitted no news of the international peace movement, which Mr Sayre conveyed. Later he concerned himself in getting food to Professor Hoffmann and his friends during the starvation period.

Under Hitler Dr Hoffmann was not allowed to leave Breslau because he had the reputation of being 'one of the worst pacifists in Germany', though no one denounced him. During the air raids an Allied bomb demolished his library, but he survived to minister to the German residents though he could not get permission to leave Poland to attend the 1946 F.o.R. Council at Stockholm.

Eventually the Poles, intimidated by the Russians, compelled him to go to Leipzig, where he now lives in a convent for aged nuns to whom he acts as chaplain. Though the East German Government does not like his pacifism, a State Secretary appre-

F. SIEGMUND-SCHULTZE

WILHELM MENSCHING

MAX JOSEF METZGER

MARTIN NIEMOELLER

Plate 7

IWAO AYUSAWA

K. K. CHANDY

D. D. LURA-VILLANUEVA

ARTHUR BLAXALL

Plate 8

ciated a pacifist sermon which he preached in the Catholic
church, and his living conditions subsequently improved.

WILHELM MENSCHING, the first German Secretary with Dr
Siegmund-Schültze as Chairman, has spent forty-two years as a
village pastor at Petzen, and though handicapped recently by
ill-health virtually symbolizes pacifism for Germany.

When the First War began he was a missionary in South-
West Africa. In 1916 he and his wife were driven from their
mission station, and finally arrived as prisoners at an English
mission hospital. There a British doctor, Sir Albert Cook of
Uganda, laid a friendly hand on his shoulder and said: 'Be calm;
we are not enemies but brothers'.

Mensching wrote later: 'Since that Englishman so spoke to me,
a German, in time of war, I have been unable to forget the fact
of brotherhood'. Soon he learnt more about it for he was interned
in India, and studied Gandhi's technique of non-violence. He
published two books on the race problem, *The Fourth Continent*
and *Coloured and White*.

Under Hitler after the voluntary dissolution of the F.o.R., he
proved both brave and resourceful. He never said 'Heil Hitler!',
and harboured and fed a Russian soldier who had escaped from
a prison camp, though German troops were billeted at his home.
Perpetually suspected by the Nazis, he was never imprisoned
because he was much beloved in his neighbourhood. The Nazi
Mayor assured a visiting Gauleiter that he was an honest man
unconnected with the underground.

Mensching combated Nazi propaganda by spending his summer holidays in a succession of different districts, announcing
his visit beforehand, and by preparing attractive biographical
pamphlets on the Jews. These had popular titles such as
A Bedouin Chief, and were based on the Old Testament. He also
produced eight-page booklets known as the *Erbgut* Series, with
such reassuring names as *Our German Heritage*. A biographical
note of the author appeared on the jacket, but inside were
extracts from the moral and religious writings of Luther, Kant,
Schweitzer, and kindred writers. These widely-circulated booklets were published by the Quaker Centre at Pyrmont.

After the war Wilhelm Mensching established a peace education centre at Petzen now widely known as the *Freundschafts-*

I

heim. The British military government supplied two Nissen huts as a beginning, and the Americans helped with food, shoes and money. Today there are three permanent buildings, and each year young people from different countries, races, religions and political backgrounds gather there for work, study and worship.

One of Dr MAX JOSEF METZGER'S pictures radiates the same infectious gaiety as those of Dick Sheppard at St Martin-in-the-Fields. His portraits are refreshingly free from the solemnity which sometimes impairs the witness of F.o.R. leaders. Yet because they convey that 'other-worldliness' characteristic of Maurice Maeterlinck's 'Predestinés', they appropriately represent the martyred prophet of Christian unity who went tranquilly to his death under the Nazis 'with countenance transfigured'. At the Bilthoven Conferences of 1919-20 Max Metzger became an F.o.R. founder, and was perhaps the noblest and holiest leader which the Fellowship has been privileged to enrol.

In December 1944 *Reconciliation*, struggling to penetrate the blanket of silence which shrouded Occupied Europe, printed a tragic item of news: 'A month ago we heard . . . that Monsignor Max Josef Metzger had been shot'. So impenetrable was the sombre curtain of war that this modern saint, known as Brother Paulus, had actually been beheaded in Brandenburg Prison eight months earlier (April 17th). Though Dr Metzger was 'eradicated' for all that he believed and professed, the 'occasion' was political; he had drawn up for submission to Dr Eidem, Protestant Archbishop of Uppsala, a scheme for a new German government embodying reconciliation and understanding if revolution should conclude the war. He entrusted this document to a Swedish woman who proved to be a Gestapo agent. As any suggestion that the war might end in a Nazi defeat rated as treason, Dr Metzger's fate became a foregone conclusion.

Max Josef Metzger was born in 1887 in the Black Forest and became a Roman Catholic priest. In 1917 he published a pamphlet, *Peace on Earth*, which made him suspect when the Nazis came. In addition to the I.F.o.R. and the German Catholic Peace Movement, he founded at Meitingen the Society of Christ the King, or the White Cross, an organization of priests and laity which worked for the regeneration of church and society.

He was also deeply troubled by the divisions in the Christian Church, and in 1938 established the Una Sancta Brotherhood to work for Christian unity.

The following year, in prison for the first time, he wrote a letter to Pope Pius XII (probably intercepted by the Gestapo, as no reply was received), which contained the following prophetic words:

'When the Reformation in Germany became an unhappy revolution, the Holy Spirit called for a true Council of Reform to meet in Trent. It was a wise and humble thought of the Pope to invite Protestants to this Council. Has not the time come today to repeat this experiment, trusting in the Lord who stretches His protecting Hand over His Church? It seems to me that your Holiness might choose some twelve men and commission them to get in touch with representatives of separated Churches . . . Only a great venture of faith, humility and love can solve the problem of the fate of Christendom.'

Today, twenty-five years later, thanks to the great inspiration of Pope John XXIII and the kindred spirit of his successor, an Ecumenical Council has sat in St Peter's, and a Secretariat similar to that envisaged by Brother Paulus is continuously at work.

Dr Metzger's prophetic initiative and sacrificial love survive to inspire the Fellowship today. The S.P.C.K. published a biography of him by Lilian Stevenson in 1952, and on April 15, 1962, a BBC Home Service programme based on his life was written and produced by the Rev. Paul Oestreicher.

The profound contrast between Metzger and MARTIN NIEMÖLLER—the disciplined fighter trained both to obey and to command—illustrates how many are the roads to the pacifist faith. Niemöller came to it the hard way, through denial and doubt. In *Christians in the Arena* Allan Hunter gave his story the appropriate title, *A Conscience That Grew*. It was only after a conversation with three German physicists in 1954 had presented him with a choice between the Christian way of life and the acceptance of nuclear weapons, that Niemöller joined the F.o.R.

Born in 1892, Niemöller as a boy had a passion for the sea which took him into the Kaiser's Navy as a cadet in April 1910. His conscience began to trouble him in 1917, when he was ordered, and refused, to shoot the victims of an Allied troopship sunk by his submarine. But the subsequent defeat of Germany seemed to him a 'dark disaster'.

In 1924 he decided, at thirty-two, to study theology, and became a Lutheran pastor. As Pastor Franz Hildebrandt has pointed out in The Bridge magazine, this late start gave him the theological outlook of a younger generation.

His initial support for Hitler, as the apostle of German resurrection, changed to opposition when the Nazis with brutal jingoism began to 'eliminate' clergy of Jewish origin, for he did not admit the right of the State to interfere in the Church and mobilize it for the dethronement of Christ. This opinion caused him to found the Confessional Church (as a group within the Evangelical Church) to maintain the purity of the Christian creed. Nearly 7,000 pastors joined this movement, which has substantially changed with Niemöller through the years, and he was arrested for his activities, prosecuted and acquitted, but kept in Dachau. There, for six long and lonely years, he prayed for peace.

His survival of the war is a puzzle which may have been due to Nazi fears of a strengthened resistance movement if he was killed, or to the desire to use him as a valuable hostage. By some miracle he escaped the final Nazi order to kill all prisoners rather than resign them to capture, and he finished the war (with former Austrian premier Dr Schuschnigg) in an Allied internment camp on the Island of Capri.

When Niemöller finally returned home he dedicated himself to Church work and to preaching Jesus as the Prince of Peacemakers who never counted the cost of His mission. Speaking in USA, he endorsed the view that the German nation as a whole should plead guilty to Hitler's crimes. Though this opinion was not popular with all Germans, he was elected President of the Evangelical Church in Hesse and Nassau—an eight-year appointment which to the surprise of many was renewed in 1961. The post-war drive to rearm Germany carried him close to pacifism, but as late as 1950, when he preached for Dr Hunter before the Hiroshima cross of charred wood in California's Mt. Hollywood Church, he was still acknowledging a difficulty in making up his mind, for he is, writes his friend Heinz Kraschützki, 'a fighter, not a man of quiet meditation'.

His acceptance at Evanston in 1954 of the belief that his ordination vow 'enlists us in the services of reconciliation' was perhaps underlined by an acute experience of personal tragedy. In August 1961 a car accident in Denmark, where he and his family were travelling to a Norwegian holiday, killed his devoted wife and their housekeeper, and took him into hospital for six weeks with severe concussion. He recovered in time to attend the Third Assembly of the World Council of Churches at New Delhi in November, where he became one of its six presidents. Today, as Allen Hunter puts it, he has spiritually passed 'the point of no return'; the rebel passion has at last overcome his early impulse towards force. In 1959 he himself had described his spiritual journey: 'I am not ashamed of the fact that I have changed my convictions in my lifetime—not from a lack of character, I believe, but because I have learned. Let us hope that those who are our present leaders will still be able to learn too.'

Some years ago Martin Niemöller introduced HEINZ KRASCHUTZKI to Professor Heinrich Vogel of Berlin with the words: 'This is an old friend of mine from the time we were together in the Navy. The First World War opened his eyes about the nature of militarism. For me, I am sorry to say, a second one was necessary.'

At Wilhelmshaven in 1915 Heinz Kraschützki, born in Danzig in 1891, met a Commander, Charles Hincheldeyn, who said to him: 'We are guilty of the war, that is why we are going to lose it'. He introduced Kraschützki to the books of the educational writer Friedrich Wilhelm Foerster, and to revolutionary (and prohibited) publications about the war's origins such as Grelling's J'accuse. Temperance work with the lower ranks of the Navy taught Heinz Kraschützki their opinions and prepared him for the coming revolution. The crew of his mine-sweeper elected him on to the Soldiers' and Workers' Council at Bremerhaven. After the revolutionary period he left the Navy and went into business.

Already an opponent of militarism, he was converted to pacifism by the suffering of the Ruhr children during the French occupation in 1923. He joined the German Peace Society and became Editor of its weekly paper, Das Andere Deutschland. As this sometimes published news about the clandestine rearming of Germany, proceedings for revealing military secrets were taken against him, and he moved to Spain. In 1934 he was expatriated by order of the Nazi Government, became stateless, and during the Spanish Civil War was sentenced to life imprisonment. He remained in jail till 1945, when he left Spain, found his family in Berlin, and remarried his wife who had been compelled to divorce him in order to retain their children.

In 1947 he was elected to the Council of the War Resisters' International, lectured for a time at a Potsdam college, and then became a prison social worker until his retirement at sixty-five in 1956. He now regards his chief duty, despite suspicions of 'fellow-travelling', as that of maintaining contact with the East German peace movement. In spite of the Berlin situation, he describes himself as 'a hopeless optimist'.

Outstanding Members

Dr RUDI DAUR, a contemporary of Wilhelm Mensching, is Pastor of the chief Lutheran Church in Stüttgart, and like Mensching refused to say 'Heil Hitler' throughout the Nazi period. He was offered the German Secretaryship of the F.o.R., but declined owing to his wish to concentrate on youth work in his parish, where music, social service and church unity are his major concerns. For a year Mr Sayre's son 'Bill' lived with him helping in youth work.

In December 1950 *Reconciliation* reported Rudi Daur as preparing for a South German Pastors' Conference. At the F.o.R. Annual General Meeting at Stüttgart in May 1961, the speakers included an Indian and a Nigerian, and the Conference ended with a great public service in Dr Daur's large church.

As Pastor at Kaulsdorf, near Berlin, Dr HEINRICH GRUBER helped many Communists as human beings. Under Hitler his 'Boro Grüber' managed to smuggle 5,000 Jews out of Berlin. He also went to Goering to protest against the transfer of mothers and children to Polish concentration camps.

When Eichmann sent for him and inquired why, having no Jewish blood, he helped the Jews, Dr Grüber quoted the parable of the Good Samaritan. This reply took him to Dachau concentration camp, where he had a heart attack in the winter of 1941-2 and was left unconscious amid a pile of corpses. The companions who rescued his half-dead body were atheistic Communists, who hid him under their beds to save him from cremation. Almost unbelievably, thanks to the intervention of a Nazi physician whose conscience he had disturbed, Heinrich Grüber survived the war, and returned to his post in Berlin.

In the nineteen-fifties his collected sermons, *Dona Nobis Pacem*, were published in Germany, and more recently a collection of essays called *Hatred Cross-ed Out* was dedicated to him by the Christian editor, Rudolph Weckerling.

In 1943 EVA HERMANN, a German Quaker greatly influenced by the American Friend Thomas Kelly, was convicted of helping the Jews in her neighbourhood and imprisoned at Mannheim. Her husband, KARL, was sent to another prison. They remained in jail until American troops arrived two years later, and now live in Marburg. Eva wrote some memorable letters from prison, which she found a place of inward liberation. One, translated by Dr Daniel Coogan of Haverford College, USA, under the title *In Prison—Yet Free*, appeared in *The Friends' Intelligencer* in 1947.

Eva wrote in this letter: 'When one's existence which has seemed quite secure suddenly melts away, . . . when every security fails and every support gives way—then one stands face to face with the Eternal and confronts Him without protection and with fearful directness. . . . When imprisonment has lasted a certain time it ceases to be punishment. One has removed one's self from ordinary life and slowly begins to find a new standard.'

A teacher born in 1891, MARIE PLEISSNER still lives in Chemnitz (now Karl-Marx-Stadt). After teaching from 1911 to 1914, she came to pacifism and politics through First War experience. Membership of the German Youth Movement and the World Youth League brought her into touch with the F.o.R. and especially with its member, Eleanor Harrison. Later she was influenced by Wilhelm Mensching.

In 1934 she lost her job through refusing the greeting 'Heil Hitler!' She attended the 1939 I.F.o.R. Conference in Denmark, and was denounced to the Nazi authorities after war began. Solitary confinement followed at Ravensbrück concentration camp, from which she was released after nine months. In 1945 the Russians foiled her attempt to start a Fellowship group in Chemnitz. She has continued to work in the spirit of the F.o.R.

and has been a member of the City Council of Karl-Marx-Stadt for some years.

HERMANN STOHR, a martyr in the magnificent Metzger tradition, was beheaded by the Nazis after long imprisonment on June 21, 1940, aged forty-two. Many encounters between the Gestapo and F.o.R. members disappeared into silence with the death of the victim—'known only to God'. Hermann Stohr is one of the few about whom some knowledge survived.

A former naval purser, he graduated in political science in 1923, offered his services to Dr Siegmund-Schültze, and became local director of the F.o.R. office which was then incorporated in the East Berlin settlement. He wrote several books on social service. One fine survey of American foreign aid, *So Half Amerika (1936)*, revealed the spiritual background of this work.

Called up in the Second World War he refused any service under Hitler, was dismissed by the Wehrmacht, and sentenced to death by an ordinary court. A few friends were permitted to bury his maimed body, and one, Erich Gramm, recorded some details. Four F.o.R. members and three Gestapo officials attended the funeral. The pastor, Fellowship member DR HARALD POELCHAU, who conducted the service, began a sermon which the Gestapo officials forbade. He then started to quote the text: 'Well done, good and faithful servant . . .'. An official shouted 'Stop that!' and all was silent except for the singing birds. Dr Poelchau then concluded with the Lord's Prayer, pausing impressively after each significant phrase.

As a chaplain at Moabit prison Harald Poelchau was a friend and messenger of the Gospel to thousands of prisoners jailed by Hitler, and particularly to those who had been associated with the conspiracy of July 20, 1944. He has related his experiences in a book recently published by 'Unterwegs' Verlag in Berlin.

ELIZABETH VON THADDEN represents in this history the women martyred under Hitler. A stately woman from an old Pomeranian family, she was born in 1890. Her father, the chairman of the local Council at Mohrungen, East Prussia, later became substitute for Dr Siegmund-Schültze as President of the *Soziale Arbeitsgemeinschaft*. Elizabeth herself joined the F.o.R., and in 1927 founded a Protestant girls' boarding school at Schloss Wieblingen, near Heidelberg.

In 1941 new state regulations obliged her to give up the headship, and she began work for the Red Cross. Here she was in a position to act as *liaison* between various German friends and Dr Siegmund-Schültze, whom she met at Basel station. Dr Heinz Kloppenburg reports that she once invited him to attend a discussion on how to feed children after the war had ended. When he arrived, the meeting was over—but all those present had been arrested by the Gestapo.

On July 1, 1944 a Nazi People's Court sentenced Elizabeth to death after a period of imprisonment in Berlin and Ravensbrück. She experienced a series of cruel inquisitions, but said nothing to incriminate members of Una Sancta and the Confessional Church. The prison chaplain, Pastor Ohm, who accompanied her to the door of the execution chamber on September 8, 1944, reported that her steps were sure and her bearing steady.

The present German F.o.R. secretary, Oberkirchenrat HEINZ KLOPPENBURG, was born in 1903, the son of a merchant navy ship's master who became unemployed when the Versailles Treaty deprived Germany of all sea-going ships. After working as a commercial apprentice, and conquering tuberculosis, he studied theology under the influence of Karl Barth and Martin Buber, and was the first 'senior' of Karl Barth's first Bonn seminar (1930). In 1932 he became the pastor of a Lutheran church in Wilhelmshaven, but in 1937, owing to his opposition to Nazism, the Gestapo forbade him to preach and his church dismissed him. He then became a friend of Martin Niemöller and a leader of the Confessional church.

He is now well known not only as editor of the *Junge Kirche*, the monthly Protestant journal which more than any other church magazine promotes the work of the Confessional church, but because of his outstanding service in ecumenical efforts for peace between East and West. Thanks to him there is growing co-operation between Christians in West and East Germany, and between German Christians and those in both Western and Eastern Europe. He is a founder and vice-president of the Prague Peace Conference, and owing to many visits to Eastern churches, he has become an expert in Eastern church life. In 1961 he was

a member of the German delegation to the World Council of
Churches in New Delhi, and has also taken part in the Puidoux
Conferences which have resumed theological discussions inter-
rupted for nearly 400 years. In the secular field he opposes
German rearmament and nuclear weapons, and works for demo-
cratic adult education.

FRAU IRMGARD SCHUCHARDT is one of the most active mem-
bers of the German Fellowship, which she joined after the
Second World War. She lives in Berlin-Friedeman, is now the
Berlin chairman, and has often attended I.F.o.R. conferences.

Other noteworthy members of the German Fellowship include
FRAU ASTA BRUGELMANN, a Cologne Friend who followed
Wilhelm Mensching as German secretary in 1948; AGNES
MARTENS-EDELMANN, a Dresden teacher and Quaker who was
an early F.o.R. member and later experienced the Russian occupation; PAUL KRAHE, who resigned the secretaryship in 1954 to
work for refugees; ALBRECHT MEYER ZU SCHWABEDISSEN, an
industrialist who helps the Fellowship to carry its financial
burden; DR HANS MAIER, a geography teacher who succeeded
Paul Krahe; and PROFESSOR WALDUS NESSLER, the Fellowship
leader in Leipzig and an influential educationist. Professor
Nessler, who died in 1954, could not continue his F.o.R. work in
the Soviet Zone, but kept contact with the office in West Berlin.

In post-war years the I.F.o.R. contributed financially to peace
work in Germany, but in the last five years the Versönungsbund
has given generously to the work of the International Fellowship. This is largely due to the efforts of the Versönungsbund
treasurer, OTTO HERRNFELD, who served in German submarines
during the last war, but has since devoted his energies to peace.

This brief history of the German Fellowship reveals that,
costly as the creed of compassion in this century of violence has
everywhere been to its practitioners in terms of prison, persecution, obloquy, loss of position, and the surrender of worldly
success, it has nowhere demanded the same measure of heroism
as it required from the German martyrs who laid down their
lives under the Nazis in the cause not of political domination
but of human pity. Their anonymous sacrifices, registered only
in the Book of the Recording Angel, have furnished a superb

reinforcement to mankind's spiritual heritage of courage and faith.

II. AUSTRIA

The so-called Peace Treaties which followed the First World War left Austria humiliated and impoverished. Vienna, once the proud centre of an unwieldy empire, became a huge head without a body; an administration with nothing to administer. Ruined but unresentful, the Austrians remained dignified in defeat. Politics and religion have traditionally been intermingled in their country, though the population is predominantly interested in art and music. During the nineteen-twenties economic distress brought not only a low standard of living but party hatreds, though these are not typical of the peace-loving people.

As early as 1920 a F.o.R. centre was established in Vienna by BEATRICE HOYSTED, an English woman who drew the Austrian peace groups together and won the confidence of her fellow workers. When she died in 1931 the Fellowship remained for a time without a leader, though it was associated with the names of JOHANNES UDE, and later of Kaspar Mayr.

The contact between Dr Ude and the Fellowship does not appear to have been close. A somewhat contentious man, he had differences of opinion with Dr Metzger in Graz regarding the work of the Catholic 'Blue Cross'. At one period he attempted to become President of Austria, but secured only 6,000 votes out of 400,000. He is however an outstanding pacifist by conviction, and in 1939 was prosecuted by the Gestapo in Graz for objecting to the persecution of the Jews.

He was declared a traitor, and worked for a time as a parish priest in the Upper Austrian Alps, but suddenly disappeared at the outbreak of the Second War. Rumours spread of his execution, but in 1960 a letter to Percy Bartlett from Kaspar Mayr reported that these stories were legends. For a time Dr Ude had been Professor of Morals in the University of Graz, but seldom agreed with his bishop. He has since retired and lives in the village of Grundlsee. His book *Du Solls Nicht Toten* (Thou Shalt Not Kill) takes the radical position, but is not endorsed by any ecclesiastical leader.

KASPAR MAYR himself was born in Bavaria, but lived for many

years in Vienna. During the First World War he came to believe that the reality of Christ and the reality of modern war were irreconcilable. He represented the secretarial centre of the German Catholics in the Fellowship, and was especially close to Hermann Hoffmann. The chief practical piece of work in which they were able to co-operate was the effort, by repeated visits and in the magazine *Die Brücke* (*The Bridge*), to inculcate the spirit of reconciliation on the western border of (Catholic) Poland in the years of stress before the Second World War. When war began the whole area was twice overrun, and the work could not continue.

From 1924 to 1928, Kaspar Mayr worked with the I.F.o.R. Secretariat in London. He was then sent to Eastern Europe, and moved with his family to Vienna. Between 1928 and 1934 he worked from Vienna in the Balkans, in Poland, and in the German-Polish conflict over the Danzig Corridor. By 1934 the F.o.R. could no longer afford to pay for his services, but he remained in Vienna. At this time Hitler forbade the Fellowship to continue the conciliation work between Germany and Poland.

Kaspar Mayr then worked for 'Catholic Action' (a movement run by lay members within the Catholic Church) and became co-editor of *Schönere Zukunft*. In 1938 he was prosecuted and imprisoned for short periods, both for 'subversive activities' and for his position in the Church. The Catholic Church was not openly persecuted, but individuals were harried according to the amount of opposition they showed to Hitlerism.

In 1945 the Russians occupied Vienna, and Kaspar Mayr and his family survived the bombing of the city after a narrow escape. Their eldest son Richard had been killed in Russia. Three years later Kaspar Mayr reported to the I.F.o.R.: 'Progress is slow; so far no group is visible'.

But the arrival of the Russians gave an opportunity for some practical demonstrations of non-violence. Most of the inhabitants, when visited by Russians, adopted a defensive attitude, but the Mayrs, in spite of their son's death, opened the door spontaneously, announced 'We are your friends', and invited them into the house. Hildegard Mayr has written of this period: 'In confronting them unarmed on his own doorstep, and in making them feel his love, Kaspar Mayr disarmed their hatred and aggression, and thus defended his family in the most efficient way. Though willing rather to give his own life than to take that of his adversaries, God permitted his power of the spirit repeatedly to change the attitude and heart of the occupying forces.'

When the war ended the Mayr family began to build up young people's groups to discuss the spirit and technique of non-violent resistance. Thinking them of no importance the occupation forces disregarded these groups, which amalgamated under the name of 'Christopher Jugend'. This body came under the F.o.R. when the Four-Power Administration was established at the end of 1945. In 1950 Kaspar started a periodical, *Der Christ in Der Welt* (which still continues), in order to develop a non-violent philosophy among Catholics and to gather supporters into the F.o.R. In 1951 he made a tour of Germany, hoping to encourage co-operation between the F.o.R. and German Catholic pacifists. In this after-war period, Catholic theological study conferences were held annually.

With the signing of the Peace Treaty in May 1955, Austria faced a new political situation. The Austrian F.o.R. Committee had to act speedily in order to bring its proposals before the Parliament and Government, which had agreed on general conscription. Their main purpose was to ensure the right of conscientious objection, and they began by sending a Memorandum to the Government, Parliament, and also the Church authorities. The next step was to draft a suggested law for conscientious objectors, and submit it to Parliament, the Church, and the Military Commission. Personal letters went to bishops and other authoritative individuals, and the idea of conscientious objection as a respectworthy political attitude thus became known.

The following year Kaspar Mayr reported to London: 'The F.o.R., in co-operation with the Service Civile and the Society of Friends, succeeded, . . . in so far as the Government provided "a law for a non-combatant service for C.O.s". Attempts to improve this law will be continued. We received the support of both the Catholic and Protestant Church.'

In 1957 a new Centre was officially opened with an office in Vienna, to serve both as an F.o.R. office and a basis for the development of international relations between East and West. At an East-West Conference held that year, a group of Polish Catholics were able to come to the West to meet their fellow

Christians. A second Conference in 1958 brought members of the Catholic, Protestant and Orthodox Churches together for the first time to study Christian non-violence. That year Kaspar Mayr published a handbook on peace called *Der Andere Weg*; he also officially retired and became a voluntary chairman, while his daughter Hildegard took his place as leader of the Vienna Centre. He died in December 1963 after a long life of outstanding service to the cause of peace.

HILDEGARD MAYR, an attractive young woman, began her work as I.F.o.R. travelling secretary in 1953. She had once thought of becoming a nun but instead, during her university studies, she met Jean Goss, the young vice-president of the French F.o.R. They were married at Easter 1958, and continued their Fellowship work together.

(See Chapter 8, *Peace Leadership in France*, pp. 159-61, for the work of the Goss-Mayrs as joint F.o.R. travelling secretaries.)

III. CZECHOSLOVAKIA

The pacifist tradition in Czechoslovakia goes back even further than the great Comenius (Johann Amos Komensky, 1592-1671), a pioneer writer on education and the last bishop of the old Church of the Moravian and Bohemian Brethren, whose theological work was much influenced by the German mystic, Jakob Boehme. In the fourteenth century King George of Bohemia had tried to organize a Peace League of Christian princes who would take their disputes to a Court of Arbitration, and early in the fifteenth century the preachers of the Hussite Wars were opposed to the use of weapons.

These historic precedents created a favourable atmosphere after the First War for the League of Nations and the Czech peace societies which supported its ideals; it was not therefore difficult for HEINRICH TUTSCH to start a Fellowship group in 1922 in Prague, which also became the centre of the International Youth Service. As late as 1938, Prague was one of the cities visited by Embassies of Reconciliation in their endeavours to prevent the Second World War.

The first chairman of the Czech Fellowship was FRAU PAVLA MOUDRA, who survived until 1941. After the death of Heinrich Tutsch from tuberculosis in 1931 and his widow's departure to

live in London, the leadership of the group came into the hands
of PREMYSL PITTER, assisted by two devoted colleagues, OLGA
FIERZ and JAN KUCERA. The first two now live in Switzerland;
the third is still in Czechoslovakia.

Premysl Pitter and Olga Fierz formed a remarkable team
between the wars in Prague, where he founded a religious social
settlement for children in the slums of the city. It was known as
Milicuv Dum after Jan Militsch, forerunner of Jan Hus and a
pioneer social worker. When Henri Roser visited this home in
the nineteen-thirties, about 130 workers' children played there
daily. At this time Premysl represented both the F.o.R. and the
War Resisters' International.

Born in Czechoslovakia in 1895, Premysl came from a Roman
Catholic family but soon reacted against it. He was deeply
affected by the Czech struggle against Austro-Hungary. His
parents died when he was fifteen, and he enlisted in the 1914
war but was quickly disillusioned. In this 'Hell' (his own word)
he began to think: 'How can we who call ourselves Christians
kill our brothers? I refuse.' He became a medical orderly, and
when the war ended he organized a group of Czech soldiers to
bring some of its victims into hospital.

Czech independence made possible his return to Prague and
he became a student in the Protestant faculty of theology, but
his now radical Christian attitude, reinforced by the discovery
of Tolstoy's writings, made it impossible for him to remain at
the university. Before he was called up for military service, he
wrote a celebrated letter to President T. G. Masaryk: 'I am
unable to serve as a soldier and therefore I return my military
papers to you, the Commander-in-Chief. Not until I read your
great work, *The World Revolution*, did I come to the firm
decision to take this step. I am returning my military book
because the knowledge that I am part of the military organization is intolerable to me . . . This does not mean that I am not
ready to go to prison at once in this cause. But I doubt that this
would be the right way to convince heretics of this type and to
destroy their ideas . . . There are names on my side . . . upon
whom you too are calling, Mr President — Jesus, Chelcicky,
Tolstoi, and among the living thinkers of the world we have
sympathizers too, such as Gandhi, Romain Rolland.'

In March 1925 Premysl was sentenced to three months

imprisonment on the charge of encouraging objectors to military service, and carrying on anti-militarist propaganda. This sentence was never carried out, and after the amnesty proclaimed for Czechoslovakia's 'jubilee' in 1929, it was remitted on condition that he was not sentenced again within two years. During May 1925 Premysl toured Latvia and Estonia for the F.o.R. with Lilian Stevenson and Matilda Widegren of Sweden.

His Children's Home was opened in 1935, and in 1939 it received £200 from the I.F.o.R. fund for the relief of refugees. In order to give it his full attention, Premysl resigned from the chairmanship of 'New Jerusalem', an association aiming at the regeneration of people in every social sphere. He himself, a fair-haired man with a strong profile and benevolent eyes, is a vegetarian, non-smoker and non-drinker. To help Milicuv Dum he now delivered a series of addresses, flaming with youthful enthusiasm. These brought him thousands of supporters, and his magazine Sbrateni (Brotherhood) had a circulation of 10,000 copies.

During the Nazi regime, Premysl and Olga Fierz continued their work uninterrupted throughout the war, though the Gestapo combed the organization to find Jewish children. Some were discovered and sent to the gas chambers. Premysl asked more than once if he could accompany and comfort them on their last journey, but the request was always refused. One day a leading Gestapo official sent for him. Premysl did not deny helping Jewish children, but insisted that as a Christian he was obliged to do this work. The official commented: 'You have not lied to me so you can go'. In spite of his constant danger, food secretly contributed by well-wishers was distributed to the children of 100 Jewish families.

After the war the Germans were thrown out, and Premysl persuaded the Czech Government to let him have four fine country mansions which the Nazis had acquired for themselves. Here he gradually brought 370 Czech-Jewish children from concentration camps, and with Olga Fierz's help nursed them back to health. Later, over two years, he rescued more than 400 German children from Czech internment camps. In all this work he had the help of a Jewish doctor named Voegel, whose wife had been put to death by the Nazis. He said to Premysl: 'My work is with children, so we must not allow images of hatred to grow in our minds'. In 1946, helped by Jan Masaryk with whom Premsyl was friendly, Mr Sayre visited Milicuv Dum, and took eighty letters from the children to their relatives in Germany. In 1951 Premysl was declared 'politically and ideologically unacceptable' by the new Communist regime. Realizing that their work for the children, most of whom had been reunited with their parents, was virtually finished, Premysl and Olga Fierz left Czechoslovakia. For a time he lived in London, but eventually the World Council of Churches accepted him for pastoral and welfare services among Czech refugees at Valka Camp near Nuremberg, where he worked with indefatigable devotion for some years.

K

Chapter 8

PEACE LEADERSHIP IN FRANCE

Peace work in France during the past fifty years has taken especially two forms: witness against conscription, and positive experiments in the work of reconciliation. Both national and, at times of especial danger, private conferences have reinforced the constructive experiments.

The chief difficulty of French conscientious objectors has arisen because in France, unlike other Western countries such as Britain and the United States, there was no recognition of the rights of conscience relating to military service. From the time of the French Revolution conscription has been regarded as a normal claim on all male citizens, and the refusal to serve in peace or war was an illegal act involving heavy penalties. Only recently has public opinion been ready to demand a revision of the law in the interests of spiritual liberty. For this reason a Bill to allow alternative civilian service, proposed by a Socialist politician, M. Richard, in 1932 made no progress though some Protestant churches supported him. Catholic F.o.R. members and workers in the I.V.S.P. also endeavoured to obtain this legal change, but the Church as a whole failed to secure agreement to the idea of conscience as sacred. Finally, on December 12, 1963, the French Parliament granted Frenchmen the right of conscientious objection.

Conscientious objectors however have long borne their witness, and a number have been sentenced for terms of up to two years. In most cases this was repeated several times. Though the French code of military justice made a general allowance for 'extenuating circumstances' with the intention of occasionally reducing the penalty, most objectors received maximum sentences, and no provision existed to prevent them from being called up repeatedly after their sentences had expired.

By 1929, military preparation was compulsory in twenty-one educational institutions and optional in 300. Notwithstanding these regulations, a campaign began in favour of conscientious objectors, and in 1933 a circular issued by the Ministry of the Interior called attention to its influence upon young soldiers.

Immediately after the First World War a movement led by Marc Sagnier, known as *La Jeune République*, exerted considerable influence on Catholic peace workers. One of its purposes was to restore the faith in humanity which had largely disappeared under the impact of wartime cruelty and hatred. In 1920-21 an international reconstruction unit which included representatives of six nationalities—Swiss, Hungarian, German, British, Austrian and French—took up work in the devastated area of Esnes, near Verdun.

At the time the experiment appeared to be unsuccessful, since the French occupation of the Ruhr brought a new phase of Franco-German antagonism; after the debris of war had been cleared and two wooden houses built, the Prefect of the District suppressed the work as untimely. But the inspiration was not quenched, and the Verdun experiment ultimately led to the International Voluntary Service for Peace founded by Pierre Cérésole and supported by the F.o.R. In 1928 this new body enrolled over 700 men and women from all over Europe for the relief of distress in Lichtenstein.

Five years earlier, meetings addressed in France by Oliver Dryer had some religious and philosophical consequences. A number of theological students, after leaving Paris, formed study groups in Strasbourg, Colmar, Montpelier and Lille, and made contacts with like-minded Germans. In 1925, fifty French and German students took part in a fortnight's walking tour, and subsequently held a small conference in Paris with Jacques Martin, the secretary of the Paris group. Three years afterwards Pasteur Henri Roser became French secretary, and combined this work with running a workers' settlement in a Paris suburb.

During the nineteen-thirties a number of conferences took place, and a crusade was organized in several towns and villages in 1932. About this time the French movement began to publish a monthly magazine, *Les Cahiers de la Réconciliation*, which attracted about 900 subscribers.

The I.F.o.R. office moved from Vienna to Paris in 1933, and

Henri Roser was appointed general secretary, with Daniel Hogg as an assistant. Just before the Second World War broke out the office was moved from Paris to London, but a national conference of the French F.o.R. proved to be possible in the summer of 1939, and in December private meetings were still taking place in a worker's house. With the end of the 'phoney' war in the spring of 1940 the real testing time for French pacifists began, though in February Hélène Schott, the stenographer in the Paris F.o.R. office, was still carrying on under the guidance of André Trocmé who was able to continue his parish work in the Cévennes.

Opportunities of pacifist witness, except for individuals, then disappeared until the spring of 1945, when large public meetings were held in Lyons and Nîmes. But the continuous reconstruction of the French F.o.R. did not begin until the next decade. In July 1952 a conference took place at Versailles with Joan and François Chevalley as the new secretaries. Later gatherings arranged there at the *Maison de Réconciliation* included Catholics, Protestants, Mennonites and Quakers. One conference held in March 1957 followed the publication of an impressive brochure, *Les Chrétiens l'Evangile et la Guerre*.

In the same year a *Comité de la Résistance Spirituelle* found support from both Protestants and Catholics owing to the behaviour of both French and Moslem troops in Algeria. The leaders of this committee included Henri Roser, André Trocmé, Jean Lasserre and Daniel Parker. They issued a card to young men fighting in Algeria which stated that the Church itself takes responsibility for a soldier who declines on conscientious grounds to join in acts of torture, André Trocmé, with Lanza del Vasto, the founder of the Gandhian *Communauté de l'Arche*, led a demonstration in 1960 at the military atomic centre near Anfragon. During May, following a conference on non-violence in June 1959, a protest campaign began against the scandal of French concentration camps reserved for North Africans.

Many French pacifists, who included Jean Goss, served their apprenticeship to non-violence in this campaign. In co-operation with the *Action Civique Non-Violente*, they held fortnightly demonstrations of prayer and silence outside the Ministry of Justice.

In January 1961 *Reconciliation* reported that, after much

thought and preparation, the French F.o.R. had publicly declared that young men with conscientious scruples against serving in the Algerian war should proclaim their objection, behave as conscientious objectors, and be ready for 'non-violent civil action' to bring pressure on their governments. As there was still no law in France permitting conscientious objection, those who refused military service were automatically imprisoned, sometimes for years on end. The law also forbade persons not liable for military service to advocate conscientious objection by others.

Witnesses reported that the power of the spirit made itself deeply felt in the demonstrations at the Ministry of Justice. Simultaneously the French Fellowship called a growing number of young men to serve in the work camps for Algerian refugees.

The first widely-known modern French protagonist of peace has been HENRI ROSER, born at Pantin, France, in 1899 to a family with a tradition of missionary and religious service. His father, educated in Alsace under the German regime, had refused to swear fidelity to the German Emperor and went to France. Henri, the third of eight children, planned to become a missionary himself.

He graduated from the Sorbonne in 1918, and had then to undergo the three years of military service prescribed for all Frenchmen. Though doubts soon sprang from the incompatibility of this training with the Gospel teaching, he managed to stifle his conscience and finish his three years. The war ended just as he reached the front, thus saving him from being killed or wounded.

In March 1921, his training completed, he was demobilised with the rank of sub-lieutenant in the Reserve. He began his theological studies in the Paris Missionary College with the intention of taking a post in West Africa; he also became engaged to the daughter of a History Professor in the University of Geneva. At this period he started to preach the Gospel outside the gates of Paris, and was once charged for speaking in the street where a drunken man insisted: 'You shall not speak of Jesus Christ here'.

Again his conscience was troubling him, for it suggested that he should refuse military service which might mean prison or exile. His fiancée Claire Seitz shared his spiritual struggle, and supported him at every stage.

At the time that the French invaded the Ruhr in 1923, Henri decided that his country could no longer be permitted to count on him as a reservist officer. He told his parents and the Director of the Missionary Society that he had determined to return his papers to the French War Ministry, and resolved to prove to the head of the mission school that he was not insane. Some days after his decision he was encouraged by hearing Oliver Dryer speak of the F.o.R., but in between he spent many hours of lonely disquiet and sometimes wondered if he were indeed going mad.

During these difficult days he had to meet compelling arguments from persons who disagreed with him, such as a university professor and the mother of a son fallen in war. Attempts by such critics to make his fiancée persuade him to change his mind met with no response. His great moral authority today springs from his position as the first French Christian pacifist to bear witness between the wars.

The Missionary Society now refused to give him any appointment, and ten years later, like his friends Philippe Vernier and Jacques Martin, he was refused ordination owing to the conscription law. He therefore began work with his wife, whom he married in 1925, in a small parish in the Ardeche. Shortly afterwards he became French secretary of the F.o.R., and moved to the slum area of Aubervilliers outside Paris.

During the 'twenties he travelled alone to many German cities, where he made a number of good friends. He has since recorded that Northern France, which had experienced invasion and suffering, was more favourable to this type of *rapprochement* than the comfortable South. In 1933, while he was talking to German acquaintances in Essen (Ruhrgebiet), three policemen took him into custody as 'a danger to the German State'. Already, like many other pacifists, he had begun to be 'stoned by both sides'.

As the Second World War came nearer, Henri's personal peril increased. Though the War Ministry had long ago cancelled his commission as a Reserve infantry officer it had never punished him further, but on September 4, 1939, he surrendered himself. Three days later he refused to obey a military order, and on

December 19th a tribunal sentenced him to four years' imprisonment. Shortly afterwards he learned that no obstacle would now be raised to his ordination, but the Ordination Committee of the Church could not arrange this while he was in prison.

Six months later, when the Germans had broken through the Maginot Line, the warden of his prison freed all the inmates lest they should be taken to forced labour in Germany. Henri, told to 'get out and go to the devil', walked fifty kilometres through the night towards the Cévennes village of Le Chambon-sur-Lignon where the four Roser children had been taken to security in a home. Claire Roser also escaped from Paris on the luggage carrier of a motor cycle, and managed to join her children. A month afterwards, as by a miracle, Henri himself arrived there after returning to Paris on a bicycle to try to find his wife.

The American F.o.R. offered to arrange a lecture tour for him, but as 1940 piled up its tragedies his conscience summoned him back to his humble parishioners in Aubervillers. His place, he felt, was among his people; it seemed to him vital to work out a dignified relationship, which avoided both servility and insolence, between them and the invaders, and try to discover what creative accomplishments the power of love might bring. At that time Hélène Schott of the F.o.R. office went back to her native Alsace. The office could not be reopened, but the work of reconciliation need not end.

Henri Roser now returned to his ministry, and as the salary possible for the poverty-stricken congregation was too small to support him and his family, he earned his living by translating documents for a medical academy. In this way he continued to live in France throughout the occupation.

At this time he compiled a treatise, *Reflections of a Pastor in Occupied France*, which a friend later carried to the United States. There it was translated by Edith Lovejoy Pierce, and published by the New York Fellowship. He arranged his meditations under three headings, 'Steadfastness', 'Action' and 'Charity'. He also received a prize from the *Atlantic Monthly* for an article entitled 'Communion', describing an incident on a train from Cracow to Paris in which a sacramental understanding was established between Roser and a Russian peasant woman though neither could speak a word of the other's language. In addition he translated a work by Leonhard Ragaz, the Swiss theologian who wrote in German, and thus interpreted him to

French-speaking countries. After 1943, underground meetings of the F.o.R. were held every month in Paris.

Henri and his family survived the many dangers — Allied bombing, the final fighting, and the acute food shortage—which threatened French citizens during the last months of the war. In October 1944 a small gathering of the Fellowship again became possible. Released at last from the atmosphere of falsehood which had surrounded him, he wrote his friends in the I.F.o.R. that 'now we are taking up again freedom of life and thought, and giving thanks'.

In February 1945, acknowledging a gift from the American Fellowship's war victims fund, he reported that he was working in a camp at Drancy among suspected persons, some guilty of collaboration and others innocent. During this year he was finally ordained, with forty pastors in attendance, and after ordination put in charge of the École de Colportage for mission preachers. Today he is leader of the British-founded and American-supported McCall Mission in France which trains evangelists among workers. This mission controls sixteen settlements in large French cities, and represents a modern form of the settlement movement in France. Two of his pastors have carried the F.o.R. message to Eastern Europe.

Henri Roser has always been a dedicated traveller. In 1934 he toured Austria and Czechoslovakia, visited Spain in 1937 during the Spanish Civil War, and was in Vienna in 1938, three days before Hitler marched into the city. After the war he went further afield, attended the World Pacifist Meeting in India in 1949-50, and in 1951 went with Antonio Loureiro on a tour of South America, visiting F.o.R. centres in Chile, Argentina, Uruguay and Brazil. Further journeys followed to Hungary, Madagascar (twice), Abidjan (Ivory Coast of Africa) and the Cameroons.

Before joining the McCall Mission, Henri Roser was associated with the Church of Saint-Esprit, of which he was pastor from 1952-6. Now he is connected with several organizations which include the French Society of the Blue Cross (working for the rehabilitation of alcoholics), and the French Committee of Le Service Civil Volontaire International, of which he is President. In 1960, at the request of l'Action Civique Non-Violente, he organized two non-violent demonstrations at Vincennes and in the Champs-Elysées to protest against the internment of North Africans without trial. Still more recently his time has been occupied with representations in favour of the statute, passed at the end of 1963, to establish the rights of French conscientious objectors.

ANDRE TROCME was born to a Huguenot family in 1901 at St Quentin, one of the first French towns to be invaded by the Germans in 1914. His mother, who died three years before the war, was German, and his wife, Magda Grilli Trocmé, is the daughter of an Italian who married a Russian woman born in Siberia to a deportee of the Decembrist Revolution. Fellow F.o.R. members know André Trocmé as a fine, scholarly preacher with an attractive smile who is equally at home in French, German and English.

A religious revival in the Protestant church at St Quentin led to a local early study of non-violent resistance, and in 1923, when André was preparing for the ministry, he took part in founding the French section of the F.o.R. When he was only sixteen the idea of pacifism had come to him through a German officer from Breslau, billeted in his parents' home during the Battle of the Somme, who was in effect a conscientious objector determined never to kill. Subsequently the German went back to the front and the Trocmés never heard from him again, but the effect of their conversations remained.

André was not yet, however, a convinced pacifist, and like Henri Roser allowed himself to be drafted into the Army. But the struggle with his conscience became acute, and during an expedition to Morocco to deal with a local rebellion he abandoned his rifle and went unarmed into the desert. When his officer discovered this non-violent protest he sympathized with André's scruples, but warned him that if the group of soldiers was attacked he would be brought before a military court as a deserter. The group was not attacked, but André now recognized the logic of his own position.

He finished his pastoral training in France and later at the Union Theological Seminary in New York, where he met his future wife. For eight years, in which they married and had four children, he was pastor of a mining and steel workers' parish in Northern France, and in 1934, after being eliminated as a pacifist from several lists of candidates for church positions.

he was invited to the small parish of Le Chambon-sur-Lignon in the Cévennes where several thousand Huguenots had lived since the Reformation.

To British visitors this beautiful mountain village suggests the New Forest lifted to the height of Snowdon and surrounded by still loftier peaks. Here André was not required to sign a declaration that he would refrain from advocating conscientious objection, and thus became the first pacifist minister in France. In his first year, in co-operation with Pastor EDOUARD THEIS, he founded the Collège Cévenol, an international secondary school preparing students for the university. The college developed quickly until it held 350 pupils and became widely known.

After the Second World War broke out, Le Chambon became a sanctuary for Jewish and other political refugees from all over Europe, and eventually attracted the attention of the Gestapo and the Vichy police. Many refugees had to be smuggled across the frontiers; others were arrested. These included André Trocmé himself; for five weeks he was interned in a French concentration camp and, subsequently threatened with death by the Gestapo, went for a time into hiding. His chief problem after his return was to resist Vichy's injustices, but also to maintain the technique of non-violence. The Trocmés and their followers never associated with the Maquis, though he remained on good terms with its leaders, since their methods of resistance were totally different.

When the war ended he resumed his normal occupation as a pastor, working in association with the Reformed Church and the F.o.R. Several Fellowship conferences have been held at Le Chambon, and André, appointed shortly after the war as an F.o.R. travelling secretary, toured Southern Germany under the auspices of the German Fellowship. At an F.o.R. meeting at Cologne in 1948 a former Jewish refugee at Le Chambon asked André to convey his thanks to the peasant woman who had hidden him; he also met one of the military police who arrested members of the Maquis, and is now a convert to the F.o.R. Of these experiences André Trocmé subsequently said that although, at a given moment, a man may be unable to see the way out of his predicament, in terms of later events the methods of God become clear.

Owing to the wartime work for refugees at Le Chambon the American Congregationalists became interested in the school. Through them a generous couple named Sangrée, who had been looking for a European centre in which to invest their money and enthusiasm, gave large donations towards founding the College Cévenol. André Trocmé hopes that several similar centres of pacifist teaching may be established in Europe.

In 1950 André and Magda Trocmé moved to Versailles, where a house was rented for use as an F.o.R. office and centre. Four years later a book compiled from his Paine lectures in USA, *The Politics of Repentance*, was published in English.

When the war in Algeria began soon afterwards the Trocmés went there, and for three weeks of 1955 André lived in the Moslem quarter of Algiers. There a French doctor said to him: 'Send me ten and tens of young doctors and nurses who will go to villages I know', and André persuaded ten French students to begin this work. They went two by two in the apostolic fashion, showing the love of Christ in action rather than attempting the task of conversion. This undertaking was the origin of the service subsequently known as 'Eirene'.

On a later journey by André and Magda to Algeria, they learned that the large-scale torturing of rebels had been organized in thirteen centres. A visit to the headquarters of the French General Massu established the truth of these accusations, which greatly increased hatred and fear among the Arabs. The Trocmés intervened with both the General and his wife on behalf of the rebels.

In 1960 André Trocmé became pastor of the St Gervais parish of the Reformed Church in Geneva. A few months earlier he had received a D.D. degree at Bethany Biblical Seminary in the United States, for which the citation ran: 'A man of forgiving love in the midst of hatred; a reconciler in the midst of estrangement; a voice of hope in the midst of despair; a man of God knee-deep in human need—the Rev. André Pascal Trocmé'.

It will have become apparent that peace witness in France has taken a somewhat different form from that of Britain, the United States, and even Germany. Owing to the long non-recognition of conscientious objection by French law and the severe penalties imposed on objectors, resistance to the military machine has fallen, not on groups, but to a handful of exceptionally courageous individuals such as Henri Roser and André Trocmé, who have carried on their own shoulders the burden of the struggle to change the relevant legislation. Though occasional protests against legal injustice have taken place in great cities such as Paris, Lyons and Lille, anti-war resistance has not, as in other countries, been conducted from metropolitan centres, but has been concentrated mainly on the Huguenot village of Le Chambon in the Haute Loire.

A third outstanding witness against compulsory military service, who has also been associated with Le Chambon, is PHILIPPE VERNIER, a pastor of profound religious quality who has three times accepted long periods of imprisonment in the cause of spiritual freedom.

Philippe Vernier, the son of a Madagascar missionary, was born in 1909 at Tananarive in Madagascar, where his mother, formerly a teacher in Nîmes, taught him until he was twelve. He then went to school at Nîmes from his grandparents' home, and in 1925-6 graduated in theology at Paris. During his studies he came into contact with Henri Roser and other members of the French F.o.R., and was already a pacifist when he began work under Pastor Henri Nick as an assistant minister in the working-class quarter of Fives in the city of Lille.

In 1932 Philippe Vernier had completed his studies and was due to be called up for military service. He decided to tell the Army that he intended to refuse this service, and to propose marriage to Henriette Dubois, the daughter of an early pacifist who died in 1916 and had based his position on Bible teaching. Her mother showed Philippe M. Dubois's diary to indicate how her husband had reached his own conclusions.

In June 1933 Philippe was arrested for his refusal on Christian grounds to accept the Army's demands, and sentenced to a year's solitary confinement. At the trial his superintendent minister, Pastor Nick, said of him: 'He has nothing that is his own. He served without pay and in order to serve was ready to give up even his studies which he had pursued brilliantly. . . . He does not fear death, is not attached to life, and has several times risked it to save others. He pays little attention to the judgment and opinion of men, but is anxious not to displease God.' The minister went on to describe Philippe as the organizer of holiday

camps, the tireless teller of exciting stories to boys, and a song
writer and flute player beloved by all children.

After his liberation in April 1934, Philippe was re-arrested in
fifteen days for the renewed refusal to serve in the Army. This
time he was sentenced to the maximum penalty of two years'
solitary confinement in Fort St Nicolas, Marseilles, where his
cell measured only nine feet by six. The authorities made every
effort to weaken his morale; he was visited only by persons who
disagreed with his stand, and allowed to receive only seven
letters a week of the many which reached him after his case had
been publicized by Henri Roser. On his behalf Pastor Roser
collected 2,000 signatures from French citizens of all classes.

At first Philippe was permitted no books, but his family
insisted that the prison authorities must allow him his Bible.
Eventually he obtained permission to compose short daily read-
ings for young people, 'Avec le Maître', later translated by Edith
Lovejoy Pierce under the title With the Master. These beautiful
brief devotional studies, seventy-four in number, were based on
short texts such as 'For My Name's Sake', 'Yet I am not alone'
and 'My time is not yet come'. Eventually they formed a wartime link between the many Christian pastors and pacifist
leaders upon whom silence was imposed by political catastrophe.

In July 1935 Nevin Sayre presented to the French Chargé
d'Affaires in Washington a petition for the release of Philippe
Vernier, signed by young Americans from forty states, and forty
colleges and universities. Philippe had now become an embarrassment to the Army, and in December 1935 they offered him
hospital service in Morocco under a Protestant chaplain. He
accepted and went to Meknes, but the military leaders refused
to allow him to minister to the soldiers and the civil authorities
prevented him from preaching in church or conducting Sunday
school. He was reduced to weeding the courtyard and holding
occasional classes for children. On returning from Morocco he
endeavoured unsuccessfully to be ordained in France; he was
then offered a missionary parish at Quaregnon in Belgium and
was ordained there in January 1939.

In September 1939 the French military authorities recalled
him to France to serve in the war, and with his brother Pierre
he refused to take part. Philippe was then imprisoned at Nîmes,
where he was almost starved, and Pierre in Marseilles. They

would probably have been shot had not their Paris lawyer succeeded in establishing that it was not at the front that they refused to serve.

The brothers were tried in Marseilles on February 22, 1940. Philippe was sentenced to four years' imprisonment and Pierre to two, and they were sent to the great prison at Clairvaux. In June 1940 a German bomb fell on this prison, and the prisoners dispersed. The Verniers made their way to Le Chambon, where Philippe's wife, who had escaped there with their two young daughters, was already teaching. After a few months there Philippe was able to secure new identity papers, and spent the rest of the war in his Belgian parish where he combined his pastoral responsibilities with work as a miner among the men of his congregation. In 1946 he managed to organize an international volunteer work camp—the first of its kind in Belgium—at St Ghislain, a small town two miles from his parish which had largely been destroyed by Allied bombs.

Philippe was again arrested in 1952 because he had never been officially pardoned, but he was released after intervention by his friends. Two years later, having been a loyal witness for the Fellowship in Belgium for several years, he moved back to France where he received a call to a parish at Maubeuge. Here he has since continued his rôle of an inspired evangelist, and a simple and popular preacher in spiritual communion especially with young people.

Other friends and supporters of the Fellowship well known in France include Jacques Martin, Jean Lasserre, Jean Goss, Daniel Parker and Etienne Mathiot.

JEAN LASSERRE, who has been described as 'The Josephine Butler of France', courageously organized a campaign against brothels covering the whole North of France, directly after the Second World War. To the surprise of the French military, he was able to prove that venereal disease actually decreased where brothels and the compulsory medical inspection of prostitutes had been abolished. Owing to the success of his crusade, a law prepared by the indefatigable work of Daniel Parker (see p. 161) was passed in 1946 forbidding the establishment of houses of prostitution.

Born in 1908, Jean Lasserre spent his early years in Lyons.

Then, for five years, he studied theology in Paris and New York, where he obtained his degree. In 1932 he became a minister of the Reformed (Protestant) Church, and until 1961 worked among the coal miners and steel operatives of Northern France. During the Second World War, he shared in the anti-Nazi Resistance.

In 1949 his Church asked him to draw up a report to the North Synod on the problems of war, based on the two main reports produced by the World Council of Churches in Amsterdam. His report was accepted, and a study commission set up. It had however inspired him with a desire to investigate further the problem of the Christian's participation in war, and this led to a period of historical research. Thus he discovered the weakness of the tradition that a Christian must serve in the Forces, and joined the F.o.R.

Jean Lasserre then brought his considerable learning and wide experience of life to the writing of his book *La Guerre et l'Evangile* (*War and the Gospel*), published in French (1953), German (1957) and English (1962). He now became an active member of the I.F.o.R., and has been editor of the publication *Les Cahiers de la Réconciliation* since 1957.

From 1953 Jean Lasserre was a pastor in a working-class area of St Etienne, building up a reformed community in a suburb destroyed by bombing in 1944. Some years later he began to take part in non-violent demonstrations against the French internment camps for Algerians, and on behalf of a legal status for conscientious objectors. He also joined a group of fifteen pacifists who sought to bear witness by a three-days' fast in the UNESCO Headquarters in Paris, and has several times been arrested for short periods.

In September 1961 he became Regional Secretary for the French-speaking countries in the I.F.o.R., and has lectured in Belgium, France and Switzerland as well as joining marches against nuclear weapons. He is a dedicated and distinguished member of the French Fellowship.

The two young F.o.R. members, JEAN GOSS and his wife HILDEGARD, the daughter of Kasper Mayr of Vienna, have come to be regarded especially as the Roman Catholic evangelists of the Fellowship. They have recently travelled in Southern Europe and in several countries of Eastern Europe.

In 1940, when only twenty, Jean Goss experienced a remarkable revelation of the reality of Christ. Soon afterwards he became a prisoner of war, and was in close contact with other captives from many countries. Conscious of God's love, Jean endeavoured to love these associates 'as himself', but soon realized the limits of this emotion. He discovered then that only Christ had set no boundaries to His love, which had inspired all His actions. This led Jean to write a thesis concluding that he must love the Germans. One or two of its readers were interested, but more were scandalized.

When released from imprisonment he sent his thesis to Pierre-Henri Simon, François Mauriac, and his bishop the Cardinal Suhard of Paris. Finally one left-wing Catholic said to him: 'But you are a conscientious objector'. When he inquired 'What's that?' his acquaintance sent him to Henri Roser, who talked to him of non-violence and the work of Gandhi. Through Pastor Roser he came to know many radical pacifists, of whom one especially, Anne Boirard, influenced him greatly. Finally he returned to the War Ministry his military account-book and his war decorations, presented to him with several citations for gallantry.

In 1949 Jean Goss was elected a vice-president of the French F.o.R. and became acquainted with Father Lorson S.J. Father Lorson told him of the ecclesiastical ruling accepted by Cardinal Ottaviani — *Bellum est omnino interdicendum* ('war is condemned without reserve'), since the values of war destroyed the transcendant message of the Gospel. In 1950 Jean went to Rome, and sought all over the Vatican for Mgr Ottaviani (not yet a cardinal). He finally had two hours' conversation with him and a further talk with Mgr Cordovani, chief translator for the *Osservatore Romano*. Other fruitful contacts followed up to the time that Pope John XXIII was elected, summoned the Vatican Council in 1962, and produced the famous Encyclical *Pacem in Terris*.

A year or two earlier Jean Goss had married Hildegard Mayr. Together they dedicated themselves to a life devoted to the creation of peace between nations, the Churches and the people. The Vatican Council gave them an unprecedented opportunity to interest the whole Catholic Church with a testament of non-violence which they had prepared under Catholic theologians at the personal suggestion of Cardinal Ottaviani. Many remarkable letters reached them from members of the Council, of whom one of the most active wrote: 'I am overjoyed by the fine apostolic work with which you have helped the Council during your stay in Rome . . . We were in the preparatory phase and that is why your initiative has been so important. I thank God for having called you to apply the Gospel teaching to the problems of our time.'

Since that period Jean and Hildegard have travelled continuously, sometimes with their twin children Etienne and Myriam. They have been encouraged by letters from Cardinals Feltin (Paris), Liénart (Lille), and Bea and Ottaviani (Rome), and by the support of the International Pax Christi Movement. Besides visiting all the Catholic countries of Europe, they spent much of 1961 in Moscow, and of 1962 in Latin America, where they visited Colombia, Chile, the Argentine, Uruguay and Brazil. Each Christmas they report their progress in long circular letters. For the Second Vatican Council in 1963, they prepared a substantial thesis, *Propositions Concerning Peace and War*.

DANIEL PARKER, a civil engineer and the son of a Methodist minister, Louis Parker, was born in Paris in 1901, and became associated with the F.o.R. through Henri Roser, Edouard Theis and André Trocmé.

From 1925 he worked as an engineer with the Methodist Mission at Dahomey on the Ivory Coast of West Africa. After his return to France he campaigned actively, like Jean Lasserre, against the system of *maisons de tolérance* from 1937 until the law abolishing these houses was passed in 1946.

Already, through studying a thesis *De l'Unité Chrétienne* by a student pastor Y. M. Crespin, Daniel Parker had become convinced that the Gospels, the Acts and the Pauline Epistles implied the acceptance of non-violence. In 1949 he wrote a short book, deliberately presented very simply, which the French Fellowship published. At a public conference Professor Raymond Charles, a well-known Biblical specialist, declared this book to be 'absolutely irrefutable'.

In 1962 Daniel Parker brought out, in the Faith and Works Edition (Geneva and Paris), a more mature publication, *Le Choix Décisif*, which faced the menace of atomic war with a decisive vigour but great simplicity. This set out to be a genuine

L

'ecumenical' work, taking into account the recent evolution in the position of Protestant and Catholic theologians. His book has been read not only by Catholics and Protestants but by Jehovah's Witnesses, of whom one wrote from prison in the name of ten comrades to thank the author for the hours of comfort which his book had brought them.

During the dark years of the Algerian war, most of the meetings of the *Comité de Résistance Spirituelle* took place in the apartment of Daniel Parker and his wife. Occasionally he joined other F.o.R. members in demonstrating against the Algerian war, the internment camps, and nuclear weapons, while demanding a civilian service for conscientious objectors. At present Daniel Parker is at work on another ecumenical book with Christian unity as its purpose.

JACQUES MARTIN, five years junior to Daniel Parker, comes from a religious family and was early attracted by social and international problems. He joined the French Christian Socialist movement and the Federation of Christian Students, of which he became the Paris secretary in 1929. Much impressed by the experiences of the 1914-18 war generation, he became deeply convinced that a wide gulf lay between a Christian life, and the world of violence and injustice of which war is part.

Destined for the ministry, Jacques studied theology in Paris and became a young member of the F.o.R. He shared its travels and conferences, helped to produce *Cahiers de la Réconciliation* (1936-7), and came to realize that non-violence is the only possible attitude for a true Christian. Nevertheless, for family reasons, he performed his military service, but gave up his pastoral work and studied philosophy in Germany and Paris.

In 1933 he was again called up for military service, and this time refused to go. He was arrested and sent to prison for one year. Another summons and another year's imprisonment followed in 1935. He then endeavoured to enter the ministry, but his Church would not accept pastors who were conscientious objectors. He therefore joined Pastor Roser as a voluntary preacher in the Paris suburbs, and in 1938 became secretary for the Society Against War and Militarism.

During the Second World War Jacques Martin joined the Resistance Movement, and associated with young people in the

Maquis. In their company he helped German refugees from Hitler, anti-Hitler Germans under the Occupation, Jews, and others sought by the Gestapo. In all this work he was concerned to show that resistance should not be confused with arms and violence but, as Gandhi had shown, should be made against all forms of oppression.

Pursued and arrested by the Gestapo, Jacques became the object of a bargain by the Maquis which recognized the spiritual value of his non-violent witness. A few hours before he was due to be executed, a group of French farmers ransomed his life for a thousand sheep.

In 1946 he appeared quietly at the first post-war I.F.o.R. meeting in Stockholm. He subsequently revived the Christian Socialist movement, of which he became secretary, and in the service of the *Cimade* arranged for the resettlement of displaced persons through the Ecumenical Council of the Churches. He earns his living as Director of a Protestant Library in Lyons.

PASTOR ETIENNE MATHIOT, a long-standing F.o.R. member from Belfort, helped refugees to cross the nearby Swiss frontier during the Algerian war. He was imprisoned for eight months for hiding an Algerian refugee and helping him to escape to Switzerland. After serving five months of his sentence he was released, and joined Henri Roser at the McCall Mission in Paris.

Now that the right of conscientious objection is recognized in France, more pacifists are likely to declare themselves publicly, and to pay their tribute to the small band of pioneers so conspicuous for their solitary courage.

Chapter 9

CONTINENTAL CRUSADERS

Apart from France, with its characteristic adventures and problems, the history of the Continental Fellowships has been that of a network of small groups, isolated in their own countries, yet closely associated within the movement. In some of these groups the Fellowship has been virtually identified with national religious pacifist associations, such as Holland's *Kerk en Vrede* and Denmark's *Kristeligt Fredsforbund*. The groups have varied in size and effectiveness from Holland's well-organized 2,200 to tiny handfuls of dedicated pacifists as in Belgium and Italy, and even to organizations known mainly in terms of an outstanding leader such as Pierre Cérésole of Switzerland and Mathilda Wrede of Finland, whom Leonhard Ragaz described as 'a kingly being'.

HOLLAND

Holland, the birthplace of the International Fellowship, has fought staunchly for liberty of conscience since the sixteenth century. Because of this stern tradition, Dutch conscientious objectors have mostly been absolutists, who amounted to about 1,000 after the First World War. Though alternative service was introduced in 1923, many pacifists preferred a prison sentence.

The first I.F.o.R. Conference in 1919 took place at Bilthoven owing to the Brotherhood work of KEES (CORNELIS) BOEKE, the Dutch violinist compelled to leave England when the war began, who reclaimed a lovely stretch of Utrecht pinewood from villadom, and set up a Brotherhood House. Many meetings followed the Bilthoven Conferences in 1919 and 1920; Lilian Stevenson looked back to a crowded audience of 400 in a Rotterdam auction-hall where former enemies sat side by side.

Boeke had earlier started open-air meetings to talk about Brotherhood, but Holland was not yet ready to go so far in wartime and he was arrested. When released he went on preaching his message until the authorities finally grew tired of him. He and his wife Betty, the daughter of Richard Cadbury, continued to go their own way regardless of the State in spite of repeated imprisonments; they discarded all possessions, and used no money until by 1930 the attempts to control them through prison came to an end. They survived the Second World War, and in 1951 Lilian Stevenson published in *Reconciliation* a vignette of Kees at seventy-two—'loveable, brilliant, perplexing, sometimes inconsistent but always sincere'.

Soon after the Bilthoven Conference, Kees's Brotherhood movement put its energies into *Kerk en Vrede*, a religious peace movement which called on all Christians to oppose the crime of war. It was led by Professor G. J. Heering, author of *The Fall of Christianity*, the Rev. J. B. Th. Hugenholtz, and Pastor J. J. Buskes. By 1933 (before Hitler) this organization had about 8,000 members, of whom 350 were ministers. Under its initiative the first International Congress of anti-militarist ministers and clergy (a predecessor of the modern Puidoux theological seminar which includes the Historical Peace Churches, Quakers and I.F.o.R.) was held in 1928. Three other international meetings (Zürich 1931, Basel 1935, and Edinburgh 1937) followed this Conference.

PROFESSOR GERRIT JAN HEERING (1879-1955), had been born in the Dutch Indies, where his father was a Protestant minister. He went to Leiden University, in which he was subsequently Professor of Theology until his retirement in 1949, and then to a Remonstrant Seminary. From 1904 to 1907 he was a pastor at Oude Wetering, where he met and married Alide van Bosse, and went on to Dordrecht and Arnhem. When he became the first President of *Kerk en Vrede* in 1924 he commented that this voluntary appointment had cost him all his half-friends, but gained for him many new whole ones. Five years later he published his great book, which expressed his own burning desire to eliminate the conception of war from Christian thought, and awaken the Church to her prophetic mission. He was a spiritual aristocrat who took for his motto the words of Arminius: '*Terar dum prosim*' ('so long as I live, let me be spent'). Death came to him on the fiftieth anniversary of his wedding.

Dr Heering's chief colleague in *Kerk en Vrede*, PASTOR J. J.
BUSKES of Amsterdam, was imprisoned for a time during the
Second World War but had been released by September 1945,
and appeared in 1949-50 at the World Pacifist Meeting in India.
In 1954 the I.F.o.R. asked him to go to South Africa and meet
leaders of the Africaans-speaking Dutch Reformed Church.
During his visit of nearly three months in 1955 he had a long
talk with the Moderator of this Church, and attended the
biennial meeting of the South African F.o.R.

Just before the outbreak of the Second World War a conference of members from eighteen countries met at Lunteren to
consider the pacifist's rôle in a violent world. Soon afterwards
the curtain of wartime silence obscured occupied Holland,
behind which Fellowship matters could be discussed only in
small groups, and the magazine had to cease. In 1942 *Kerk en
Vrede* was suspended, and its secretary, PASTOR J. B. HUGEN-
HOLTZ, put into a concentration camp after arrest and imprisonment for his work in assisting Jews persecuted by the Nazis. He
was released by September 1945, when the present writer met
him at The Hague.

A year later *Kerk en Vrede*, with Professor Heering as president and Pastor Hugenholtz again acting as one of its secretaries,
was re-established, and affiliated to the F.o.R. In 1947 it arranged
a Regional Conference in Amsterdam. In December 1948, 300
people attended another Amsterdam meeting, and the following
year the organization made a spirited protest against the war in
Indonesia. Under the chairmanship of DR HANNES DE GRAAF,
who was himself a missionary in Indonesia for eight years and
was imprisoned by the Japanese, the organization has become
influential, and celebrated its thirtieth anniversary in 1950. In
1955, Dr de Graaf was appointed Professor of Ethics in the
University of Utrecht. Among his interests, which he shares
with Krijn Strijd, Study Secretary of *Kerk en Vrede* since 1961,
is the growing Pacifist Party, represented in both Houses of the
Dutch Parliament. As a Russian scholar he has also maintained
close relations with the Orthodox Church for many years. Else,
his daughter, became I.F.o.R. Youth secretary in 1964.

Kerk en Vrede has itself established Youth Committees in
Amsterdam, Utrecht and The Hague, of which the members
undertook to spend part of their holidays in social work and to

give a proportion of their pocket money to 'Eirene'. In March 1954 its Executive sent a letter to the Protestant Churches in the Netherlands urging a positive pronouncement on their moral and spiritual attitude to nuclear weapons. In 1962 this brought a statement from the Dutch Reformed Church clearly saying 'No' in all circumstances to the use of nuclear arms. By the summer of 1962 the reconstituted membership had reached 2,500, which included 275 pastors, while the readers of its periodical *Militia Christi* numbered 3,800. This association regards its principal task as that of taking the Bible teaching on peace and war to the churches and other religious bodies, and of showing war preparation to be irreconcilable with the Gospel message.

For its former slogan, 'War is contrary to the Will of God', it now prefers to emphasize a more constructive version, 'Peace is the Will of God'.

SCANDINAVIA

In Scandinavia, a civilized and enlightened section of Europe, conscientious objection to war was early accepted as a rational phenomenon. Alternative service was established in Denmark in 1917, Sweden in 1920, Norway in 1922, and Finland in 1931. The work offered involved afforestation, road-making, and farmhouse building, but many conscientious objectors found these tasks negative, and saw no point in undertaking such service merely to keep themselves out of prison.

The F.o.R. in Sweden began just after the First World War, and from 1918 was represented by the League for Christian Citizenship (*Forbundet for Kristet Samhallsliv*). The co-founders were Natanael Beskow and Ebba Pauli. Most of its 900 members took a radical pacifist position and a number were conscientious objectors. The group took various steps, such as the publication of books and pamphlets, to achieve its aims, and still existed in 1939.

The Birkagäden Settlement in Stockholm, especially designed for the education of working-class groups, worked closely with the League. It gave steady financial support to the I.F.o.R., and helped especially with an Armenian colony founded by Karen Jeppe, a Danish missionary, which was an early F.o.R. project.

Dr Beskow, President of the League for Christian Citizenship, was for many years chairman of the I.F.o.R. Council.

Owing to the special position of Sweden as a neutral country in the Second World War, the Swedish F.o.R. did not share the experience of other Scandinavian countries in organizing underground propaganda and joining in resistance movements against the Nazis. It was able to carry on its ordinary work, and organized annual conferences at Andust in 1940 and Karlstad in 1941. In June 1941 some F.o.R. members talked of forming a 'death battalion ' of Christians for removing time-bombs and helping civilians during possible raids. Both during and after the war, Swedish pacifists suffered from a bad conscience owing to their country's prosperous neutrality while their Scandinavian colleagues were enduring martyrdom and death.

In 1942 Dr Beskow reported that the Fellowship was able to maintain its teaching without hindrance, in spite of a hardening of opinion against conscientious objectors. Two years later Dr Beskow resigned his presidential position at the age of seventy-eight, and Pastor Samuel Thyssel took his place. The Swedish Fellowship organized the first post-war I.F.o.R. Conference at Stockholm in 1946. Three years afterwards its annual conference took place at Arild. In 1952 Dr Siegmund-Schültze, visiting Stockholm for the F.o.R., appealed to the King of Sweden to call a conference of governments, peace workers and experts to seek a basis for better relations. The proposal was well received, and two years later the first Northern F.o.R. Conference was held at Karlskoga for sixty-five Swedish members and thirty-five from Norway, Denmark and Finland. Rektor Eeg-Olofsson took the chair, and a Northern F.o.R. Council was formed.

The great Fellowship personality of Sweden, and indeed of all Scandinavia, was NATANAEL BESKOW (1865-1953). Ole Olden of Norway once said that only Dr Beskow's friend Nathan Soderblom could compare with him in Swedish church history. The difference between them was not of status but of personality; Dr Soderblom had a scientific mind and specialized in the history of religions; Natanael Beskow, while intellectually gifted, was also a poet and artist married to a painter, who became famous in her own right as the author and illustrator of charming children's books.

As a young man Dr Beskow found it difficult to decide on a

career. He interrupted his theological studies to enter the Swedish Royal Academy of Art, where he met his future wife Elsa. In 1898 he eventually took his theological degree, but he had a conscientious objection against ordination in the Swedish Church. His creative gifts made it difficult for him to accept any conventional position; he was an accomplished portrait painter, a moving preacher, and the writer of some of the loveliest hymns in the Swedish language.

Eventually a number of his friends built a large chapel for him in Djursholm, a garden suburb of Stockholm, where he preached in accordance with his convictions and influenced the whole of Swedish social and political life. He was headmaster from 1897 to 1909 of a coeducational grammar school in Djursholm; started the first Swedish settlement at Birkagäden in the slums of Stockholm with Ebba Pauli and Dagny Thorvall in 1910; and in 1916 became the principal of a workers' college. Nevin Sayre has described this remarkable personality as 'a tall man of rugged yet gentle face'. In 1942 he was awarded the Wallin medal, given every third year in memory of the hymn writer Archbishop Olaf Wallin. His home was one of the happiest ever known to his many guests.

Dr Beskow died, aged eighty-eight, in 1953, having outlived his radiant wife by only a few months. In his final years he had become almost blind, with a tall erect figure like that of an Old Testament prophet. In 1940, at the age of seventy-five, he had said: 'Whether I live or die, I am the Lord's. I do not know how it is on the other side, and I do not need to know. But I know that I am His, then as well as now. That is enough.' On October 17, 1953, his friend Archbishop Erling Eidem conducted his simple funeral service in Djursholm Chapel.

Of Dr Beskow's chief colleagues in the F.o.R., EBBA PAULI died in July 1941 aged sixty-seven; she had been for many years an invalid burdened with much suffering but, as Dr Beskow wrote of her, 'she had learned to keep illness and pain within narrow bounds'. Much of his own work had been made possible by his friend Pastor SAMUEL THYSSEL, an able administrator. Another supporter, Dr BIRGER FORELL, who had greatly helped the I.F.o.R. while chaplain to the Swedish Embassy in Berlin during the Nazi period, died in 1958 aged sixty-four. He had rendered great service to refugees from the East seeking new homes in the West.

No clear-cut distinction existed in Norway between F.o.R. members and others working for different bodies dedicated to peace and social service. The famous wartime Resistance Movement, often quoted as a classic example of non-violence, included most Norwegians deeply concerned for peace and their country whose varied affiliations were difficult to disentangle. The Resistance tended to divide into several different departments— religious, educational, juridical, but also military. The 'teachers' front' was led largely by Rektor Holmboe, Arnulf Nygaard and Einar Holgaard, who took his own life in the Gestapo prison at Oslo; the 'religious front' had two leaders, the one, Bishop Berggrav, described by a Norwegian F.o.R. member as a 'semi-pacifist', and the other, Professor Hallesby, a militarist.

The chief Norwegian F.o.R. member for many years was OLE F. OLDEN, a high school master who at the end of the First World War proposed that Norway should give up any claim on Germany for damage done by U-boat warfare. The religious press and student bodies widely discussed his proposal, and the Norwegian claim was abandoned, though the Germans undertook to pay a limited sum, finally about six million Kroner, to help needy relatives of the lost men.

In 1922 Ole Olden established a monthly magazine, *Verden Venter* ('The Waiting World'), edited by three high school masters, to propagate the ideals of the Fellowship. It reached a circulation of about 1,000, and after 1931 became the official organ of the Norwegian Peace Union (*Norges Fredslag*). Two years later Ole Olden visited the United States for study, and returned to Norway in 1937 to found another publication, *Kvekeren*. During the war he was imprisoned as a hostage and held for a time in Grini concentration camp, but was released in 1943. Three years later he attended the Swedish F.o.R. annual meeting, and helped to revive the F.o.R. in Norway.

In 1947, in recognition of his services to education and his spiritual resistance to Nazism, Ole Olden was made a Knight of the Order of St Olaf. Soon afterwards he was invited to supervise a rehabilitation camp for the hundreds of Jews from D.P. camps whom the Norwegian Government admitted to replace the Norwegian Jews killed during the occupation. He subsequently became the chairman of different joint peace organizations, and was the ILCOP representative of Norway in Geneva. His own description of his contribution to the Norwegian peace movement was the one word 'stability'.

Dr Olden, who died in 1963, once described an F.o.R. colleague, EDWIN LISTOR, as a 'minor prophet . . . great alike in body and spirit'. During the Second World War Dr Listor was in both Norwegian and German concentration camps and for a time lay under a sentence of death. He had endeavoured to form a Norwegian F.o.R. branch just before war broke out, and in 1946 attended the Stockholm meeting, where he made contact with Percy Bartlett. In 1947 he was recalled to Madagascar, where he had previously served with the Norwegian Mission. He took up work for the F.o.R. again on his return in 1952.

Other well-known Norwegian friends of the F.o.R. include Captain OLAF KULLMAN, a former naval captain who with Lilly Heber formed a branch of the War Resisters' International in 1938 and died in a German prison camp during the war; HAKON WERGELAND, a poet, preacher and church historian who had been a headmaster of teachers' training colleges, and Pastor FORBECH who with POLYKARP PETERSEN restarted the Norwegian F.o.R. in 1951.

The most distinguished F.o.R. contact in Norway has been HALVARD M. LANGE, an assistant secretary in the London F.o.R. office when Oliver Dryer was secretary. After a period of promoting and speaking for the F.o.R. he ceased to be a pacifist, and eventually became Norway's Foreign Minister on Trygve Lie's appointment as Secretary-General of the United Nations. He held his important diplomatic office longer than any of his predecessors, and has been a champion of the North Atlantic Treaty Organization. He seeks to end Soviet pressure on Finland for military co-operation, and though not a member for many years is still friendly to the I.F.o.R.

The story of the F.o.R. in Norway has typified that of many small countries of Northern Europe—experimental peace-making before 1939; virtual eclipse, with the imprisonment of leaders, during the Second World War; and valiant efforts for reconstruction since 1945. The present Norwegian secretary is HELGA GULBRANDSEN, and RICHARD EDVARDSEN is the Youth secretary. He has been imprisoned for refusing Civil Defence service, which is compulsory in Norway. Both report increased interest. The chairman, Pastor RAGNAR FORBECH, arranges annual peace services in Oslo Cathedral, and edits the Fellowship's 'Peace magazine', *Fredsbladet*.

In Denmark the predecessor of the I.F.o.R. was *Kristeligt Fredsforbund*, founded in 1913 by a young librarian, HOLGAR LARSEN who subsequently became chairman of the Danish F.o.R. until 1920. He also established a magazine, *Fredsvarden*, which first appeared in 1913 and became an important publication during the strong urge towards peace of the 1920s. Holgar Larsen died in 1945, but his wife Astrid was still associated with the F.o.R. in 1959.

The combined organization passed through three important phases, the first being connected with the successful struggle for the law permitting alternative service passed in 1917. During this period the membership increased, largely owing to the efforts of PETER MANNICHE from the International People's College at Elsinore. Many young pastors became conscientious objectors, and other F.o.R. members joined the I.V.S.P. as volunteers.

The second phase centred round the international conference at Nyborg Strand in 1923, where French and German groups met for one of the earliest attempts made after the First World War to find forgiveness and understanding. A third phase was associated with a small Scandinavian conference, led by Natanael Beskow, held in 1940 a few weeks before the occupation.

Denmark experienced a milder form of occupation than the other invaded countries and emotions were less passionate, though conversations with or concerning the Jews were suppressed as far as possible. *Fredsvarden* continued to circulate, and gave news to its readers of Christian pacifists in other countries. By 1946, members of the Fellowship were undertaking work among the 200,000 Germans interned in Denmark.

The Danish Fellowship was represented at the Stockholm I.F.o.R. Conference of 1946; 'none of us who were present', Margrethe Thorborg has written, 'shall ever forget the last evening when we standing in a ring joined hands, and when Beskow could say in their language (to those) who had suffered most during our days together: *"Nichts kann uns trennen"* '.

After the Second World War came a temporary decline in enthusiasm, but recently some young and energetic members have brought more life to the Fellowship. Its membership numbered 145 in 1952 and about 160 in 1954. Since 1920 it has had four chairmen in succession to Holgar Larsen, the first being CHRISTIAN SVELMØE-THOMSEN from 1920 to 1936. In that year he died at the relatively early age of fifty-four and his widow Kirsten followed him in 1940.

Christian Svelmøe-Thomsen was for twenty years the pastor of a workers' parish in the centre of Copenhagen, and joined the F.o.R. as soon as it was founded. He became a minister in 1912, when alcoholism was one of the worst features of Danish social life. His parish contained many small restaurants where alcoholics abounded. A very hard worker, and a temperance campaigner who concentrated on the social aspects of peace work, he was one of the earliest and most consistent supporters of the International People's College at Elsinore.

The parish held a population of 5,000, and he could name and describe each member. His house was always open to students, and he and his wife welcomed there many international personalities, such as Professor Heering, Natanael Beskow and Mathilda Wrede. The first small church of which he was pastor stood in a court behind an ordinary living-house, and was a pioneer example of the so-called Small Church Movement in Copenhagen. Ultimately sixty such churches were established.

Towards the end of his life Christian Svelmøe Thomsen collected money for a new large church near his old one. He raised the sum he needed by simple requests, without recourse to charity balls and other modern methods of acquisition. His manner was never pretentious, but he practised what he preached, and behind his *Forbund* existed the ideal of brotherhood which he typified by his great faith and strong personality. The Cross was the centre of his life, and in his pacifism he sought to interpret the Sermon on the Mount. He died shortly before his new Bethlehem Church was opened, but its bells were rung at his funeral, and an inscribed stone is dedicated to him in the church. Immediately after his death his wife, herself a theologian, a translator, and the editor of *Fredsvarden*, carried on his work.

His successor, ELLEN PETERSEN, a headmistress, was chairman of the Fellowship during the Second World War until 1952, and MARGRETHE THORBORG followed her until 1958. Today the organization has 300 members and 700 readers of its magazine, and is chiefly concerned to relate the message of pacifism to the Gospel teaching. Some members have done relief work in Africa, and the whole group co-operates with the War Resisters' International in seeking better conditions for conscientious objectors, and in the endeavour to get work for 'Eirene' and other social organizations accepted as alternative service. Witness has been made chiefly in words, and the development of the idea of non-violent resistance has been very recent.

The present chairman is SOGNEPRAEST JUUL GAARN LARSEN, of the twelfth-century church of Viby, Aarhus. His son, Svend Paul Gaarn Larsen, is a professional journalist who has served both as European Youth secretary and as editor of *Fredsvarden*.

Finland became an independent Republic with a democratic constitution in 1919. After the Bilthoven Conference of that year, MATHILDA WREDE, the Elizabeth Fry of Finland who had attended it, founded the small Finnish group, and FELIX IVERSEN became the first chairman.

The little organization soon encountered the opposition of the church, swayed by the Army. Since the nationalistic awakening of Finland in the nineteenth century coincided with a period of pietistic revivalism, the Church was never pacifist. As the F.o.R. depended on a few isolated workers it did not long remain a united body, though individuals continued their witness.

Apart from Mathilda Wrede, its prominent early members included Oscar von Schoultz, Pastor Stenwall and Greta Langenskjöld. They organized propaganda on conventional lines, such as pamphlets, lectures and the circulation of leaflets, until the nineteen-thirties, when Gandhi's ideas on non-violence gradually became known after his visit to England in 1931.

The Fellowship, a bilingual group reconstituted in 1939, always maintained good relations with Sweden in spite of the dispute over the ownership of the Aaland Islands (submitted to the League of Nations soon after the First World War). Much inspiration came from Sweden, and especially from Natanael Beskow, Samuel Thysell and Jonas Lindskog. In their desire to follow social developments outside their own country, Finnish F.o.R. members encouraged prominent foreign visitors such as Dr Siegmund-Schültze, André Trocmé, Oliver Dryer and Canon C. E. Raven, Ole Olden from Norway, and Ellen Petersen and Margrethe Thorborg from Denmark.

The Fellowship's records included two important Baltic Conferences, the first, led by Natanael Beskow, in 1928, and the second ten years later just before the outbreak of the Second World War. An unusual feature of this conference was its encouragement by the Finnish Government, then appreciative of pacifism, which caused the conference to be the best attended of any in the country. Like the Fellowship's other northern countries, the Finnish group was especially concerned to present the challenge of pacifism to the Church.

The Helsinki Fellowship succeeded in meeting periodically throughout the Second War, and had twenty to thirty members in 1954. In April 1949, M. KALLIEN, the Finnish Minister of Defence, assured André Trocmé during his visit to Finland: 'We will never sign a pact that will involve us in fighting against any other nation whatsoever . . . We would sooner accept the terrible consequences of a Russian occupation.' Towards the end of that year M. Kallien visited India, where he became a prominent member of the World Pacifist Meeting. The present Finnish secretary, DERYCK SIVEN, a Quaker schoolmaster, in co-operation with Jean Goss, and Els de Graaf recently led a team of young Christians at the Communist World Youth Assembly in Helsinki.

MATHILDA WREDE (1864-1928), the founder of the Finnish Fellowship, was one of Scandinavia's greatest social reformers. Long before she died on Christmas Day 1928, she had become known throughout Northern Europe as 'the Friend of Prisoners'. The daughter of a Finnish provincial Governor, born at Vasa on the West Coast, she was completely trusted by the whole prison population and was often summoned to help in penal crises.

At the early age of nineteen she had recognized her vocation, and when barely twenty obtained a permit to visit all the prisons in Finland. These included the four convict prisons of Kakola, Sornas, Tavestehus and Villimanstrand.

Thus began thirty years of dedicated work, in which she visited men and women in their cells, accompanied to the frontier prisoners exiled to Siberia, and kept a careful watch on all discharged prisoners. Kakola, with its 500 inmates mostly serving life sentences, was her special concern. She brought to her work a knowledge of country life and an understanding born from the deep silences, the dark forests, and the vivid nights of a northern land. Fearless in the presence of violence and insanity, she astonished the prisoners by her confidence in them, and this trust became a powerful factor in their redemption. Early in her career she realized that convicts did not require moral homilies, but a sympathetic listener with whom to talk.

During the 1914-18 war, Finland was rent with civil war and revolution. Though by birth and tradition Mathilda belonged to the 'Whites', she loved the poorer people from whose ranks the 'Reds' were recruited. She refused to take sides, and offered her powers of reconciliation to both. On a table in her room she kept a red and white flower in one vase, saying that both needed the same sunshine and water to bring out their beauty.

Mathilda was a tall, upright, fragile woman, with an indomitable spirit which kept her alive during the final years of suffering and ill-health. Large-hearted and generous, and impatient with injustice, she moved, as one elderly prisoner said, 'between bound and free, bringing the peace of God'. In the Fellowship of Reconciliation, she saw a field in which the principles that inspired her work for prisoners could be applied on behalf of all humanity. Ideas such as hers are acceptable to the Fellowship everywhere; in all countries its members are opposed to capital punishment and concerned for prison reform.

Among Mathilda's colleagues and disciples, OSCAR VON SCHOULTZ had been an officer in the Russian Army before Finland became independent, and was there influenced by the teaching of Tolstoy. Pastor EDVIN STENWALL, who emerged as a leader in the nineteen-thirties, was episcopal candidate for the diocese of Borgå which cares for the Swedish minority in Finland, but withdrew before the election took place. He had long been a social pioneer, and is one of the more striking personalities in the Scandinavian peace movement.

GRETA LANGENSKJOLD, chairman of the Fellowship in succession to Felix Iversen, is a schoolteacher by profession and a well-known poet and Quaker, who contributed two hymns in praise of peace to the Lutheran Protestant hymn book. After her retirement on grounds of age, Pastor ERIK EWALDS, a State Church

Minister from 1945, became Fellowship chairman until he moved to Sweden in 1961. A sympathizer, though not actually a member, is Pastor SIGFRID SIRENIUS, who studied social work in London, and started the settlement movement in Finland.

SWITZERLAND

The F.o.R. in Switzerland, like that of Finland, has been known chiefly in terms of one outstanding pacifist. The Swiss champion was PIERRE CERESOLE (1879-1945), the founder of Service Civil International, who represented Switzerland at Bilthoven in 1919 and worked for some months with Kees Boeke.

Some peculiar difficulties, such as the geographical divisions of the country and the use of four languages, have restricted both the size and the effectiveness of the Swiss Fellowship. Long after the foundation of the I.F.o.R. no Swiss branch had been formed, though groups such as the associates of Leonhard Ragaz existed with the same ideals. His influence in Switzerland was considerable, and the Zürich pacifists were deeply divided after his death.

In 1924 the Swiss Centre for Peace Action issued a petition for the establishment of a recognized civilian service, but though 40,000 persons signed the request, it was rejected by the Government. Later the former 'Union of anti-militarist pastors' developed into a Church Peace Union for Switzerland similar to Holland's *Kerk en Vrede* but smaller.

The Swiss F.o.R. began to take shape about the time of the Saanen Conference in 1945, with OTTO LAUTERBURG as the first chairman. The main architect of the new group was F. Siegmund-Schültze, who made his home in Zürich during the Second World War, but the Swiss police did not want him as its chairman because he was German. Many members felt that the right work for the F.o.R. was to present the pacifist message to the established churches; the need for such testimony was recognized especially in French-speaking Switzerland.

In German Switzerland two other bodies were closely connected with the Fellowship. One was *Kirchlicher Friedensbund der Schweiz* (the Swiss *Kerk en Vrede*), of which the aims were close to those of the F.o.R. The other organization, inspired by Frau Gertrud Kurz, is a strong and growing body which attracts many young people. Her association emphasizes Christianity

M

and service rather than pacifism, but she has been put forward by her country as a candidate for the Nobel Prize.

These two organizations, with the F.o.R. and the Friends, constitute the Christian pacifist wing of the *Conseil Suisse des Associations pour la Paix*. At present these groups are associated in a campaign for the official recognition of the rights of conscience. Other activities of Swiss pacifists include support for 'Eirene' and for the work of Danilo Dolci, and association with *L'Aide Suisse aux Regions Extra-Européennes*, which include Nepal, Nigeria, Tunisia and Lybia.

The present chairman of the Swiss F.o.R. is Pastor EMILE JEQUIER of La Chaux-de-Fonds, and the secretary was ELIZABETH MONASTIER of Lausanne until March 31, 1963, when after thirty-four years of service to the F.o.R. she was accidentally killed by a car as she came from a meeting of Friends in Geneva. The present secretary is DANIEL PACHE of Missy.

The difficulties of the Swiss group arise especially in German Switzerland, where Zürich is a centre of East-West tension, and widespread apathy exists elsewhere owing to material comfort and self-satisfaction. In French-speaking Switzerland, with a lively group in Geneva, the nearness to France with its Algerian problems has opened the eyes of many Christians to the real meaning of war. The 1960 Lausanne Ecumenical Youth Conference sent many Swiss delegates back to their parishes to work for aid to under-developed countries, a main concern of the Fellowship.

The recently-formed Lausanne group has studied the writings of Jean Lasserre and the French *Cahiers de la Réconciliation*, which now has a Swiss circulation of nearly 300 copies. In Geneva many students have refused military service, and the Swiss F.o.R. Committee emphasizes the importance of 'Eirene' owing to its practical trend towards reconciliation. One member, Pastor W. Beguin, obtained leave from his Neuchâtel church to serve with 'Eirene' as director of its work in Morocco, and succeeded in getting this type of service recognized as a form of church ministry.

Though PIERRE CERESOLE died in 1945, his name is already a legend and his *Service Civil* (formerly known to English-speaking countries as the International Voluntary Service for Peace) has become an international movement, though the

Secretariat remains in Switzerland. Pierre Cérésole derived his own inspiration from JEAN BAUDRAZ, a schoolmaster from Vaud whom Pierre introduced to Muriel Lester at Bilthoven, saying: 'I want you to meet my friend; he is the man who in Switzerland showed us the way'.

Baudraz, who had instinctively given up Bible reading during his annual military service, forced himself to face his own position when the First World War broke out. Returning one morning to the barrack, he laid his belt and gun at the captain's feet, saying, 'I can wear them no longer'. The captain took out his watch and said, 'If you don't pick up your things before the hour strikes, you will be arrested'. Baudraz did not move, and after prolonged examination was sent to an asylum. In a month his sanity was recognized, and he went before a court martial.

The president of the court was Major Arnold Cérésole, from a well-known Swiss family. He sent Baudraz to prison, but at lunch that day told his guests of the strange trial. Among the guests was his cousin Pierre, the ninth child of Paul Cérésole, president of the Swiss Confederation in 1873. Pierre said nothing at the luncheon, but later realized that his own position was the same as the schoolmaster's, and shortly afterwards announced publicly that military service and Christian discipleship were incompatible.

He was imprisoned, but his story made headlines throughout Switzerland. In jail the idea occurred to him of an international peace army which would fight not other men but the traditional enemies of man—flood, famine, earthquake and war. In this inspiration lay the germ of large-scale future developments such as 'Eirene', the World Peace Brigade, and the U.S. Peace Corps established by President Kennedy. But his beginnings were humble, though in the early years of the League of Nations he appeared at Geneva to explain his proposition 'for peoples overtaken by disaster'.

Pierre started his 'pick-and-shovel peacemaking' by rehabilitating the villages devastated on Dead Man's Hill at Verdun. This form of service for any place in special need continued every summer after 1920 for many years. The places helped by his volunteers, who worked hard and lived frugally, included the Rhondda Valley in South Wales during the depression of the 1930s, Bihar in India after the earthquake of 1934, and Spain during the Civil War. After twelve years of literal spade-work, he and his friends lobbied Swiss M.P.s in support of a Bill enabling conscripts to offer constructive rather than destructive service, and obtained the support of twenty-five per cent. Throughout his international experiments Pierre continued his struggle with the Swiss Government. Though the administration remained unmoved, his ideas took root in Holland and Scandinavia, and influenced the American Friends Service Committee, which adopted a policy of establishing work-camps in centres of tension. Pierre joined one of these, and also worked for two months with Gandhi at one of his ashrams in an isolated village. The two men, so markedly different in habits and technique, came together through their mutual concern for humanity.

Pierre was a handsome and very tall man, with a high forehead, intent eyes, and dark hair brushed back over his head. His clean, precise features gave the impression of having been carved in some sympathetic material such as soft wood. Once during the Second War he crossed the frontier into Germany without a passport, and was arrested. For this and other actions he spent several periods in prison. The last, for three months, undoubtedly hastened his end.

On the evening of his release, February 21, 1945, the symptoms of a serious heart condition showed themselves, and this first attack was followed by others. He died on October 24, 1945, having written from prison the previous January: 'We cannot live without the splendid values which the Army has monopolized. We must recover this treasure of sacrifice and service, and the only way to do this is the way of the Cross'. The writer Romain Rolland said of him: '*Pierre Cérésole est la plus haute conscience de la Suisse. Ces consciences la sauvent l'humanité.*'

The remaining European countries have had no continuous F.o.R. history, but some outstanding individuals from different centres have maintained a constant witness.

Small groups have existed for about four years in Italy, though military service there is still obligatory. They have been strengthened by visits from André and Magda Trocmé, and Hildegard and Jean Goss. Among its leaders have been Guido Graziani and Hedi Vaccaro in Rome, Pastors Tassoni and Lupo

Silvano in Bergamo, and Milly Stracuzzi, the present secretary, in Florence.

In Belgium small groups began as long ago as the nineteen-twenties in Antwerp and Brussels, but no mass movement with a pacifist programme has ever been possible. The best organized peace groups, all having some contact with the little Antwerp centre, have developed in Flanders, but the F.o.R. flourished first when Philippe Vernier was living in Belgium. After Philippe moved to France, ERNEST MEURICE took his place as Belgian secretary. A well-known individual pacifist has been MAGDA YOORS-PEETERS of Antwerp, the wife of a famous artist in stained glass. Another is Baron Antoine Allard, member of a well-known banking family. The work is now developing under the joint chairmanship of Jean van Lierdes and Abel Mascaux. The joint secretaries, Abbé Paul Carrette and Alphonse Masquelier, have arranged three annual conferences at Lustin, and develop the work on an inter-church basis. Lectures have been given by Hannes de Graaf of the Netherlands in Flemish regions, while Jean Lasserre, F.o.R. secretary for French-speaking areas, visits groups from time to time.

Spain can claim one lone pacifist in Professor JOSE BROCCA, who during the Spanish Revolution organized rescue work and shelter for orphaned children. He and his wife ran a home for young Spanish refugees at Prats-de-Mollo in the Pyrenees, but this was closed when the European war began. Brocca refused to leave his children's colony, and was interned for a time in a French camp. Eventually his life was saved through the intervention of Nevin Sayre and the New York F.o.R., and with the help of the Friends he was eventually able to emigrate to Mexico.

The Goss-Mayrs visited Spain and Portugal in 1961, but no group has been established in either country.

In Russia, as far back as 1903, members of religious sects were prepared to face any penalty rather than take part in war, and the question of exemption for conscientious objectors came up in the Duma in 1911. About a thousand refused to fight in the First War. Under Soviet rule their treatment has varied in different regions from alternative service to death sentences for desertion. A Tolstoyan group under V. G. Tchertkoff, with which Russian F.o.R. members were associated, existed until 1929, but it was then deprived of its premises and the work had to cease. A Tolstoyan community was however allowed to settle at Konzuezle in Siberia and to work on a collective farm. Pamphlets propagating non-violence are liable to confiscation and Russian pacifists are unable to attend international conferences, but the Goss-Mayrs managed to convey the Fellowship message to Moscow in 1961. (Further details of their work are given in the chapters on France and Austria.)

Some groups sympathetic to F.o.R. ideals existed in Baltic countries between the wars and in 1939 a Baltic regional conference took place at Tallinn, but all these developments ended with the Second World War. In the Balkans, many Nazarenes, Adventists and members of other sects have suffered imprisonment and even death for their beliefs, but these countries have now become inaccessible to most travellers. Poland has been easier than the rest, and the Goss-Mayrs visited the country within recent years.

Chapter 10

THE COMMONWEALTH STORY

CANADA

The impulse to form a Canadian Fellowship arose from visits to Canada by Dr Richard Roberts, the Rev. Leyton Richards and Canon C. E. Raven, who described the European movement. Before this, small isolated bodies of pacifists had grown up across the country which ultimately became part of the F.o.R. In Montreal, J. M. C. DUCKWORTH of the Y.M.C.A. and the Rev. J. LAVELL SMITH led one group, and another was formed in Vancouver after the Rev. Allan Hunter, of Hollywood, California, had attended a Christian Student Movement Conference there.

Saskatoon had the largest group, with a membership roll of thirty in 1937-38. Its most dynamic member was Professor CARLYLE KING of the University of Saskatchewan. In a 1961 letter to the present secretary of the West Canadian Fellowship, Mrs MILDRED FAHRNI, Dr King wrote: 'We called ourselves F.o.R., I think, chiefly because we liked the sound of it; it seemed more positive than Peace Pledge Union or War Resisters' International. We had no written statement of purpose, but we had unity of purpose although we had come to pacifism by a variety of roads. There were Doukhobors who had left the faith, Friends who had no Meeting, Bahaists, Jews, Mennonites, United Church people, and others without formal Church or religious connection. . . . My impression is that . . . United Church clergymen provided the most energetic leadership.'

In September 1938 the United Church Conference met in Toronto. This gave an opportunity for some thirty people to gather at the Diet Kitchen on September 27th and resolve to establish a Canadian branch of the F.o.R. The meeting named a National Committee, mainly from Ontario and Montreal. Without their knowledge or consent, Professor King and a theological student, CLEO MOWERS, who afterwards became a Lethbridge editor, were appointed to the committee, and the other members were asked to communicate with Dr King.

As nobody did so, he and Cleo Mowers appointed themselves the National Executive and sought approval from the others. Their colleagues were only too happy for them to do the work, and for the first two years the group was conducted from Dr King's house. They launched the F.o.R. by drawing up a memorandum dated October 24, 1938 recording its formation, and enclosed a statement of its basis and aims. In drafting this Dr King bore in mind some advice received from the Toronto Friends meeting 'to avoid the use of the negative-sounding word "pacifist" '. He also felt that Canada, with its small population, had room for only one pacifist organization, and therefore drew up the statement so as to make it acceptable both to Christians and to those who were pacifists on other grounds.

Their statement began as follows:

'The Fellowship of Reconciliation is an association of men and women who believe in the non-violent settlement of all conflicts between individuals, groups, classes, nations, races, and religions. Its members believe that hatred is increased through return of hatred; that peace is not achieved by fighting; that the use of violence raises more problems than it solves. . . . Many of the members have joined because of their desire to follow unswervingly the way of life exemplified by Jesus; some have received their inspiration from other religious leaders; and some have reached their faith in love and non-violence in still other ways.

'In practice their faith expresses itself in the following ways:

'(1) They try to show respect for human personality . . .

'(2) They advocate the treatment of offenders against society, not by retaliatory punishment, but in ways calculated to restore the wrongdoer to co-operative citizenship with his fellows;

'(3) They strive to build a social order in which none will be exploited . . .

'(4) They refuse to sanction war preparations or to participate in any war—rather they work to remove the causes of war . . .

'The Fellowship is open to all who accept the above principles.

. . . Its objective is twofold: (1) to educate our fellows to a belief that there are better methods than those of war and violence for settling conflicts between classes, nations, races, and religions, and to urge those methods upon our fellows: (2) to bring comfort and encouragement to peace-minded people who feel themselves to be in a hopeless and helpless minority in their community.'

When the Second World War began, a vigorous group of ministers from the United Church of Canada took a strong pacifist position. Amongst them were Dr J. M. Finlay, Dr J. Lavell Smith, the Rev. Harold Toye, the Rev. R. Edis Fairbairn, the Rev. Clare Oke and the Rev. J. W. E. Newberry. These were among the seventy-five signatories of the United Church clergy who publicized a statement on October 21, 1939, under the title 'A Witness against war'. This expressed their aversion to all wars and their commitment to the pacifist position. Later a further seventy-five approved the statement. In 1943 there were still 111 ministers, mostly from the United Church, on the F.o.R. list, and about 300 members.

On December 9, 1939, the Toronto *Financial Post* made a sustained attack on the F.o.R. in a long front-page article which alleged that its leaders were Communists or Communist-inspired. Cleo Mowers, by now a journalist, was told by his employer, the *Star-Phoenix*, that he must give up his job or the F.o.R. Dr King received his resignation early in 1940 and could find no one to replace him.

Another difficulty now faced the struggling little organization, owing to an unfortunate element of bigotry in the I.F.o.R. itself. Some members of one influential Fellowship with which the Canadian movement had hoped to associate took the view that its enlightened liberal statement was not 'Christian' enough. Strange as this outlook might seem in a body that was coming increasingly to regard Gandhi, a Hindu, as the patron saint of non-violence, the I.F.o.R., at its Council meeting in June 1939, rejected the Canadian application.

When Professor King reported this setback to his National Committee in August and offered to resign, he was unanimously asked to continue. The Committee took a similar attitude in 1940 when he again offered his resignation after Cleo Mowers had been obliged to leave. Dr King carried on single-handed for another two years. At that time several F.o.R. ministers lost their pulpits owing to their pacifist position, but in April 1942 a letter to *Reconciliation* from Quebec significantly reported: 'Our group meets regularly. The Government itself has put no pressure upon us; in the Church it is the local officials who have failed to uphold our right of conscience.'

During that year the Rev. Lavell Smith moved to Toronto, and with the Rev. J. W. E. NEWBERRY took over the Executive work. In 1943 the Rev. JAMES FINLAY of Toronto succeeded Lavell Smith, and ALBERT G. WATSON was appointed secretary. The Statement of Aims was revised, and the Canadian Fellowship finally received into the I.F.o.R. Professor King, justifiably unrepentant, recently added a final word:

'From the beginning I took the position, based on our Saskatoon experience, that the F.o.R. in Canada ought to embrace all pacifists (there were so few of us) and that therefore the Statement ought not to exclude those who were not committed Christians. Looking over my lists and reading the dozens of letters in my files, I find it sadly ironical that when the test came so many of the Christians defected, while "the others" did not.'

In October 1943, *Reconciliation* began as a bi-monthly printed publication of the Canadian F.o.R., though after several years a mimeographed monthly Newsletter replaced it. The organization now seeks to bring together *all* pacifists who take a positive position, and has recently issued the statement: 'Peace is not a passivity, a state of rest, a lull between wars. It is an activity, the art and practise of turning enemies into friends. . . . Only positive acts of good-will, justice and generosity can overcome evil and make possible an abundant life for all men.'

The Canadian Fellowship has been largely an educational movement, working sometimes within the Churches but also apart from them. It works closely with the Society of Friends. At present it is co-operating in protest demonstrations with such groups as the Canadian Committee on Radiation Hazards, and one of its main purposes today is to try to help such groups to recognize the necessity of adopting the full pacifist position.

In 1958 the work of the F.o.R. was divided into a Western area of which Mildred Fahrni is secretary in Vancouver, and an Eastern area with EDNA BARNETT, and now MARGARET BOOS in Toronto. A National Executive Committee maintains contact between them and a monthly letter serves both branches. Service projects have been carried out in both India and Korea. In Vancouver a Fellowship House provides a centre for social work and discussion groups, and another is planned for Toronto.

Mildred Fahrni, the energetic Vancouver organizer, worked for evacuated Japanese in New Denver, B.C., during the Second World War. She gave voluntary care to about 1,300 living in a centre for whom the Government provided no secondary education. In January 1949, before the division of the work, she succeeded Albert Watson as Executive Secretary.

At the end of that year she attended the World Pacifist Meeting in India and undertook some tough travelling by jeep in Orissa. After her return to Canada she spent six months of 1952 in building up the office where she is now established. During 1961 another long journey took her to South India. Before leaving she joined a march and a meeting conducted by Vinoba Bhave in Cooch Bihar. His final words to her were: 'Until there is a voluntary surrender of privilege we cannot talk of world peace'.

AUSTRALIA

In this great continent the vast distances between capital cities (e.g. 1,000 miles between Brisbane and Melbourne, and 2,000 between Melbourne and Perth) made contacts very difficult before the days of air travel. Even now the great geographical divisions and small populations have rendered impossible the building of a really national F.o.R. But small groups linked with other peace organizations, such as the War Resisters' International and the Peace Pledge Union, have existed in major cities. A few 'mergers' have been made, such as the Victoria Pacifist Movement, which combines an earlier Christian Pacifist organization and the War Resisters' International.

One famous early incident in Australian pacifist history was the Referendum on Conscription in 1916 and 1917 under the Labour Prime Minister, Mr W. M. Hughes, who had returned from a trip to Britain, where Lloyd George was then Premier, determined to introduce conscription in Australia. But he had reckoned without the Federal Constitution, in which the Defence Act allowed citizens to be conscripted for Home Defence but not for service outside Australia. Mr Hughes thought that this provision might be overridden by the all-comprehensive War Precautions Act, but his Government refused to support him and insisted upon holding the Referendum which the Constitution demanded before anything contrary to its provisions could occur.

In two Referendums the anti-conscriptionists won a notable victory for democratic independence, and kept Australian records free from such persecution of conscientious objectors as occurred in Great Britain, the United States and New Zealand. Among the courageous opponents of conscription was the Hon. Samuel Manger, the owner of a Melbourne emporium which was subsequently boycotted by his opponents, and the Rev. Leyton Richards, then holding an appointment in Australia. The country remained without conscription until 1948, when it was introduced for the Army, and still continues. It was instituted for the Air Force in 1950, but discontinued in 1957. In 1953, owing to F.o.R. action in Sydney, boys of seventeen to eighteen called up for National Service, whose claims as conscientious objectors had been rejected by the courts, were allowed the right of appeal.

Since the Second World War the pacifist Councils of the different States have affiliated with the World Peace Council; these absorb most persons interested in work for peace, including some F.o.R. members. Comparatively little concern has been apparent; a comment in *Reconciliation* in 1935 recorded that 'the apathy of the average Australian with regard to theoretical problems makes progress difficult'. Since McCarthyism in the United States cast its sinister shadow across many countries, the idea that peace is a 'naughty' word and its exponents are 'suspect' persons is less liable to modification in large isolated areas than amid the constant changes of central communities. Two wars have made Australians more liable to boast of their fighting qualities than of their will to peace, which is largely an academic question in territories so remote from probable sources of attack, and so relatively untouched, apart from battle casualties, by the international conflicts of this century.

Notwithstanding these special difficulties, four branches of the Fellowship are functioning in Australia today, each being a State branch and an independent entity. The oldest is that of New South Wales, which started after the First World War and has about 150 members. This branch holds an annual meeting and, since 1948, a Remembrance Service in Wesley Chapel in Sydney's Central Methodist Mission on August 6th, World Peace (Hiroshima) Day. In 1960 the group conducted a twenty-four-hour vigil in the grounds of St Andrew's Anglican Cathedral to challenge the conscience of passers-by on the subject of nuclear war.

Among its conspicuous members have been Dr FRED WILLIAMS, who recently died but in his lifetime sent large consignments of pacifist literature round the world; Miss MARY BYLES, the first woman solicitor in Sydney, who has published two books, *Footprints of Gautama the Buddha* and *Journey into Burmese Silence* (1962); and JOHN FALLDING of Cheltenham, N.S.W., the secretary of the branch, who represented Australia in 1949-50 at the World Pacifist meeting in India.

The Victoria branch has an extremely active Melbourne chairman in the Rev. REX MATHIAS, who took his Diploma of Religious Education at the Selly Oak Colleges in Birmingham, England. His secretary, BETTY FAIRBANK, is the senior in charge of the office of the Methodist Federal Board of Education. This branch began in 1952 and by 1961 had thirty-three full members, nine sympathizers, and thirty-three 'interested' associates. They concentrate on the study of such classics as the late Professor G. H. C. Macgregor's *New Testament Basis of Pacifism*, and on the work of reconciliation in such tension-centres as South Africa and the former Central African Federation.

Most of the members are university students and teachers who owing to their liability to move have not been permanent enough to have much success in getting their speakers into church organizations and their letters into the press. They keep in touch through a news bulletin; and in 1960 began to hold fortnightly meetings, and established a library of books on race relations. They have had contacts with the American F.o.R. and especially with Mr J. N. Sayre, A. J. Muste and Alfred Hassler. The branch has also tried to give some help to the struggling South African Fellowship.

One outstanding Melbourne member, Mrs. ELEANOR M. MOORE, the former honorary secretary of the Women's International League for Peace and Freedom (Australian Section), who died in 1949, published in 1948 a comprehensive historical study called *The Quest for Peace*. Though based on Australian events with special reference to Melbourne, this book dealt with such wider topics as imperialism, the anti-conscription Referendums of 1916 and 1917, the two World Wars, the League of Nations, the Women's International League, Collective Security, Disarmament, the United Nations, and the causes of war.

A third branch, which has no regular meetings, exists in Western Australia, with a president, the Rev. R. F. SUTTON, in Perth, and a secretary, Mr. L. D. WILKINSON, in Mt. Lawley. On Hiroshima Day it holds a combined service or meeting on the premises of the Central Methodist Mission to which members of all Churches are invited. In 1959 this branch made a successful experiment with a large open-air lunch-hour meeting in the centre of Perth, with a relay of thirty-two speakers. Over the past three or four years the members have organized an all-night Prayer Vigil for peace on New Year's Eve. In this connection letters have been sent to the Prime Minister and other leading politicians.

A fourth branch opened in 1961 in Brisbane, Queensland, where Mrs E. R. COALDRAKE was one of those responsible for reviving an earlier organization which had existed in that huge State just before the Second World War. Her husband, the Rev. FRANK COALDRAKE, started an Australian monthly pacifist magazine, *The Peacemaker*, which is now published by the Federal Pacifist Council of Australia.

From different centres Australian pacifists sent food parcels to European pacifists during the Second World War; they also helped to care for the 2,000 internees sent out from England, and started a movement for prison reform based on the inside information received from conscientious objectors.

In 1942 the Pacifist Councils of New South Wales and Victoria appointed JOAN CHADWICK as their travelling secretary for three months, but in 1942 she was refused a permit to travel from Melbourne to Sydney and back. She nevertheless managed during that year to establish a Tasmanian Pacifist Fellowship.

Following a visit by Philip Eastman, I.F.o.R. general secretary, in 1961, the Fellowship appointed official 'correspondents' in the different States. These included the Rev. Harold E. Rowland (Congregationalist) and the Rev. Norman Crawford (Anglican), chairmen in New South Wales and South Australia respectively. The correspondent in Tasmania is Ronald Darvell (Quaker).

NEW ZEALAND

A very early attempt was made to establish a Fellowship in New Zealand; old records show that the Rev. PERCY PARIS conducted an Auckland branch study circle in 1917. When the circle disbanded for lack of support, the members sought affiliation with the British F.o.R. Another abortive attempt was made in Auckland in 1932, but at that time the influence of Barthian theology was powerful, especially in the Presbyterian Church. This influence virtually destroyed pacifist thought for the time being, since neo-Calvinism and Christian pacifism are poles apart.

Though it has never formally called itself a Fellowship, the Christian Pacifist Society of New Zealand is in all essentials a section of the I.F.o.R. This Society, a wholly indigenous body, grew out of pacifist thought and discussion in the Methodist Youth Movement between the wars. The secretary, A. C. BARRINGTON, drafted a Covenant to submit to the Movement which presented the members with three choices: first, absolute pacifism; secondly, the refusal of combatant service only; thirdly, a desire to work and pray for peace without any commitment regarding war service.

In 1936 this Covenant was submitted to the Methodist Conference through the Youth Board. The Board decided that the only real issue was that of absolute pacifism, so it submitted this provision alone to the Conference. The Conference rejected it, though some forty Methodist ministers and hundreds of others had signed the Covenant. 'I have wondered since', A. C. Barrington wrote twenty-five years afterwards, 'whether the move in the Board was too subtle for my simple nature, and was intended to produce that result.'

After this rejection A. C. Barrington and his distinguished colleague ORMOND BURTON, who long before the Second World War became well known as a remarkable preacher both inside and outside his church, called a meeting to discuss the formation of an international pacifist society which ultimately grew into the Christian Pacifist Society of New Zealand. The Rev. Alan Brash, later secretary to the National Council of Churches, was an early Presbyterian member.

Ormond Burton was a Gallipoli war veteran decorated by both the French and the British, who awarded him the Military Medal. He became a militant pacifist owing to the spiritual consequences of his experience and its aftermath, which showed him that the ideals for which he and others had fought were not to be implemented by cynical governments. Although he became the official historian of the New Zealand Division's First World War campaigns, he insisted before the book appeared on his publishers recording in an Appendix his changed views and his refusal to fight in another war. He has since been described as 'the Martin Niemöller of New Zealand'.

The two founders of the Christian Pacifist Society had not then heard of the F.o.R.; they learned of it through some British Anglican Pacifists living in Christchurch who lent them copies of the F.o.R. magazine *Reconciliation* (then called *The Christian Pacifist*). From this they realized that in their concern for peace they were not alone.

A. C. Barrington was either secretary or president of the Christian Pacifist Society until 1961, when he became overseas secretary. He represented New Zealand at the World Pacifist Meeting in India in 1949-50. Besides travelling all over India he visited Pakistan, where he and Vera Brittain, at a time of great Indo-Pakistan tension, interviewed Begum Liaquat Ali Khan, Miss Fatima Jinnah and several Government Ministers. He regards his most constructive achievement as the Riverside Community, a prosperous apple-orchard and fruit-growing farm run by Christian pacifist families at Lower Moutere, near Nelson.

In 1946, despite much rough treatment during the Second World War, the Society had approximately 550 members. A monthly magazine, *The New Zealand Christian Pacifist*, has been published since 1945, replacing a cyclostyled *Bulletin* which A. C. Barrington founded and edited. When he was in prison, his colleagues kept it going. It was the subject of many prosecutions, searches, and confiscations; Ormond Burton's most severe sentence of two and a half years' imprisonment was imposed for an issue in which he reported A. C. Barrington's success in the Court of Appeal against a Supreme Court conviction (also for material appearing in the *Bulletin*).

Many other members of the Christian Pacifist Society were prosecuted and imprisoned between 1939 and 1945; in February 1943 over seventy members of the Society were in jail for continuing to write and speak against the war. The police refused the use of halls for meetings, and when the Society persisted in holding an open-air meeting in Wellington in January 1942, the speakers were arrested and sentenced to three months' hard labour, and the secretary, A. C. Barrington, to twelve months for 'subversive statements'.

Detention camps alone offered an alternative to military service; there was no legal provision for alternative service or complete exemption. Ormond Burton was the only Methodist minister imprisoned, though a younger Presbyterian minister and poet, Basil Dowling, served a prison sentence for three months. Eventually the Methodist Church expelled Ormond Burton, for he was one of a group of twelve pacifists who organized a determined campaign to take New Zealand out of the war; on the day war broke out he had addressed a large crowd outside the Parliament and was arrested with two other speakers. This meeting set the pattern for everything that followed.

The Finance Minister, Walter Nash, later told Ormond Burton that if there had been fifty instead of twelve resisters, the Government would probably have been obliged to withdraw from the war. Its action might have meant that Canada and Australia would have gone out too, since their war resisters would have been strengthened. In New Zealand the big unions were beginning to support the pacifists; hence the Labour Government was afraid of them though the Conservative Opposition was not.

The Christian Pacifist speakers attracted large crowds, which included a number of soldiers. But the official Churches were not on their side, and those ministers who agreed with them elected to keep silent rather than 'divide the Church'. After the Methodist Church had expelled Ormond Burton, several other ministers were given six months' notice. With most of her outspoken preachers in jail or detention camp the New Zealand Church failed to make any effective peace witness and, as so

N

often happens, the silent churchmen became the national hierarchy after the war.

Ormond Burton was released from prison in June 1944 but owing to his notoriety could get nothing but manual work, and finally took a job as a cleaner at Wellington College where he scrubbed the floors. Ten years later he had become the acting headmaster of this school, one of New Zealand's largest. In 1956, after prolonged consideration, the Methodist Church reinstated him as a full minister. It was a testimony to his humility that he finally left his influential position in the school to return to the ministry, but he was no more prepared to compromise with his conscience than he had ever been. During 1962 he called for civil disobedience to prevent preparations for nuclear war. In *The New Zealand Christian Pacifist* for March 1963 he lamented that nothing comparable to their wartime witness had since taken place, but added: 'The really important thing is the sense of mission to which we are moved by the Holy Spirit'.

In July and August 1963 Ormond Burton visited England, and for a week broadcast in the BBC's early morning programme, 'Lift Up Your Hearts'. He also conducted a broadcast morning service from the Congregational Church at Ealing Green, and preached a sermon at Donald Soper's church, Kingsway Hall. Recently, on the basis of his prison experience, he wrote at the request of the New Zealand National Council of Churches a book of prayers and meditations for prison chaplains and prisoners.

Branches of the Christian Pacifist Society of New Zealand now exist in Wellington, Palmerston North, Napier, Auckland, Nelson, Christchurch and Dunedin. The National Executive is located at Auckland, and the devoted secretary is Mrs Katherine Knight, a member of the Society of Friends, while the president is a Methodist, the Rev. E. A. Crane.

If this story of the Commonwealth branches of the F.o.R. appears to be largely one of tiny groups and ineffective endeavours, the newness and sheer size of the territories involved must constantly be remembered, together with the dogged courage of individuals attempting to galvanize a dead weight of apathy unknown in the small countries of Europe and the busy crowded cities of the United States.

It is unnecessary to underline the special difficulties of South Africa, no longer a Commonwealth country but one of those areas, like the Southern States of the USA, in which crises are continuous and the dangers of potential disaster a constant challenge to Christians.

SOUTH AFRICA

Though South Africa left the Commonwealth in 1961, it had been included for so many years that it belongs to this chapter. Its policy confronts the F.o.R., like other religious organizations, with one of its toughest problems. In addition to the crescendo of restrictive laws which, under the three recent Prime Ministers, Drs Malan, Strydom and Verwoerd, operate *apartheid* and relegate all black and coloured South Africans to second-class citizenship, there is tension between the English-speaking British and the Africaans-speaking Boers. Another problem is the officially-inspired fear of communism which attributes all criticism of the Government to communist influence.

This fear, half genuine and half a deliberate excuse for repressive measures, led to the arrest in 1963, on charges brought under the Suppression of Communism Act, of the F.o.R. Chairman in South Africa, the Rev. Arthur Blaxall.

The South African Fellowship has roots which go back to 1919, when a Quaker Mission led by William Henry and Harriet Alexander visited South Africa with gifts of seed to enable dispossessed Boer farmers to start afresh. They also pleaded the cause of Europe's starving children, and established branches of the Save the Children International Union. Scattered individuals joined the British F.o.R., and Olive Warner published a pacifist magazine, *The Ambassador*, from Johannesburg. In 1926 the young British writer, Winifred Holtby, visited South Africa to plead the cause of peace through the League of Nations, and eleven years later two other visitors from abroad, John Mellor and Rufus Jones, found a few peace groups in existence such as the Peace and Arbitration Society of Cape Town. Canon Raven's newly-published *War and the Christian* exercised considerable influence over these groups. One continued to meet in Port Elizabeth till after the outbreak of the Second World War, and Rev. and Mrs James Elder held meetings which eventually led to the formation of an F.o.R. branch in Grahamstown in 1942.

When John Mellor again visited South Africa in 1948, he welcomed the help of two keen F.o.R. members from Cape Town, Dr and Mrs Muir Grieve. ELLA ELDER offered to act as secretary and faithfully continued this work till 1960. Her daughter is now treasurer. Percy Bartlett, as international secretary, subsequently regularized the spontaneously-formed branch, and MARY BUTLER of Cradock sent out a roneod newsletter ambitiously entitled 'Reconciliation in South Africa'. Groups sprang up in Cape Town, Pretoria, Durban, Port Elizabeth and Pietermaritzburg (which originated as a branch of the War Resisters' International).

Two examples of concerted action were a wartime protest against the call-up of Dutch citizens resident in South Africa, and a post-war speaking tour by Muriel Lester. But during this tour racial problems began to cause disunity, as some members felt that these were not the concern of a peace organization. Interest in the F.o.R. declined as race tension grew, until in 1952 Nevin Sayre came from the United States to pull the branch together, and ARTHUR BLAXALL, finally a member, became chairman-secretary. In 1956 the total scattered membership numbered only 150, but whites and non-whites now worked together on a basis of equality and brotherhood which was characteristic of few South African organizations.

In spite of problems of distance comparable with Australia's (Johannesburg is 1,000 miles from Cape Town), conferences were held in these cities at two-yearly intervals. Douglas Steere of USA and J. J. Buskes of Holland undertook speaking tours. An important pamphlet called 'How to be a Christian in South Africa' and a report by Pastor Buskes had wide circulations. But in spite of letters to the press, book reviews and articles, the effort to maintain interest in peace and disarmament tended to be swamped, like most causes in South Africa, by the fierce political and racial struggle which for the majority of members had priority over everything else.

In the attempt to improve human relations as such, a keen group of young Pretoria members initiated a multi-racial Work Camp movement at the Wilgespruit Fellowship Centre in Roodepoort. During 1956 the Rev. ARTLEY PARSON, a retired American Episcopal Church minister aged seventy-six, arrived to help Arthur Blaxall as mobile secretary at his own expense.

Other events affecting the Fellowship and its witnesses were the
Treason Trials beginning in 1957; the formation in the same
year of an F.o.R. group in Southern Rhodesia where Leighton
Yates of Salisbury is now I.F.o.R. correspondent; the attempt to
bring a Christian spirit into the celebrations of the fiftieth anniversary of the Union in 1960; the election of Robert Mize, of
the US Episcopal Pacifist Fellowship, as Bishop of the Anglican
diocese of Damaraland (S.W. Africa); and the award of the 1960
Nobel Prize to Chief Albert Luthuli in 1961.

Chief Luthuli, who stood close to the F.o.R., is an outstanding
Christian who has continuously fought a non-violent battle for
his own people and for several years was president of the now
banned African National Congress, Luthuli's influence has
spread widely not only throughout South Africa but across the
world.

ALBERT LUTHULI belongs to a Christian family of Zulu chiefs
and took up teaching as a profession. He was educated at Adams
College, an American missionary secondary school in Natal, and
had taught in African schools for fifteen years when he was
called to become chieftain of his tribe. After he was elected
president of the A.N.C. he immediately fell under Government
suspicion, but continued to oppose both *apartheid* and the
extremist members of the Congress. Following the Defiance
Campaign of 1952, the Government announced to his tribe that
he had been deposed from the chieftainship. In December 1956
he was arrested and brought to the Treason Trial, but his indict-
ment was subsequently quashed. After the Sharpeville shooting
in 1960, he publicly burned his pass as a protest against the
Government's policy. For this he was heavily fined and sent to
prison.

During the summer of that year the present writer and her
husband succeeded in visiting him in Pretoria Gaol—though
assured by the staff of the British High Commissioner that this
was impossible—as the result of a direct request to the Pretoria
police. When released Chief Luthuli was put under restriction
in a village near Durban and forbidden to address public
meetings.

Two years later he was awarded the Nobel Prize, the first
African to be thus honoured. Some doubt hung over the possibility of permission being given him to go to Norway to receive

the prize. Owing to the pressure of world opinion he was eventually allowed to leave Africa for only ten days, but on his way through London he managed brief talks with such friends as Bishop Ambrose Reeves, Philip Noel Baker, M.P., and other supporters in Parliament. In Norway King Olaf congratulated him on his award, and his dignified and moving speech in reply made a deep impression.

In October 1963 the University of Glasgow elected Albert Luthuli as their new Rector, but he was not permitted to leave South Africa for the installation ceremony.

Other outstanding supporters of the South African F.o.R. have included Manilal Gandhi, Bishop A. H. Zulu, Bishop Robert Mize of Damaraland, Dr and Mrs Muir Grieve of Cape Town, Scarnell Lean of Johannesburg, and the Rev. Michael Scott.

MANILAL GANDHI, following his father's teaching, greatly valued the F.o.R. and attended its general meetings, but was never a full member because, as a Hindu, he was not surprisingly unable to accept the unique character of Christ's witness to the power of love. After he died his centre, Phoenix in Natal, declined in influence, and with his wife's return to India the paper Indian Opinion, founded by the Mahatma, ceased publication.

BISHOP ZULU, now assistant in St John's Diocese in the Transkei, was for several years, as Canon Zulu, the chairman of the Durban group of the F.o.R. He has become convinced that the pacifist interpretation of Scripture is correct and offers the right policy for a liberation movement in South Africa.

BISHOP ROBERT MIZE of Damaraland is a convinced pacifist who belonged to the Episcopal Pacifist Fellowship in the United States; he gave an impressive Enthronement sermon in December 1960, but during his short sojourn in South-West Africa he has not so far had much opportunity to work with the F.o.R. Dr MUIR GRIEVE is a member of the Cape Town Medical School, and SCARNELL LEAN and WILL FOX, Johannesburg Quakers, are the backbone of the local group.

The Rev. MICHAEL SCOTT, now the honorary director of the Africa Bureau in London, received part of his education at St Paul's College, Grahamstown, and lived in South Africa from 1943 to 1950 after a year in the R.A.F. In 1947 he appealed to the United Nations on behalf of two tribes of the S.W. African Mandated Territory, and at the Chief's request he attended sessions of the United Nations Assembly, and was granted hearings by the Fourth Committee in 1949, 1950 and 1955. The question was eventually referred to the International Court of Justice. Though long regarded as an international F.o.R. figure, Michael Scott has publicly expressed doubts regarding the relevance of non-violence to South African politics, is not now a member of the Fellowship, and might perhaps not regard the term 'pacifist' as suitably applied to himself.

The chairman of the South African Fellowship, the Rev. ARTHUR BLAXALL, was born in 1891 and trained for the ministry at St Augustine's College, Canterbury. He went to Keble College, Oxford, with a scholarship in 1914, tried to join the Army, was rejected on health grounds, and went to Serbia with a hospital unit for the rest of the war. He returned to Keble, was ordained in 1921, and in 1923, at a friend's invitation, became curate to a church in Cape Town. The welfare of deaf and blind coloured children claimed his interest; under the Earl of Athlone's patronage he opened a school for them in Cape Town, and ten years later founded a similar institution in Johannesburg.

While engaged in this work he met Muriel Lester, through whom he joined the F.o.R. At first he felt unable to adopt the full pacifist position, but gradually came to believe that such problems as he and others faced in South Africa could only be solved at the deepest Christian levels. He took over the F.o.R. in 1952 with the help of Ella Elder who had kept it alive between the wars, and was appointed I.F.o.R. secretary for Southern Africa in 1961. In 1962 long speaking tours took him east, west and south of Johannesburg to meet African and European leaders. He appears in chapter 13 of Alan Paton's Cry the Beloved Country as the superintendent of the Institution for blind, deaf and dumb Africans at Ezenzeleni, near Johannesburg.

In 1963, when on the point of leaving for the All-Africa Church Conference in Uganda, he was arrested on charges under the Suppression of Communism Act, and was detained on bail at his home in Roodepoort, Transvaal, until October 7th, when he was tried at the magistrates' court in Johannesburg. He was sentenced on four counts of aiding banned organizations (Pan Africanist Congress and the Pan African Congress), and for possessing two banned publications, *New Age* and *Fighting Talk*. All but six of the twenty-eight months' sentence were suspended for three years, and after representations were made to the Minister of Justice, Arthur Blaxall was released on parole following twenty-four hours in prison.

Philip Eastman and Bishop Zulu were among those who testified at his trial. The South African Fellowship at a conference of members in December 1963 appointed new officers based on East London, where there is a growing witness.

Arthur and Florence Blaxall left South Africa for Great Britain in February 1964.

Chapter 11

THE FELLOWSHIP IN ASIA

CHINA

The F.o.R. in China was always a somewhat nebulous body; its experimental activities were continuously interrupted and finally overwhelmed by the revolutionary and military events which battered the country between Sun Yat-sen's proclamation of a Chinese Republic in 1911, and the final triumph of Chinese Communism in September 1949. The attempt to trace the Fellowship's story is no more than a spasmodic endeavour to follow the progress of an errant spark in a huge field of stubble with non-existent communications between the different sections.

Such organization as there was grew up mainly among missionaries, and centred round the personality of Henry Hodgkin, joint secretary of the National Christian Council in China between 1922 and 1929. This endeavour consisted of more or less unrelated groups in several centres, made up largely of foreign missionary leaders but with a few like-minded Chinese members. Conspicuous among these was Dr P. C. Hsu, a Christian internationalist who in 1924 returned from three years of study at Union Theological College in New York to find the F.o.R., in his own words, 'very popular'. In June 1925 the Peking group published a statement advocating immediate steps towards the abolition of extra-territoriality, and the removal of all foreign troops from Chinese soil.

Just before Henry Hodgkin left China, soon after General Chiang Kai-shek had succeeded Sun Yat-sen as Republican leader and established his capital in Nanking, an F.o.R. Conference was held in that city and a committee of about five members was formed. These included Leonard Tomkinson of the Society of Friends and two Chinese Christians, Y. T. Wu and Francis Wang. Dr P. C. Hsu, who in his schooldays had been an enthusiastic follower of Sun Yat-sen, attended the conference but declined to join the committee.

Its chief result was the foundation of a small magazine, *Wei Ai* ('Love Only'), the Wei Shi Association being the name of the F.o.R. in Chinese. This magazine continued for some years in which Y. T. Wu emerged as a pacifist leader, but in 1937 he came under the influence of Reinhold Niebuhr, whose ideas were incompatible with those of the F.o.R., and abandoned his pacifism. This drastic step ended the paper, and the committee dissolved. It had however been in touch with the influential Tsengs of Hong Kong, a brother and sister who represented China at the World Pacifist Meeting, and after the Communist victory emigrated to Formosa and became associated with Taipeh University.

Other meetings using the name of the F.o.R. were held periodically in Shanghai and also in the summer resort of Kuling. Their keener members included Frank Millican of the Chinese Literature Society, who subsequently transferred his allegiance to Moral Rearmament, and Frank Rawlinson, the Editor of the *Chinese Recorder*, who lost his life in the bombing which occurred during the first Japanese-Shanghai fighting in the nineteen-thirties.

Another group met in Anking, the provincial capital of Anhui, for several years before 1935, and was the only one with mainly Chinese attenders and meetings usually conducted in the Chinese language. The organizers of this body did not insist that its members should all belong to Christian churches; at one time the secretary was a Chinese living in a Buddhist temple. The Ahung of the Muslim Mosque also attended one meeting. Among its other activities this group undertook a survey of the living conditions of apprentices and of the city's charitable institutions, most of which had started under Buddhist inspiration.

The Fellowship also lent its name to a body which met in Chengtu both before and during the Sino-Japanese war, though most of the attenders, such as Wallace Wang, chaplain to West China Union University, did not formally belong to the F.o.R. Even P. C. Hsu was apparently never an actual member, though in May 1931 *Reconciliation* described him as 'Chairman of the F.o.R. groups in China'.

From 1931, when the Japanese began their career of large-scale conquests and occupied Manchuria, few F.o.R. members, whether Chinese or foreign, openly opposed the War of Resistance. After 1937, with the flight of the Chiang Kai-shek government first to Hankow and then to Chungking and the conquest by Japan of the whole Chinese coast, the F.o.R. became completely disorganized. A few local groups carried on, but the membership was predominantly foreign.

After the Second World War, when Britain and America had renounced all their rights and privileges in China, Dr Winburn Thomas, an American missionary living in Shanghai, attempted, in 1948, to revive the F.o.R. One meeting took place in the home of Bishop Roberts, an Anglican; the Bishop was absent but his wife, a Roman Catholic convert, showed deep concern for the reorganization of the Fellowship. Y. T. Wu was present, and though he stated that he could not now 'go along' with the F.o.R., he did supply a statement prepared before the war on the Chinese organization as a basis of membership.

This initiative could not be followed up owing to the rapid development of revolutionary politics. There was no question of any Chinese F.o.R. surviving the establishment of the People's Republic, and the work, such as it was, had to be carried on by American Fellowship members. The possibility of some ultimate quiet revival is not however wholly out of the question, for contrary to popular belief, Christianity has not totally disappeared in Communist China.

The Roman Catholics, directed by the Vatican to oppose the Communists in 1949, were condemned as counter-revolutionaries and had to flee the country, but the Protestant Churches, not being centrally organized, had no authority which could declare anti-Communist opposition. The missionary societies none-the-less felt that the presence of foreign missions would prejudice the position of Chinese Protestants and therefore withdrew. Meanwhile the People's Government compelled the Chinese Protestant churches to sever their connection with the parent churches overseas and the missionary societies which had supported them, and both Protestants and Catholics were officially debarred from running educational institutions which were now the monopoly of the State.

The Christian churches in China were thus confined to purely religious activities and had to rely exclusively on their own followers and internal resources. But they did not die. In 1950 forty Chinese Christians started a movement for a self-supporting and self-administering Chinese Christian Church. Four years later a national committee was formed in Shanghai by more than sixty denominational groups and church organizations, and now has hundreds of thousands of supporters.

In 1959 a Chinese woman with an American mission school background (Mrs Derek Bryan) returned to China to find the Anglican, Congregational and Baptist churches carrying on as before and the Baptists flourishing. *Reconciliation* for 1961 published an article entitled 'China Revisited', by Nancy Lapwood, which described how she and her sister joined a congregation of 450, including many young people, in the Community Church of Shanghai. Though she acknowledged that it is not easy to be a Christian in China today, she referred to the existence of two large Protestant Theological seminaries in Peking and Nanking, and reported the institution of joint services and a considerable sale of Bibles.

She emphasized especially the importance of Westerners realizing that Chinese Christians now identify themselves with their own people, accept the social order, and feel pride in its achievements. They tend to repudiate the social and political ideas formerly incorporated in missionary teaching, and to re-interpret Christianity in Chinese terms.

Victor Purcell's recent history of China[1] expresses the view that Christianity may have a future there if it divorces religion from all social activity and ceases to regard itself as the spearhead of Western civilization. The Protestant churches, he reports, have nationalized 'themselves into a few branches or denominations, and the Government grants them the finance necessary for their maintenance. The question now', he concludes, 'is whether the century of intensive missionary effort by European Christians has given the Chinese Christians the necessary spiritual impetus to ride the storm or whether (as the Communists expect) Christianity will wither away.'

The leading Chinese Christians connected with the F.o.R. have been Dr P. C. Hsu, Y. T. Wu (alternatively described by Francis

[1] Victor Purcell, *China*, Ernest Benn, 1962.

Price Jones as Wu Yao-tsung),[1] and Christopher Tang. Other Chinese mentioned in the few surviving records are Y. C. Tu; Miss Liu En-lan; Dr Wu Yi-fong, the President of Ginling College; Dr Wu Lui Chuan, President of Yening University; and Dr Li Chao Huan of Shanghai.

Dr P. C. HSU, after his enthusiastic support for Sun Yat-sen, came into contact with Christianity in 1913 while still at college, and was converted. After his return to China from New York's Union College in 1921, he became a Christian internationalist and faced the pacifist issue for the first time. His uncle and virtual father in Chekiang Province, a profound and scholarly Confucian of conservative tendencies, eventually joined the Revolution and became a Christian.

An article by J. Stewart Burgess in *The Christian Century* for April 19, 1944, describes how Dr Hsu joined the Christian Church after prolonged and intensive inquiries, and became known to the 40,000 students of Peking University as a brilliant young Christian who gave a fresh and vital interpretation of the new religion to which he had dedicated himself.

Subsequently he made a marked contribution to the building of the Christian movement in China. After studying philosophy and theology in the United States at Columbia University and Union Seminary, he joined the young theological faculty of Yenching University, Peking. Here he taught social ethics and organized the Yenching Christian Fellowship, a faculty-student experiment. When Japan began her career of Chinese conquests in the nineteen-thirties, he took part in a group which organized a Retreat for Chinese and Japanese Christian leaders, and volunteered his help to the Rural Reconstruction Movement afterwards sponsored by Madame Chiang Kai-shek.

During the Second World War Dr Hsu did translation work for the Council of Churches in China, and taught at the University of Chengtu. In February 1944 he met with a fatal accident while travelling by road to Chungking in a postal truck. The truck overturned, pinning him—a very small man—beneath the mail bags, and he died two days later. At the time he was engaged on plans for establishing an ashram in Central China

[1] Francis Price Jones, *The Church in Communist China*, Friendship Press, New York, 1962.

and for completing the translation of Hocking's *The Meaning of God in Human Experience*.

Y. T. WU, the editor of *Wei Ai* and chairman for a time of the Chinese F.o.R., came from a non-Christian Canton family and was converted to Christianity as a student in Customs College, Peking. He was ordained by the Congregational Church in June 1920, and studied in New York at Union Seminary in 1924 and again in 1937. Between these dates he had served from 1929 to 1932 as Executive Secretary of the student division of the American YMCA, and then became National Literature Secretary of the Association Press, sponsoring the publication in Chinese of important works on Christianity. It was during his second period at Union Seminary that he gave up his pacifism under the influence of Reinhold Niebuhr.

In 1949 Y. T. Wu was drawn into the Communist-sponsored peace movement, and in 1952 in a magazine described his former adherence to pacifism as 'a beautiful dream'. But he did not abandon his hopes for world peace, and on his return to China from Communist peace conferences in Prague and Paris he devoted himself to the task of preparing the Christian Church in China to accept the new regime. He clearly felt that this was the only alternative to its complete destruction.

The third outstanding Chinese supporter of the F.o.R., CHRISTOPHER TANG, joined the Fellowship at Hankow under the influence of Muriel Lester in 1933. She records that as a schoolboy he had refused to take part in a patriotic procession which was shouting the slogans: 'Down with the foreign devils! Down with the Japanese!' He survived the persecution which followed this episode, and at college again became a solitary witness by refusing compulsory military drill. This cost him his degree, and for a time he joined a Christian community in Kyoto where he humbly acted as cook.

In November 1961, in a letter to Nevin Sayre, he described his attempts from 1946 onwards to revive the Chinese F.o.R. Eventually he started a group in Hong Kong after a visit there by Muriel in 1951, but it did not survive his departure from the island in February 1952.

JAPAN

Soon after the F.o.R. began in England, a small number of

Japanese Christians and foreign missionaries met in Kamakura and established an informal group. But the Japanese Fellowship was not formally organized until 1926, when it was constituted under the name 'Yuwakai' (Society of Friendly Harmony) with the Rev. Michio Kozaki as chairman, Katsuo Takenaka and the Rev. T. D. Walser as secretary-treasurers, and Gilbert Bowles and Yuri Watanabe as standing committee members.

From 1931, when the Japanese invaded Manchuria, the dominant militarism of the country created increasing difficulties for the peace movement. Soon after the outbreak of hostilities, TOYOHIKO KAGAWA—never a member of the F.o.R. but widely revered as a pacifist saint—asked China's pardon for his nation in an address to the students and faculty of Cheeloo University in Tainan, Shantung. With the attack on Pearl Harbour in 1941, the Sino-Japanese conflict became merged in the Second World War, but the Fellowship continued its precarious existence with the help of American missionaries. In 1944, the year before the collapse of Japanese militarism, it was however dissolved by the Army with other peace organizations.

Japan then suffered the atomic bombing of Hiroshima and Nagasaki, which was followed by the strange stories of Claude Etherly, one of the American pilots who took part. He began a career of minor crimes said to be due to his unquiet conscience, and the Japanese F.o.R. treated him with great charity as a 'victim of war'. In 1964 however a book published in America by G. P. Putnam (The Hiroshima Pilot, by William Bradford Huie) 'exposed' Etherley as a fraud who was never nearer to Hiroshima than a reconnaissance plane 200 miles away when the bomb fell. The author maintained that journalistic ingenuity and a credulous public in search of a 'symbol' for its guilt created the Etherly legend. Nevertheless the possibility remains that he was a genuine victim of schizophrenia, and the whole truth about him may never be known.

After General MacArthur's occupation of Japan, Harry Silcock, a British Quaker, visited Japan in 1948, and with several Japanese Christians laid new foundations for the establishment of a peace group. The following year Nevin Sayre, then chairman of the I.F.o.R., visited Japan with his wife Kathleen, and the Fellowship was revived. Iwao Ayusawa was elected chairman; Mrs Tomi Kora vice-chairman; Paul Sekiya vice-chairman and executive secretary; and Bunichi Kagami treasurer. Two additional secretaries were Hideo Kagami and Hiroshi Sakamoto.

The new organisation laid down two principles as guidance for its future:

1. We refuse to co-operate with any international or civil war, or further any preparation for or exercise of violence.

2. We affirm that the love of God manifested in the love of Christ Jesus and his death on the Cross should be the standard for all human conduct, and afford the basic and ultimate power for peaceful settlement of disputes between individuals, classes, races or nations.

The Fellowship was reorganised and much developed in 1950, after Paul Sekiya and Dr Kora had visited the World Pacifist Meeting in India. By June 1952 the Tokyo group had grown to fifty, and the whole body was especially concerned to rouse public opinion against rearmament. In 1954, when the signed membership was nearing 300, delegates from twenty-seven branches throughout Japan attended the fourth Annual Conference. Two years later, while Mrs Hatsue Nonomiya carried on the work in Japan, Paul Sekiya visited the United States, Britain, Eire, France, Germany and Switzerland.

When Japan became a full member of the United Nations in 1957, the F.o.R. prepared a statement for the Japanese delegation asking that other nations should share in her disarmed status. At its tenth Annual Convention in August 1960, the Japanese Fellowship issued another statement deploring the failure of the Summit Conference and the revision of the Security Pact.

Japanese-American Relations

One outstanding feature in the history of the Japanese Fellowship has been the persistent endeavour of the American Fellowship to create friendship between the United States and Japan. From the end of the First World War up to the present, these efforts have passed through several phases. Before the Second World War, they were designed to prevent war between the two countries; after it had broken out, the purpose was to try to modify its consequences. Among the outstanding members of the American F.o.R. who shared in these experiments in reconciliation were Gilbert Bowles, Theodore Walser, Merrell Vories, Charles Iglehart, Russell Durgin, Winburn Thomas, Stanley Jones, Floyd Schmoe, Caleb Foote, Roger Baldwin, and, of course, the dominant personality of the American group, Nevin Sayre.

An early pre-war project for reconciliation was the foundation by Merrell Vories, a young American Christian who took a teaching post in a Japanese Government College, of the Omi Brotherhood at Omi-Hachiman City, Shigaken. Then, among the deliberate endeavours to prevent World War II, came an 'Open Letter to the People of Japan' in 1935, the year in which the Japanese statesman, Mr Matsuoka, publicly regretted that he had to be the person responsible for taking Japan out of the League of Nations.

The 'Open Letter', organized by Harold Fey, then the Editor of *Fellowship*, was signed by 301 American religious leaders who included Allen Knight Chalmers, Henry H. Crane, Sherwood Eddy, Harry Emerson Fosdick, John Haynes Holmes, Rufus M. Jones, Reinhold Niebuhr, Kirby Page, Clarence R. Pickett and Mary E. Wooley. The key sentences, which were widely publicized in the Japanese press, ran as follows:

'For eighty-one years our two nations have maintained friendly relations. . . . We write this letter of goodwill at this time because this cherished bond might be menaced by a plan announced by our Government . . . to hold manoeuvres of a large fleet in the North Pacific. . . . Many thousands of our citizens, especially those who constitute the membership of our churches and synagogues, have protested against the holding of these manoeuvres. . . . In the spirit of equality and brotherhood we therefore ask you to unite with us in redoubling our efforts to maintain our historic friendship.'

A further endeavour 'behind the scenes before Pearl Harbour' to preserve the peace involved an off-the-record interview on December 3, 1941, between President Roosevelt and E. Stanley Jones, who subsequently described the abortive negotiations in an article entitled 'An Adventure in Failure', published by the magazine *Asia and the Americas* in December 1945. Stanley Jones attributed his failure chiefly to the Japanese war party, the nefarious example of Western imperialism, the discrimination

O

against Japan in the American immigration laws, the pressure of the militarists surrounding Mr Roosevelt, and the efforts of the nations—notably Britain, China, and the Netherlands—who wanted to get the United States into the war.

Once war had broken out, remedial efforts took the place of attempted reconciliation. First came the help given to Japanese-American citizens evacuated to Relocation Centres—described by Nevin Sayre as 'a shameful and unnecessary procedure which Mr Roosevelt sanctioned'. The F.o.R. also initiated and raised a Revolving Loan Fund to help the evacuees to re-settle after their release from the Centres.

In 1944, following the publication by the American Fellowship of the widely-discussed pamphlet *Massacre by Bombing* (see Chapter 4, p. 60), Mr Sayre added a postscript which aimed at preventing the use of poison gas on Japanese islands. The following year a group similar to that of the religious leaders who had put their names to the pamphlet publicly protested against the atomic bombing of Hiroshima and Nagasaki.

After Charles Iglehart and Roger Baldwin had been invited to Japan to work with General MacArthur during the American occupation, the chief initiative of the New York F.o.R. between 1949 and 1958 was directed towards obtaining clemency for Japanese war prisoners. Nevin Sayre's attention was drawn to this problem when the Rev. Eugene Hessel, F.o.R. member in the Philippines, wrote him about the hanging of one of these men. From the total of 1,160 Japanese convicted of war crimes by the United States, 332 remained on October 1, 1953. In July of that year, following persistent appeals from the F.o.R. which also approached General MacArthur and the British Prime Minister, Clement Attlee, President Quirino of the Philippines had pardoned and returned to Japan 53 of these prisoners, and commuted to life imprisonment the death sentences on 52 others who were subsequently transferred to the Sugamo Prison in Tokyo.

Following renewed endeavours by the Fellowship on behalf of these men, Paul Sekiya was able to write to Mr Sayre on January 7, 1959: 'All the war criminals under the US jurisdiction who had been pardoned for several months were given complete remission at the end of last year, so all the war criminals business has been ended'. F.o.R. members who joined in this remarkable effort included Russell L. Durgin (who died in 1956): Muriel Lester (who visited ninety Japanese prisoners in Manila and carried fifty-nine letters to their relatives in Tokyo); Bishop Lawrence of Western Massachusetts; and Dr John Oliver Nelson of Yale University. Many distinguished American ministers and social workers also co-operated. More recently the New York Fellowship protested against the Japanese Peace Treaty and Mutual Security Pact for which John Foster Dulles was mainly responsible.

In 1958, after ten years' work by the reconstituted Japanese F.o.R., Paul Sekiya issued a document summarizing its main activities as annual conventions, monthly meetings at the fifteen local chapters, seminars and study circles, visits to peace leaders at home and abroad, the issue of publications which include the monthly eight-page magazine *Yūwa*, and peace promotion work through public lectures. This document also included an interesting résumé of the group's chief difficulties, under the headings Theological (the influence of Reinhold Niebuhr's anti-pacifist theories), Ideological (confusion with Communism, which is not confined to Japan), Sociological (the difficulty of a State-conditioned people in putting conscience before the nation), and Practical (due largely to widespread apathy based on ignorance).

The latest report of the Japanese F.o.R. (1961-3) recapitulates much of the earlier document, but adds several more recent activities, such as a Christian peace conference in September 1962 which witnessed against nuclear tests and, in addition to the lawsuits filed in Washington and Moscow in 1963, may well have contributed to the recent Test Ban Treaty; the formation of a Christian Committee to oppose the use of Japan as a nuclear base; opposition to the revival of *Kigensetsu* (National Foundation Day, which might lead to a resurgence of militarism); and active co-operation in the World Federalist movement.

The Japanese Fellowship now has 272 members, of whom 243 (163 men and 80 women) are natives of Japan. Its latest office is situated at the Neighbourhood Centre, 7 Gochi, Toyama Heights, Shinjuku-ku, Tokyo.

In addition to the active and devoted Paul Sekiya, eminent Japanese citizens who have promoted the F.o.R. include Iwao Ayusawa, Michi Kawai, Jin Masaike and Hatsue Nonomiya. Besides Nevin Sayre their American supporters have included

Merrell Vories, Dr T. D. Walser, Dr Winburn Thomas, Russell Luther Durgin and Charles Iglehart.

PAUL MASAHIKO SEKIYA has been largely responsible for the vigour of the Japanese F.o.R. The eldest son of the Vice-Minister of the Imperial Household, he took his law degree at Tokyo University, studied theology at Cambridge, England, and after his return to Japan was ordained in the Protestant Episcopal Church in 1933. During the war he was conscripted into the Japanese Army, remained in Shanghai doing relief work, met British and American Quakers there, and became a Friend in 1947.

The Fellowship chairman, Dr IWAO AYUSAWA, the son of a Samurai, joined the F.o.R. as a student at Haverford College, USA, in 1917, and became a Ph.D. of Columbia University and Professor of Labour Relations at International Christian University. Before the Second World War he spent eleven years as Senior Staff Member of the I.L.O. in Geneva and four as the Director of its Tokyo office. He was Executive Director of the Central Labour Relations Board from 1946 to 1949, and as a Quaker has served for several years as Clerk of the Japanese Society of Friends.

MICHI KAWAI, who died in 1953, was a 1904 graduate of Bryn Mawr University in USA and a founder of the YWCA movement in Japan. Also of noble birth, she had built up Keisen, her cosmopolitan school in which her girls learned the facts of international life, before the military clique gained control of Japan.

In 1938, when she represented the Japanese Church with Kagawa and seven others at an ecumenical Church conference at Tambaram, Madras, she joined a discussion on the drug traffic in order frankly to acknowledge the guilt of Japan. Her lifelong dream of a Christian school which would train young women in horticulture and animal husbandry to work in Japan's rural areas developed amid the violent air raids of the Second World War, and finally took shape in 1946 at Nosen, the Horticultural Department of Keisen Junior College in Setagaya-ku, near Tokyo. The Michi Kawai Christian Fellowship Inc. carries on this work in her memory.

JIN MASAIKE, born in Aichi Prefecture in 1900, is a preacher of the Mu-Kyokai group of Japanese Christians and has been a Council member of the F.o.R. since 1950. The stirring sermons of Kanzo Uchimara directed him in his youth towards Christian pacifism, and he lost his position as teacher in a Government high school at Shizuoka for courageously protesting against Japan's aggression in Manchuria. Since then he has spent his time writing and preaching on peace throughout the four islands of Japan.

Mrs HATSUE NONOMIYA is also a Council member of the F.o.R., which she joined after Muriel Lester's visit in 1951. Born in 1889 she graduated from the Japan Women's University, where she learned a concern for international friendship under the guidance of its founder and first president, Jinzo Naruse. For fourteen years she acted as counsellor to students at her own university, and has since become vice-president of the Japanese group of the Women's International League for Peace and Freedom.

Among the American supporters of the Japanese Fellowship, MERRELL VORIES, though now a paralyzed invalid, still exercises his influence from the Omi Brotherhood where his Japanese wife, Maki Hitotsuyanagi, takes care of him.

Dr T. D. WALSER, a member for many years with his wife Gladys of the Japan Mission of the Presbyterian Church, was interned in Tokyo when the Second War broke out. After compulsory repatriation on the Gripsholm, he wrote to Nevin Sayre: 'My heart is broken, but God is Love and, with all the strength He has given me to "stick" through the past months, I expect to give myself as never before to the work of reconciliation'. After becoming secretary of the New York City group of the F.o.R., he died in Pennsylvania on August 14, 1949. A year later his wife received a 'Certificate of Merit and Token of Gratitude' for his services to Japan from the Association for Japan-United States Amity and Trade Centennial.

Dr WINBURN THOMAS, secretary to the Interpretation Services of the United Presbyterian Church's Commission on Ecumenical Missionary Relations and vice-chairman of the I.F.o.R. North American Committee, and Dr CHARLES W. IGLEHART, D.D., Professor of Missions at Union Theological Seminary and for thirty-two years a missionary in Japan, are also valuable supporters of the Japanese Fellowship.

RUSSELL LUTHER DURGIN, a 'Christian statesman' who found his life work in the YMCA movement, also associated himself with the F.o.R. He died in January 1956, and was commemorated a month later at a service in the chapel of Riverside Church, New York.

INDIA

Unlike the Chinese and Japanese Fellowships, which struggled to carry on their work amid the savage conflicts of military factions, the F.o.R. in India has ploughed a shorter and easier furrow, with the benevolent sympathy of Gandhi's disciples propagating the idea of non-violence against the background of India's ancient tradition of peace. Support has also come from the long-established groups of British Quakers who maintained their own non-violent creed during the rule of the Raj.

The early members of the F.o.R. in India were mainly British and American, since there seemed little point for Indians to start another non-violent movement when MAHATMA GANDHI's was so far-reaching and vital. Even among his closest colleagues, there was at first total ignorance of the fact that believers in non-violence existed in the West. They learned with amazement that thousands of F.o.R. members and other pacifists in many countries had endured obloquy and imprisonment for the sake of their convictions.

In 1926 the leader of an Indian Workers' Union said to Muriel Lester, who paid many visits to the Far East between the wars and after: 'We can't thank you enough for coming and letting us know about your movement. Of course we have the utmost faith in Bapu (Gandhi). He is right in insisting that non-violence is the best way. We follow him gladly but sometimes we ask ourselves, "Can this be true? Is it thinkable that we alone are right and the rest of the world wrong?" What you have told us has greatly increased our confidence.'

Thenceforth F.o.R. members received a special welcome wherever they travelled in India. Meetings and helpers abounded; Gandhi himself was never actually a member, but Indian supporters included many of his friends, such as E. W. Aryanayakam, his wife Asha Devi, Vinoba Bhave, Amiya Chakravarti (Tagore's former secretary), K. K. Chandy, Sudhir Ghosh, J. P. Joshua, John Sadiq and Gurdial Mallik. Among Western supporters were C. F. Andrews, Horace Alexander, Stanley Jones, Margery Sykes, Dr Forrester Paton and Richard

Keithahn. Dr Keithahn, an American missionary captivated by India, later established his own ashram at Gandhigram near Dindigul, in the Province of Madras.

Long before the post-war foundation of the present Indian Fellowship, contacts between British members and Indian sympathizers were continuous. In 1931, for example, following Gandhi's return to India after the Round Table Conference, Eric Hayman and Percy Bartlett visited India at the request of the India Conciliation Committee which met in the London F.o.R. office. Three years later another contact came through Pierre Cérésole after the Bihar earthquake had devastated a thickly-populated area the size of Scotland, and his I.V.S.P. took part in the work of reconstruction.

In 1941 the I.F.o.R. quarterly News Sheet—though endeavours to link F.o.R. members with India were forbidden by the British Government—quoted letters from Gandhi both to *The Times of India*, which had criticized his non-violent policy, and to Adolf Hitler. The second letter, which the British authorities would not allow to be published or transmitted abroad, reached the I.F.o.R. through Gandhi's close friend Mahadev Desai. One passage ran as follows:

'Your own writings, pronouncements and those of your friends and admirers leave no room for doubt that many of your acts are monstrous and unbecoming of human dignity, especially in the estimation of men like me, who believe in universal friendliness. Such are your humiliation of Czechoslovakia, rape of Poland, swallowing of Denmark. I am aware that your view of life regards such spoliations as virtuous acts. But we have been taught from childhood to regard them as acts degrading humanity. Hence we cannot possibly wish success to your arms. You are leaving no legacy to your people of which they would feel proud. They cannot take pride in a recital of cruel deeds, however skilfully planned. I, therefore, appeal to you in the name of humanity to stop the war.'

After the fighting had ended, some English Quakers and F.o.R. organizers suggested to Gandhi that a group of individuals representing many countries who were interested in his technique of peace-making should meet him to discuss post-war problems and the creation of world peace. The Mahatma welcomed the idea, but insisted that only those who had been, in his own phrase, '100 per cent reliable' in their witness against violence should be invited to meet him. This conference, later known as the World Pacifist Meeting, was planned for the winter of 1947, but Gandhi then decided that it would be wiser to wait until the 'British bayonets' had been finally withdrawn from India in June 1948.

The meeting was therefore postponed until January 1949, and the visitors from abroad were asked to meet him at Santiniketan, the Bengal home of Tagore and his family, and later at Sevagram, the village in the Central Provinces where he had established his latest ashram. But before the date came Gandhi had been assassinated, and though his disciples decided that the scheme must not be abandoned, it was not until December 1949 that seventy-five men and eighteen women from five continents and thirty-four countries gathered at Santiniketan in his memory.

The present Indian Fellowship arose from the World Pacifist Meeting. On January 1, 1950, when the Sevagram part of it was over, some of the delegates, who included Nevin Sayre and A. J. Muste (then president and executive secretary of the I.F.o.R.), met at Nagpur. They deputed K. K. Chandy in the south and Hero Singh in the north to attempt to organize a group which would eventually be independent and run its own magazine. John Sadiq, a member of a Christian Muslim family, who lived at Nagpur, undertook to distribute literature.

In November Muriel Lester arrived for a tour of India, and an All-India F.o.R. Conference was arranged for November 29th. On the night of the 30th, after a unanimous resolution, the Indian F.o.R. was born and the delegates stood in silent thanksgiving. The new Fellowship accepted the following Basis of Membership, which was posted to possible supporters all over the country:

'I believe that love, as demonstrated in the life and death and teachings of Jesus Christ, is the only adequate basis for personal, social, economic, national and international relationships.

'I, therefore, as a child of God, forbidden to kill, or to participate in or support any act of war of violence, pledge myself always to seek to reconcile conflicting groups in the spirit of self-giving love and to serve my country and fellowmen by means which are compatible with the laws of God.'

The working committee then drawn up included C. S. Paul as president, the Rev. R. R. Keithahn, Hero M. C. Singh, V. K. Cherian as treasurer, and the Rev. K. K. Chandy, lent by the Chapter of the Christavashram at Manganam in South India, as general secretary. In 1956 Dr J. P. Joshua of Madras Christian College became honorary secretary, with P. M. John as organizing secretary. Professor Joshua continued this work until he left for an academic post at the University of Monrovia in Liberia.

Between the foundation of the Indian Fellowship and Dr Joshua's departure for his new post in zoology, the group had accomplished much useful work. One of the first challenges it had to face was that of communal discord in Kerala, when friends and members in Travancore brought together a heterogeneous gathering of representatives from the different communities, and managed in spite of their contrasting ideals and methods to create a measure of harmony and understanding. Tension here increased when the Communists took over the Government in 1956, and exploited the bitterness of the unemployed quarter of Kerala's population, keenly conscious of the differences between 'haves' and 'have-nots'. The F.o.R. meetings helped to ease these difficulties, but many problems remain and the work continues.

Another challenge in which the Fellowship met with remarkable success was presented by the Church in Kerala. For over half a century the Malankara Church had suffered from strain and litigation, and the Fellowship, with prayer and fasting, endeavoured to unite the two warring parties. In the Advent season of 1958 they managed, in spite of a few remaining pockets of discord, to achieve their purpose. Similarly the Marthoma Syrian Church was recently split by doctrinal differences, and here again the Fellowship helped to mitigate personal animosities by persuading some leaders of the two sections to pray together.

As part of its normal work the Indian Fellowship is seeking contact with historic peace churches, such as the Society of Friends and the Church of the Brethren in the Gujerat area; they have also plans for co-operation with the Irish Presbyterian

Mission, and the Methodists and Mennonites in South India. Messages of reconciliation, with a few fruitful results, have been sent to the bishops of the Roman Catholic Church and the presbyters of most Protestant and oriental churches in India, and there is constant co-operation with the followers of Gandhi and with Service Civil International. Attempts at contacts with friends of the Fellowship in Pakistan, Burma and Ceylon began from the start, and were intensified in 1959 when the honorary secretary visited Ceylon. At New Delhi in 1961 the general secretary of the I.F.o.R., Philip Eastman, with the leading members attended the Third Assembly of the World Council of Churches.

Two honorary organizers are at work in Tamilnad and in North India, and others are planned for further areas. The Fellowship now has an official organ, *Arunodayam* (Dawn), which is also the journal of the Christava Ashram. Shortage of funds has been a difficulty because, as Professor Joshua pointed out in a Bulletin published for the Triennial Convention in 1959, the traditional practice of looking to missionary organizations for financial support dies hard, and 'Christians in India have yet to learn how to give'. But the Indian Fellowship has at least managed gradually to reduce the contribution from the I.F.o.R. Though the membership is still small (theoretically 300), there is a strong committee, with Dr s. GURUBATHAN, a former Community Development minister of Madras, as president; Bishop SADIQ of Nagpur as vice-president; and Presbyter K. K. CHANDY as general secretary and managing editor of *Arunodayam*.

In the autumn of 1963 this magazine gave recent news of the Delhi-Peking Friendship March; it also published an article by A. J. Muste answering the question 'What would you advise India to do if China attacks again?' He wrote that neither the United States nor India should meet violence with violence, and added: 'Let India develop ways of non-violent resistance. And she of all the nations of the world has had the advantage of such training under Gandhi's leadership. No nation will be able to have another under domination if that nation developed the real spirit of non-violent resistance.'

The Indian Fellowship, though young and small, may well have a further valuable example to set to the rest of the I.F.o.R., since Gandhi was spiritually nourished on both the *Bhagavad*

Gita and the Sermon on the Mount. It may lead the whole Fellowship further from the risk of such denominational bigotry as that which hampered the development of the Canadian F.o.R. The World Pacifist Meeting, from which the Indian Fellowship grew, was in the widest sense of the word ecumenical. In 1949 the Christmas Day service celebrated at Sevagram was composed from the hymns and prayers of four great religions, Christianity, Hinduism, Mohammedanism and Buddhism. Those of us who attended it felt that its comprehensive character detracted in no way from the special quality of Christian inspiration; rather it showed the Christians present that One God may be approached by many different roads.

Today, thanks to the example of Pope John XXIII and other great Christians, mankind is moving away from its former preoccupation with sectional divisions to a consciousness of unity in which each great faith contributes its share of wisdom to all the others, and each possesses its own experience of the Rebel Passion.

'True religion', Gandhi once concluded, 'is not narrow dogma. It is not external observance. It is faith in God, and living in the presence of God; it means faith in a future life, in truth and *ahimsa* . . . Religion, in the highest sense of the term, includes Hinduism, Islam, Christianity, etc., but is superior to them all. You may recognize it by the name of Truth.'

If the Indian Fellowship can carry this message to the rest of the I.F.o.R., it will symbolize both its Christian basis and Gandhi's belief in the need for toleration and constructive peace in the right living of human life.

Chapter 12

THE PEACE MOVEMENT THROUGH FIFTY YEARS: SOME CHANGES IN THOUGHT AND PRACTICE

This record of half a century would not be a human story if it had included no examples of weakness and failure: the defection, for instance, of individuals dominated by fear and self-interest when faced by such testing times as war and revolution, or occasional lapses into the bigotry and spiritual pride which are the special temptations of idealists. But on the whole it is a worthy tale of unshaken courage on the part of obscure men and women faced with prison or death, and of resolute witness by eminent leaders for whom their faith meant the loss—to some less easily sacrificed than life—of position and prestige.

Though the guiding principle of the Fellowship of Reconciliation, which is the sovereign power of love, remains fundamental and unaltered, its educational and practical work through half a century has inevitably been affected, first, by the changing public attitude towards peace and war which arises from the experience of two major and several minor wars and from drastic advances in the destructive power of lethal weapons; and secondly, by variations in the technique of war resistance to meet these new challenges. At no previous period has mankind been faced by a half-century which so paradoxically united violence and progress. Its greater and lesser wars and long series of major assassinations have been strangely combined with the liberation of more societies and individuals than ever before in history, and by the transformation of millions of second-class citizens—women, workers, and the members of subject races—to a stage at which first-rate achievement is no longer inhibited even if opportunities are not yet complete.

Between 1900 and 1914, in spite of the limited experiments in peace-making described in Chapter 2, war was normally regarded as an heroic and wholly creditable occupation. Even schoolgirls, as the author well remembers in the years immediately preceding the First World War, formed patriotic leagues designed to emphasize the superiority of their own country to every other. But by 1919, when most of these schoolgirls had lost their brothers and fiancés, the moral merits of a war-to-end-war which had extinguished a generation of young men in the first flower of their youth did not appear so obvious, and the mourning survivors began in large numbers to search for a road to peace.

It had, however, to be a 'respectable' road, on which the pilgrims endorsed the traditional use of war as a final sanction. For this sanction the Covenant of the League of Nations, while giving eloquent lip-service to the cause of peace, usefully provided. Until about 1935 the comprehensive umbrella of collective security sheltered platforms which even the members of the F.o.R. and the denominational Fellowships found not too inconsistent with their basic creed. The wide spiritual division between League of Nations supporters and the exponents of revolutionary pacifism always existed, but became clear only with the threat of a Second World War. Individuals who believed that war was wrong in all circumstances could then no longer join hands with those who were prepared to fight in the last resort.

In Britain the Peace Pledge Union founded by Dick Sheppard, rather than the older F.o.R. with its predominantly Christian creed, symbolized, for a few years, the practice of individual war resistance based on conscience which had gathered objectors all over Europe and America into the War Resisters' International. To F.o.R. members, with their belief in the power of the Cross to change hate into love, a mere pledge to renounce war seemed negative and incomplete, but at least the supporters of both groups were uncompromising pacifists, and as such, apart from a few backsliders, they accepted together the penalties imposed on would-be peace-makers in a world of victory-minded nations. More constructively, they joined in denouncing and seeking to mitigate the peculiar cruelties of the Second World War, such as obliteration bombing, and the large-scale starvation on the blockaded Continent of its weakest inhabitants—children, the old, and the sick. They also helped, whenever opportunity offered, to care for refugees and the victims of internment camps.

When victory came to the Allies in 1945 its function as a war-remover seemed even more dubious than it had appeared in 1919, since the price of victory was the invention of nuclear weapons. The policy of genocide involved in their use sprang directly from the saturation bombing which had ignored the sacredness of the human soul in the eyes of God, and presented a continuous future threat to the life of man on earth. The unpopular protests by pacifists against 'obliteration' now appeared not merely as an attempt to limit the ferocity of war, but as a plea for the continued existence of mankind.

Nuclear weapons immediately vitiated the campaigning methods of the secular pacifist societies, since the individual renunciation of war, while retaining its moral authority, had lost its political validity. Wars would not now cease if the common man refused to fight when governments possessed weapons which were capable of annihilating both the enemy and his opponent. A million citizens renouncing war would have no success in preventing it if the members of a war-minded Cabinet set out to use the hydrogen bomb. In spite of the British Campaign for Nuclear Disarmament, the American Crusade for a Sane Nuclear Policy, and their international equivalents directed against nuclear weapons, the answer to war lay, as it had always lain, in the power of the spirit. Only the domination of the souls of men by the rebel passion could save them from annihilation by the seekers of power.

The technique of the peace and pacifist movements over half a century roughly kept pace with these developing challenges. Today it is customary for pacifists to speak with some scorn of the equivocal witness made in the nineteen-twenties and thirties by the League of Nations Union, and by its post-Second War successor, the United Nations Association. But we should not underrate the useful educational campaigns which publicized the League of Nations after the First World War, for they accustomed a public moulded by militarist propaganda to the idea that alternatives to war were not only possible but desirable. Education and persuasion are essential processes; no sudden advance is possible over ground which has not been prepared.

Thus it took roughly forty years for the reborn international peace movement which coincided with the League of Nations to develop a new phase of life. In every movement a period comes when a few crusaders realize that their tactics must change. Such a period is now recognizable the world over in the revolutionary campaigns against war in which the groups responsible look back, not to the League of Nations Union or even the War Resisters' International, but to Gandhi's Civil Disobedience Movement in India and the non-violent resistance of the Norwegians against the Nazis between 1940 and 1945.

Since atomic bombs extinguished Hiroshima and Nagasaki, the developing threat of annihilation for all mankind has led a growing minority, both in and out of the F.o.R., to study the technique of non-violence. Richard Gregg's early text-book, *The Power of Non-Violence*, has been in constant use; so has *Defence in the Nuclear Age*, by Stephen King-Hall, the non-pacifist former naval commander who sees neither hope nor common-sense in modern warfare.

Within the past few years a world-wide crescendo of non-violent campaigns has not only brought encouragement to small groups trying on their own initiative to break through the impotence and frustration imposed upon them by power-wielding governments, but has provided evidence of comparable thinking by widely-separated organizations and individuals whose only link has been the power of example.

The objective has not always been identical. Martin Luther King's bus boycott at Montgomery, Alabama, was a protest against racial segregation and not, like most recent instances of non-violent action, a demonstration against the H-bomb or nuclear testing. But each of these episodes has represented a phase of resistance against the war on humanity by the possessors of power, and whatever the precise objective, the technique has been similar.

The protest might be made by an individual, such as the British M.P. Sir Richard Acland, who resigned his seat in the House of Commons to test British opinion on the H-bomb, or another Englishman, Harold Steele, who tried to get to Christmas Island in 1947; or by Americans Earle Reynolds and Albert Bigelow, who successively endeavoured to sail their small vessels *Phoenix* and *The Golden Rule* into the Pacific nuclear testing grounds, and thereby sowed the grain of mustard seed which eventually flowered into the Test Ban Treaty.

The non-violent expostulation might be passive, such as the behaviour of the English group which sat down on the pavement outside the War Office in January 1952 after the British Government had decided to manufacture atomic bombs—and thereby created a precedent for numerous other groups which during the next ten years periodically sat down in protest all over London from Trafalgar Square to the doorways of Embassies. Or it might be illegally active, such as the attempt to enter the nuclear rocket base at Swaffham, Norfolk, led by Michael Scott in 1958, and the similar demonstration initiated by F.o.R. member Kenneth Calkins at the ICBM base near Cheyenne, Wyoming.

Among many other examples of dissent by demonstration, the biggest have been the succession of Aldermaston marches which began in 1958 with a few thousand campaigners, and by the nineteen-sixties had collected nearly 100,000 marchers stretching for seven miles along the road between Aldermaston and London. Other more difficult marches have succeeded these experiments, such as Japan's massive month-long peace march from Hiroshima to Tokyo; the great march from San Francisco to Moscow led by A. J. Muste; and the attempted march over mountains and rivers from Delhi to Peking.

But important though it is that a technique has been found by which the suppressed millions in every politically conscious country can express themselves, protest is only one half of the story. The meaning of these demonstrations will have been imperfectly understood if those who watch or share in them do not begin to recognize the power of non-violence in both political and human life, and to consider what further spiritual heights this power gives us the strength to ascend.

Even though every nation renounced not only the H-bomb but all other weapons, war would not be conquered so long as any reliance on violence remained. Many years ago Gandhi recognized this fact when he founded his school of 'Nai Talim' ('New Education') at Sevagram in India's Central Provinces to eliminate the concept of violence from all life—not only political but economic, commercial, and scholastic. Only when the will to war is uprooted not merely from the councils of governments, but from the hearts and minds of men, will the Fellowship and those who share its outlook have learned how to translate effective dissent against evil into constructive assent to the power of good.

There is reason for both hope and faith in the possibility of this lesson, since in recent years has come a new and widespread realization that pacifists are not mere minority thinkers self-consciously seeking to substitute lunatic values for down-to-earth commonsense. The development of nuclear weapons has caused all citizens who possess imagination to perceive that the only commonsense lies in war renunciation; they do not now ask whether war should be rejected, but only how. At long last the rebel passion is ceasing to be rebellious, owing to an increasing perception that only through the values based upon it can the menaced human race be saved from both material annihilation and spiritual death.

The pacifist's task today is to find a method of helping and healing which provides a revolutionary constructive substitute for war. Such recent institutions as *Eirene,* Service Civil, and the American Peace Corps point the way to a society based upon compassion which could supersede the long domination of hatred, violence and greed. In so far as the Fellowship of Reconciliation can contribute to this achievement, its history will belong not only to the past half century, but to the challenging years ahead.

P

APPENDIX

From 'The Impact of the War on Religion in America', by F. Ernest Johnson. (*American Journal of Sociology*, November 1942.)

Far and away the most impressive feature of the impact of the war on the Protestant churches has been the contrast between their response to the outbreak of hostilities in 1941 and what happened upon the entrance of the United States into World War I. Then the churches quite generally conformed to the secular pattern. They 'mobilized' as did all other community organizations. The book *Preachers Present Arms*, written by Ray Abrams in 1933, tells the story, not without bias, perhaps, but in well-documented fashion. In the interval between the two wars something momentous has happened.

From a sociological point of view the pacifist crusade which swept the country in the 'twenties and 'thirties was an extraordinary phenomenon. Indeed, it is perhaps the most impressive single example of the power of propaganda for an idea that our history records. And here the word 'propaganda' is used in a purely descriptive sense to characterize a remarkable movement. Its strength lay very largely in the fact that those who became purveyors of its philosophy were among the most intellectual, liberal and socially minded, and therefore the most broadly intellectual, of the ministerial leaders. The movement had the support of some of the most ably edited religious journals, and it produced a pamphlet literature of a vigorous and convincing sort. The influence of the spoken and written word, unsupported by vested interest of any kind, has perhaps never been so strikingly demonstrated. Christian pacifism became an indubitably authentic movement, the influence of which is strongly felt in the religious life of America.

(See *The Rebel Passion*, pp. 58-9)

INDEX

CPSIA information can be obtained
at www.ICGtesting.com
Printed in the USA
LVHW010813280821
696343LV00028B/1091